Is Judaism Democratic? Reflections from Theory and Practice Throughout the Ages

Studies in Jewish Civilization
Volume 29

Proceedings of the Twenty-Ninth Annual Symposium of the Klutznick Chair in Jewish Civilization, the Harris Center for Judaic Studies, and the Schwalb Center for Israel and Jewish Studies

October 30–31, 2016

Other volumes in the
Studies in Jewish Civilization Series
Distributed by the Purdue University Press

2010 – Rites of Passage:
How Today's Jews Celebrate, Commemorate, and Commiserate

2011 – Jews and Humor

2012 – Jews in the Gym:
Judaism, Sports, and Athletics

2013 – Fashioning Jews:
Clothing, Culture, and Commerce

2014 – Who Is a Jew?
Reflections on History, Religion, and Culture

2015 – Wealth and Poverty in Jewish Tradition

2016 – Mishpachah:
The Jewish Family in Tradition and in Transition

2017 – *olam ha-zeh v'olam ha-ba*:
This World and the World to Come in Jewish Belief and Practice

Is Judaism Democratic? Reflections from Theory and Practice Throughout the Ages

Studies in Jewish Civilization
Volume 29

Editor:
Leonard J. Greenspoon

The Klutznick Chair in Jewish Civilization

Purdue University Press
West Lafayette, Indiana

Published by Purdue University Press

Manufactured in the United States of America

Library of Congress Cataloging-in-Publication Data

Names: Greenspoon, Leonard J. (Leonard Jay), editor.
Title: Is Judaism democratic? : reflections from theory and practice throughout the ages / edited by Leonard J. Greenspoon.
Description: West Lafayette, Indiana : Purdue University Press, [2018] | Series: Studies in Jewish civilization | Includes bibliographical references.
Identifiers: LCCN 2018031602 | ISBN 9781557538338 (pbk. : alk. paper) | ISBN 9781612495538 (epub) | ISBN 9781612495545 (epdf)
Subjects: LCSH: Jews—Politics and government. | Democracy.
Classification: LCC BM538.S7 I82 2018 | DDC 296.3/82—dc23
LC record available at https://lccn.loc.gov/2018031602

Cover image: vividvic/iStock/ThinkStock

Table of Contents

Acknowledgments

The 29th Annual Symposium on Jewish Civilization took place on Sunday, October 30, and Monday, October 31, 2016, in Omaha, Nebraska. The title of the symposium, from which this volume also takes its name, is "Is Judaism Democratic? Reflections from Theory and Practice Throughout the Ages." All of the papers collected here, with the exception of the study by Alan Mittleman, were delivered at the symposium itself.

The academic sponsors of this symposium represent three major educational institutions in Nebraska: Creighton University (the Klutznick Chair in Jewish Civilization, the Kripke Center for the Study of Religion and Society), the University of Nebraska–Lincoln (the Harris Center for Judaic Studies), and the University of Nebraska at Omaha (the Schwalb Center for Israel and Jewish Studies).

In large measure, the symposium owes its success to two groups of dedicated and talented individuals. First are my academic colleagues: Dr. Ronald Simkins (Creighton), Dr. Jean Cahan (UNL), and Drs. Moshe Gershovitz and Curtis Hutt (UNO). Their generosity, individually and collectively, has been exemplary.

The second group consists of administrative assistants, the individuals who really know how to get things done. In this context, I offer sincere expressions of gratitude to Colleen Hastings, who works with the Klutznick Chair and Kripke Center at Creighton; Kasey Davis, of the Schwalb Center at UNO; and Mary Sue Grossman, who is associated with the Center for Jewish Life, part of the Jewish Federation of Omaha.

As many readers of this volume know well, the road from oral presentation to written publication is filled with obstacles. Our path has been inestimably smoothed over through our relationship with the Purdue University Press. For almost a decade, we have enjoyed the professional and personable staff of the press, under the previous directors Charles Watkinson and Peter Froehlich, and now under co-interim directors Katherine Purple and Bryan Shaffer. They have made us feel comfortable in every way, and we look forward to many more years of association with them.

In addition to the academic and communal organizations mentioned above, this symposium is also generously supported by:

The Ike and Roz Friedman Foundation
The Riekes Family

Creighton University Lectures, Films, and Concerts
The Creighton College of Arts and Sciences
The Henry Monsky Lodge of B'nai B'rith
The Drs. Bernard H. and Bruce S. Bloom Memorial Endowment
And others

Leonard J. Greenspoon
Omaha, Nebraska
March 2018
ljgrn@creighton.edu

Editor's Introduction

Over the course of several millennia, humans have devised a considerable number and variety of ways to govern themselves. This is apparent from even a partial listing of forms of government (here in alphabetical order): anarchy, aristocracy, autocracy, democracy, meritocracy, monarchy, nomocracy, oligarchy, plutocracy, technocracy, and theocracy. Although the forms themselves derive from different time periods and social conditions, their names are almost always Greek: the ending "-cracy" from the Greek verb meaning "to gain or have control over" and "-archy" from the root "to be ruler over."

For many, especially in the West, democracy (however defined at its contours) has held a special place for philosophers and practitioners alike. The essays in this volume explore democracy within Judaism, from its beginnings (the Hebrew Bible) until today (especially, as the concept is being played out in the State of Israel). As with democracy in general, so it is in Judaism: questions arise at both theoretical (or theological) and practical levels.

For me, as volume editor and as its first reader, the essays collected here hold many surprises. For example, I had not previously detected the intimations of democracy in certain biblical texts. Nor had I fully appreciated the multilayered interrelations between the classical rabbis and the practice of democracy.

At the same time, I found reinforcement for my understanding that the current turmoil over the "Jewish" versus the "democratic" nature of the State of Israel was only a part, albeit a vital part, of a long-standing and vigorously argued debate among Jewish thinkers and politicians. And I was also encouraged to discover that many of the foundational ideas and ideals of the United States and other modern governments do indeed draw their distinctive features from the Jewish tradition.

As always in our volumes, we are nonpartisan. This is not to say, however, that our authors lack passion or precision. Every scholar in this volume demonstrates how much they care about their respective topics by their concern for accuracy and their recognition of relevancy in the presentation and evaluation of material.

The first two chapters place considerable emphasis on the Hebrew Bible: Joshua I. Weinstein, Herzl Institute, Jerusalem, "A Biblical Alternative to Greek Political Philosophy and the Limits of Liberal Democracy"; and Baruch Alster, Givat Washington College, Israel, "The 'Will of the People' in Antimonarchic Biblical Texts."

In Weinstein's analysis, which is chapter 1, classical Jewish sources from the Hebrew Bible forward highlight three central aims of the Jewish ideal: leaving "the house of bondage," inheriting a land of "milk and honey," and maintaining a covenant of divine intimacy. In this context, no system of governance can be viewed as successful if it loses its sense of dependence on the divine as established in Deuteronomy 8:11–18.

For Alster in chapter 2, the key biblical passage is Deuteronomy 17, which is critical of the excesses of any human king and demonstrates trust in the people to uphold the covenant with God. In his view, this is in keeping with a major theme of the book of Deuteronomy, which sees the public as responsible for its leadership.

David Brodsky, Brooklyn College, and Simcha Fishbane, Touro College and University System, take the opportunity to analyze classical rabbinic texts. Chapter 3 constitutes Brodsky's presentation, which is titled "The Democratic Principle Underlying Jewish Law: Moving Beyond Whether It Is So to How and Why It Is So." Here he establishes that the Mishnah lays out the principle that Jewish law is governed by the rules of democracy: when disputes arise, the majority rules. But, Brodsky continues, democracy is not the ultimate goal, but serves to promote other ends that he has discerned.

Fishbane's paper is chapter 4: "*Mipnei Darkhei Shalom*: The Promotion of Harmonious Relationships in the Mishnah's Social Order." For Fishbane, Judaism is not a democratic religion per se, but it does include many aspects that advocate democratic traditions, such as the principle of *mipnei darkei shalom*. The application of this principle creates an environment of peaceful and mutual respect between all people.

Another two essays feature the works of some of the most distinguished modern Jewish philosophers: Samuel Hayim Brody, University of Kansas, "Theocracy as Monarchy and Anarchy"; and Joseph Isaac Lifshitz, Shalem College, Jerusalem, "Jewish Democracy: From Medieval Community to Modern State."

In chapter 5, Brody points to Martin Buber as a religious Zionist who sought out the roots for radical political novelties in traditional Jewish texts like the Hebrew Bible. Buber focused on the premonarchic era of Israel, during which God ruled Israel directly. But, as Brody demonstrates, the resultant system resembled something close to anarchy—and this represented the original "constitution" of Judaism.

Lifshitz begins chapter 6 by looking back at the medieval political concept of the Jews, which differs considerably from the modern democratic social contract. Within this framework, he presents the political theory of modern Jewish philosophers like Martin Buber and Emmanuel Levinas as a possibility for modern Jewish democracy.

The American Jewish experience is at the center of the next two chapters. The first of these is chapter 7, titled "Linking 'Egypt with Texas': Emma Lazarus's Jewish Vision of American Democracy," by Joan Latchaw and David J. Peterson, both professors at UNO. As Latchaw and Peterson point out, Lazarus's "The New Colossus" continues to beckon millions to the shores of America. At the same time, the bulk of her poetry has been largely forgotten. By closely examining some of this poetry, they show how Lazarus portrays America and American democracy as enabling Jews to flourish: democratic America offers both refuge and homeland.

Lenn E. Goodman, Vanderbilt University, was keynoter for the symposium. He provides a significant analysis of "Judaism and Democracy" in chapter 8. He concludes that many of the key elements of the democratic ideal are rooted in the biblical text and rabbinic tradition. Among these are consent of the governed, the presumption of innocence, the exclusion of self-incrimination from court proceedings, and a commitment to the sanctity of life and the inestimable preciousness of the unique human individual.

The three chapters that follow, Lawrence H. Schiffman, New York University, Ori Z. Soltes, Georgetown University, and Alan Mittleman, Jewish Theological Seminary, offer broad views encompassing many different time periods and approaches. Schiffman's presentation, chapter 9, is "Monarchy and Polity: Systems of Government in Jewish Tradition." In this essay, Schiffman brings forth a number of texts that offer parallel lines of debate concerning the political organization of the Jewish people. Both texts and practical experience come together to guarantee that by modern times democracy would be assumed by the Jewish community to be the ideal system and model.

Chapter 10 contains analysis by Ori Z. Soltes, titled "Democracy, Judaism, Israel, Art, and Demagoguery." To the presentations by other presenters, Soltes adds considerations of art. As he illustrates, art has affirmed and challenged, defined and dissented from Israel's political-spiritual self-conception: it has offered a consummate expression of democratic principles.

The study by Alan Mittleman, titled "Dignity and Democracy: Defending the Principle of the Sanctity of Human Life," constitutes chapter 11. Throughout his essay he offers a robust defense of dignity. He concludes with this observation: if dignity is fundamental to a decent democracy, biblical conviction about indefeasible human value may well be necessary. In fact,

Mittleman asserts, without the continuing cultural power of "Jerusalem," the claims of reason might ring hollow.

No symposium on Judaism and democracy would be complete without some reference to the modern State of Israel. For the authors of the last two chapters, the State of Israel is central:

Chapter 12, titled "'The Will of the People' or 'The Will of the Rabbis'—Democracy and the Rabbis' Authority," is by Shlomo Abramovich (Bar Ilan University and visiting scholar, Beth Israel Synagogue, Omaha). In it, he looks with special interest at Orthodox communities of the twentieth century, where rabbis have very wide authority and their followers obey their decisions absolutely. He then explores differing explanations and diverse motives for such absolute obedience to the rabbis. As a result, Abramovich observes that a community led through obedience to rabbis should not necessarily be considered nondemocratic.

In her paper (chapter 13), "The Jewish State and the End of Democratic Judaism," Meirav Jones (University of Pennsylvania) acknowledges that different democratic forms have characterized Judaism in Eastern and Western Europe from medieval to modern times. She then contends that the presence of a Jewish state—even a democratic Jewish state—has changed the nature of Jewish life since 1948 such that Judaism is no longer in the hands of its constituents.

Leonard J. Greenspoon

Contributors

Shlomo Abramovich	Beth Israel Synagogue 12604 Pacific Street Omaha, NE 68154 shlomo23@gmail.com
Baruch Alster	Hatamar 96a 44865 Zufim ISRAEL alsterb@gmail.com
David Brodsky	Judaic Studies Brooklyn College 3111 James Hall Brooklyn, NY 11210 davidmbrodsky@gmail.com
Samuel Hayim Brody	Department of Religious Studies University of Kansas 105 Smith Hall 1300 Oread Avenue Lawrence, KS 66045-7615 samuelbrody@ku.edu
Simcha Fishbane	70-44 137 St. Flushing, New York 11367 Simcha.Fishbane@touro.edu
Lenn E. Goodman	Philosophy and Jewish Studies Vanderbilt University Nashville, TN 37240 lenn.e.goodman@Vanderbilt.Edu
Meirav Jones	Department of Political Science The Hebrew University of Jerusalem Mount Scopus Jerusalem 9190501 ISRAEL meiravjo@gmail.com

Joan Latchaw	Department of English ASH 192 University of Nebraska at Omaha Omaha, NE 68182 jlatchaw@unomaha.edu
Joseph Isaac Lifshitz	Gdud Hermesh 13/7 Jerusalem 9754513 ISRAEL Isaacl@shalem.ac.il
Alan Mittleman	Jewish Theological Seminary 3080 Broadway New York, NY 10027 almittleman@jtsa.edu
David J. Peterson	Department of English ASH 192 University of Nebraska at Omaha Omaha, NE 68182 davidpeterso1@unomaha.edu
Lawrence H. Schiffman	Skirball Department of Hebrew and Judaic Studies New York University 51 Washington Square South New York, NY 10012 lawrence.schiffman@nyu.edu
Ori Z. Soltes	5114 Westridge RD Bethesda, MD 20816 orisoltes@gmail.com
Joshua I. Weinstein	Katriel Tchorsh Street 4/2 Jerusalem, ISRAEL josh.i.weinstein@gmail.com

Goalkeeping: A Biblical Alternative to Greek Political Philosophy and the Limits of Liberal Democracy

Joshua I. Weinstein

Since the State of Israel defines itself, for certain purposes, as both Jewish and democratic, presumably these elements, while not the same, nevertheless can combine in a useful or even complementary fashion. Democracy, whatever else one might say about it, must be termed a form of government and, like all such forms, promotes some aims and purposes more effectively than others. From a Jewish perspective, then, the question must arise what contributions democracy—or, practically speaking, liberal democracy—can make to key Jewish goals. But what are these goals? Fukuyama's influential analysis suggests that the mutuality of egalitarian democracy, combined with the economic productivity of liberal capitalism, makes liberal democracy the optimal solution to the political problem and hence the "end of History."[1] Since freedom from slavery or domination and material prosperity express central goals of the Torah, liberal democracy can fill an important role in Judaism. But Judaism also seeks other aims, so that liberal democracy should serve it, rather than as some ultimate endpoint or man-made solution, instead as a platform or springboard for approaching the divine.

The concept of democracy, as the name suggests, emerges from the Greek logic of regime analysis. Experience of a variety of polities—multiethnic empires, traditional kingships, new tyrannies, revolutionary egalitarianisms—raised for the Greeks an interlocking set of questions that focus on the *politeia* or form of government. First, can one systematically outline all the basic forms? Rule by one, by the few, by the many? By the rich or by the poor? Under law or not? Virtuous or corrupt? To this day, most of the names in use to describe forms of government come from classical Greece: oligarchy, aristocracy, monarchy, tyranny, anarchy. Second, can one articulate rules of political causality or change from one form to another, such as the tendency of a corrupt oligarchy to be overthrown by a public-spirited popular movement? Does rule by any one person tend to deteriorate into corrupt tyranny? Does the instability of all forms lead, ultimately, to a cycle of regimes? Third, and most characteristically, which regime form is the best? Rule by the philosopher-kings of Plato's *Republic*? Obeying the laws set down by a wise lawgiver? Or is Polybius correct to judge the mixed regime—which includes elements of rule by one, by the few, and by the many and that he attributes to Republican Rome—the most stable, and hence the best? The living relevance of this last emerges most clearly from the US Constitution, which not only provides for a president (one), a small Senate (few), and a large House of Representatives (many), but also explicitly guarantees to each of the several states a "Republican Form of Government" (IV.4).[2] While the term *democracy* has received many different meanings, none of them is coherent outside this essentially Greek logic of regime analysis.

The foundational texts of Judaism display no interest in this Greek *politeia* discourse. Biblical texts, of course, display awareness of the various ways rulers exercise their authority; compare, for example, the decision-making process of Pharaoh as depicted in the first part of Exodus with that of Ahashverosh depicted in the scroll of Esther. But no biblical text itself makes a comparison of this kind nor seeks any more systematic taxonomy. In the absence of the Greek logic, language alone does not decide when a biblical *melekh* qualifies as a monarch—as opposed to, say, an elected but dominant figure like Pericles. With no taxonomy, there can be no investigation of causal interconnections and no concern for identifying the best form of government. This same systematic lack is just as evident—though raising more complex historical questions—in the corpus of rabbinic texts of Mishnah, Talmud, and midrash. Many Greek loanwords stud rabbinic language, but there is no sign of the vocabulary—and, more important, the logic—of *politeia* analysis.[3] Indeed, without imagining a "pure" or "uninfluenced" Judaism pristinely divorced from historical context, the generalization still holds that Jewish authors do not engage with the themes and logic of Greek political philosophy, in the first instance, as Hebrew speakers.[4] Since this Greek tradition forms the core of Western political thought in general, there is, in a strict sense, no comparable native Jewish tradition—as indeed the lack of a native Hebrew term for "politics" suggests.[5]

The significance of this negative conclusion can hardly be overstated. If Aristotle is right that man is "a political animal by nature," then this must include the Jews as well.[6] Jewish thinkers show no shortage of interest in struggles for power and rulership—one need only think of the authors of Judges and Kings. But this does not by any means entail that thinking in the Greek terms of political analysis comes to humans "by nature." To the contrary. Consequently, when scholars apply to Jewish texts and thinkers terms that grow (ultimately) out of the Greek political tradition—such as "elected representatives," "checks and balances," "equal rights," "separation of powers," and of course "democracy"—this must be understood as importing concepts that do not spring from the intellectual tradition of the works in question.[7] There is nothing illegitimate in this practice—despite the risk of mistakenly imputing one's own conceptual framework to the object of one's studies—but it does have the unfortunate tendency to obscure the Jewish terms and approach to collective matters of rule and authority. These latter cannot, at the risk of begging the question, even be termed "political matters." But once the Greek tradition becomes clearly identified, it can then be set aside and methodologically suspended so that the Hebrew texts have the opportunity to speak in their own terms and voice—without a Greek accent, as it were.

While the logic of *politeia* analysis neither engages nor appeals to Jewish thought overall, the logic of collective goals—what rule and authority should aim to accomplish—very much does. Whether the goal in question is the conquest of the Land of Israel, the purification of Temple worship, or the establishment of peace among peoples, many biblical characters and prophets exhort their audiences (and readers) toward large-scale collective actions. The rabbinic corpus similarly overflows with communal purposes and aims: from rescuing the aggrieved and supporting the poor, through providing public infrastructure and regulating the market, all the way to uprooting idolatry and pursuing the "paths of peace." A particularly telling talmudic passage takes up the issue of whether and how one can sort out or in any way simplify this welter of imperatives.[8] If the central questions of the Greek tradition are "Who should rule and how?" the Jewish thinkers focus primarily on "What is the aim to be accomplished? For what purpose should rule be exercised?" In this context, the distinction between the Greek and Jewish traditions can perhaps best be termed a difference of logic.[9]

If this is an appropriate characterization of the logic of Jewish thinking about rule and community, then the emphasis in analysis should be to determine what Judaism has to say about goals. Quite a bit, it turns out. In the first instance, three goals stand out with particular salience. First, Egypt serves as a negative pole, the "iron furnace" and "house of bondage" that must be left behind before any other purpose can hope for realization. Physical removal, however, does not, unto itself, suffice. The people of Israel are exhorted to leave also the ways of Egypt, lest they merely reproduce a "house of bondage" in a new location.[10] In a summary slogan, the goal is freedom from oppression. Second, as the Israelites are quick to point out, liberation without food is simply starvation. They are therefore offered not only water, manna, and quail, but eventually also land, bread, well-being of every kind, the opportunity to sit each "under his vine and under his fig tree." In a slogan, prosperity. The conjunction of these two goals forms precisely the divine plan or promise as laid out to Moses at the Burning Bush: "I will descend to save them from the hands of Egypt and to raise them from that land to a wide, good land, a land that oozes milk and honey" (Exod 3:8). This pair similarly structures the threats of suffering and retribution should Israel fail in its devotion to the covenant: "You will serve your enemies that God your Lord will send against you thirsty, hungry, naked and utterly lacking, and he will place an iron yoke on your neck until he destroys you" (Deut 28:48). Exile means losing both freedom and prosperity.

The aims of prosperity and freedom from oppression take their place within the overall framework of the covenant, of the relationship of Israel to her God. In some contexts there is haziness regarding the ends–means relations here; the Israelites at times appear to be motivated only by prosperity and freedom, for the sake of which the divine seems to serve as an effective means. But viewing God this way leads to problems—for example, of the sort raised by the accuser in the opening of the book of Job. But as far as the collective is concerned, there is ultimately little doubt that closeness to God—displayed through the pillars of cloud and fire, the Tabernacle and the Ark, or through expressions like "going before you," "coming to you," and especially "dwelling among you"—enjoys independent, indeed, ultimate status in its own right.

At the risk of imposing a ham-fisted unity on the rich variety of the Bible, and, a fortiori, of rabbinic and later strata, one can consider a "toy model" Judaism boiled down to these three aims: the negative goal of leaving "the house of bondage" (not just Egypt), the positive goal of inheriting a land of "milk and honey" (not just Canaan), and the relational goal of living in a covenant of divine intimacy (not just in Jerusalem).[11] But even this artificial simplicity suffices to generate a raft of questions and difficulties and sets up what may be termed the central dilemma of Judaism: the biblical texts show these three aims systematically conflicting with and undermining one another. Egypt, for example, is itself a land of milk and honey, but it is also a house of bondage. The wilderness makes available contact with the divine, but the menu generates recurrent complaints. Perhaps most salient is the worry that the experience of freedom combined with prosperity will extinguish awareness of the divine grounds of these very attainments: "Beware, lest . . . when everything that is yours increases, your heart grow high and you forget God your

Lord who brought you out of the Land of Egypt" (Deut 8:11–14). If even so simplified a picture leads to the conclusion that the main aims of Judaism are in practice incompatible, this raises the possibility that Judaism is not merely difficult but perhaps ultimately futile.

This central dilemma can be confronted, but not solved. Genesis shows the trade-off between freedom and prosperity already at work among other nations as well, for example when the Egyptians, but not the Canaanites, choose to sell themselves into slavery under the pressure of famine (Gen 47:13–26). One possibility is that the divine covenant—including the restrictions divine law imposes on royal prerogatives and on ownership of the Land of Israel—allows Israel to escape from an apparently universal dynamic. But even if this is correct, such an approach (once again) converts God into a means for achieving human goals—which therefore makes it more a restatement of the dilemma than its dissolution.

Liberal democracy—though appearing in the first instance as a Greek-style *politeia* form—also remains caught in the central dilemma. On the one hand, individual liberty plays a decisive role in the technological capitalism that has lifted billions out of starvation. Judaism lauds this, fulfilling as it does the first human mission of "filling the earth and subduing it" (Gen 1:28) At the same time, liberal democracies also prevent as many people as possible from suffering oppression and injustice and seem to allow for indefinite improvement in this regard. There is less slavery—both formal and not—in democracies than elsewhere. The Jewish logic of aims thus justifies liberal democracy to a very considerable degree, seeing in this form of government—in the Greek sense—a valuable means for accomplishing essential goals. But precisely as a humanly devised means, liberal democracy threatens our awareness that all human deeds are founded on divinely given capacities: "Lest you say in your heart 'My power and the force of my arm have brought me this success.' But remember God your lord, for he gives you the power to succeed" (Deut 8:17–18). Indeed, taking liberal democracy as some kind of ultimate—as the best man-made solution to the human problems—risks running afoul of even the injunction against bowing down to the works of one's own hands. Furthermore, liberal democracy also seems exposed to various kinds of perversions, corruption, and decay. It remains an open—and increasingly pressing—question whether these are best captured and ameliorated by the biblical goal-oriented warnings against success-worship and outright idolatry or perhaps better by the Greek *politeia*-oriented warnings against the tendency of democracy to decay into mob rule or tyranny.

THE GREEK TRADITION OF REGIME ANALYSIS

Methodological suspension of the Greek perspective requires first a clearer view of just what this point of view entails, and here it is useful to begin with Herodotus, who gives the earliest account of systematic *politeia* analysis. As he sets the scene, the rule of Persia has been usurped by an imposter, and in response a cadre of loyalist nobles undertakes a bold strike against the usurpers. They succeed, but finding that the heirs of Cyrus are no more, they debate the future of Persia. Otanes advocates handing power over to the many, to the middling Persians, since they are not given to the profligacy, insolence, and instability of power-mad kings, ruling instead through equality and accountable, public deliberation. Megabyzus responds that, while he agrees with the critique of one-man rule, the many are basically ignorant and foolish, tending to deteriorate into a useless mob. The best decisions will be made by the best men, who are likely to be few—an aristocracy. Darius replies that the few can go just as bad as the many, while if we take any form of rule at its best, rule by one has the advantage. It prevents factional infighting and the risk of plans leaking to the enemy. In fact, the tendency of both popular and elitist movements ultimately to lead to one-man rule proves the superiority of monarchy. Thus ends the debate. But the set speeches Herodotus presents here have all the hallmarks of Greek rhetoric, and even though he insists on their veracity, no one who knows the Greek intellectual tradition is willing to accept at face value his attribution of the debate to the Persians.[12]

Perhaps the most famous *politeia* analysis is that offered in Plato's dialogue of that name, *Politeia*—known in English as *Republic*. Here, Socrates details what he takes to be the best way to organize a city, which, as ruled by philosopher-kings, deserves the name *aristocracy*, rule of the best. But like all human things, this regime too will eventually fall into decline. Even a city focused on the pursuit of truth, Socrates explains, will eventually fail to propagate its education and will decay into a city focused instead on success, power, and glory. This latter city, in its turn, will be corrupted by pursuit of wealth into an oligarchy, which will in time be replaced in a revolutionary movement by a popular democracy. Democracy, as Socrates presents it, is typified not by focus on any one goal in particular, but rather by a refusal to focus, granting instead equal legitimacy to all aims. Openness of this kind, Socrates warns, is genuine openness and hence also openness to transgression. Eventually, he predicts, the openness in such a democracy to any craving will bring a transgressive tyrant to power.[13]

Do democracy—as Plato understands it—and Judaism go together? From the perspective of Judaism, this kind of democracy offers genuine advantages in that its openness to all ends also allows Jews to pursue Jewish ends. Jewish ends in such a democracy are just as legitimate as any others; they are equal. But this pseudoequality is necessarily temporary. All forms of government, Socrates explains, create an environment in which the young are educated, and so too does democracy create a public culture in which the norms, both written and unwritten, train and educate its young. This democratic education, however, does not aim at Jewish ends but rather at the defining democratic end: the essential equality of all purposes. So if Judaism teaches any goals in particular—aside from the equality of all purposes—Jewish education will suffer limitations, perhaps severe, in such a democracy. Judaism will become private, clandestine, or even countercultural, and the younger generation will tend to feel psychic conflicts between devotion to the aims of Judaism and to the equality of all aims as taught by democracy.[14] Such mental tension may be found among Jewish youths even in non-Athenian democracies.

Aristotle's analysis of regime types aims to be more complete and is for that reason less clear and simple. He begins from the approach reported by Herodotus—rule by one, by few, by many—and then distinguishes whether the ruling segment rules for its own benefit or for the common good. This allows him to define one "correct" and one "perverse" regime type for each size of the ruling group, so that, for example, aristocracy is rule by the few for the common good, while oligarchy is rule by the few for the good of the few. So there seem to be six basic regime types. But then he points out that, while oligarchy seems to be defined by the fewness of its ruling class, this misses its essence. Oligarchy is primarily rule by the wealthy, while democracy is rule by the poor; it is merely coincidental that the wealthy are few and the poor many.[15] Then it turns out that there are four or five different kinds of democracies, and so too of oligarchies.[16]

Among the recommendations that Aristotle puts forward, one with a very rich afterlife is the idea of a mixed regime.[17] Aristotle presents several versions here of both the rationale and the implementation, but the general thrust seems to be that, since each form of government offers different strengths and weaknesses, one should (ideally) be able to blend the forms so as to maximize the strengths while minimizing the weaknesses. Thus, for example, freedom, wealth, and excellence are each legitimate claims to a share of the rule, and each, if followed exclusively, would lead to democracy, oligarchy, and aristocracy respectively. But in an aristocracy, the great mass of men—who have little share in excellence—would also have little share in rule and would be therefore embittered. Similarly, if the great mass of freemen—the poor—were given access to the common purse, the temptation to feather their own nests would be overwhelming. But if the masses can serve in groups—such as on juries—then their strengths can be brought to bear while minimizing exposure to their weaknesses. Executive power, by contrast, such as military leadership, should rest with those who are most able. If the blend is successful—as Aristotle suggests that Sparta's was—one could name this regime either a democracy or an oligarchy, but actually neither would be strictly appropriate; the right name is the generic *politeia*.

Writing some two centuries after Aristotle, Polybius offers a stripped-down and systematized version of this kind of *politeia* analysis. Book six of his *Histories* not only follows a schema of six basic regime types similar to Aristotle's, but also proposes two laws of evolution: healthy regimes decay into corrupt ones and these in turn are ousted by the public-spiritedness of a larger group. Thus a monarch will tend to become a tyrant, and a tyrant will tend to be overthrown by a virtuous elite and its aristocracy—which will eventually decay into an oligarchy, and so forth. The instability of all forms leads Polybius to assume a never-ending cycle and to propose that the best regime is one that can escape this cycle. It must therefore be a mixed regime, balancing the strengths and weaknesses of the one, the few, and many. Polybius sees in Republican Rome—with its king-like consuls, its elitist Senate, and its popular plebs and tribunes—an instantiation of this mixture and a demonstration of its superiority.

Modern republicanism can mean many things, but in the first instance it refers to something like this interpretation of the Roman constitution. Thinkers of the later Roman and medieval periods offer many approaches that emphasize virtuous, legitimate, or even divine kingship, but from at least the Latin translation of Aristotle's *Politics* in the mid-thirteenth century, the notion gains traction in the West that proper rule is shared, limited rule.[18] By the late fourteenth and fifteenth centuries (at least), Venice, Florence, and other Italian city-states begin to develop some kind of republican self-understanding and this—on at least some readings of the evidence—eventually finds its way into an "Atlantic" republican tradition including (in various ways) English and American thinkers and politicians such as James Harrington, Henry St. John Bolingbroke, John Adams, and Thomas Jefferson.[19] The various discourses of corruption and virtue, constitutionalism, opposition to tyranny, separation of powers, and checks and balances form a rich backdrop to seventeenth and eighteenth century Anglo-American political thought, study, and dispute, but regardless of whether any given thinker works with terminology from Polybius, Livy, Tacitus, or even directly from Aristotle, one basic fact remains: the entire discussion presupposes the search for the correct or best form of government. The logic of Greek *politeia* analysis thus remains prominent—indeed, dominant—to this day, and it is this logic that will need to be put in abeyance so as to allow a clearer view of the Jewish thinkers.

THREE GOALS OF THE JEWISH TRADITION

Whatever account one gives of the rich variety exemplified in the Pentateuch, one cannot mistake the central thrust of the composite whole. From the blessings of land and progeny offered to Abraham, Isaac, and Jacob, to the blessings—and apposite curses—dealt out by Moses at both Sinai and Moab, the core issue remains surprisingly consistent. The Torah concerns itself above all else with the fertility of man, plant, and animal. Blessing, in the first instance, means children, plain and simple—immediately followed by the agricultural productivity for feeding and supporting same. As the key to all such growth resides in the rain, God can appear as sitting in the sky, all but literally opening and closing the spigot of precious water—hence, of food and life itself. While mere life is the minimal, bottom-line goal, the pinnacle or complete fulfillment of this aim and blessing comes to be expressed in various symbols: in the prophetic writings, each sits "under one's vine and under one's fig" (1 Kgs 5:5, Mic 4:4; cf. Isa 36:16, Amos 9:14, Zech 3:10); but in the Pentateuch, the preferred expression is simply to inherit "a land that oozes milk and honey" (cf. Joel 4:18).

This last expression performs such important work in the Pentateuch that it deserves somewhat closer analysis. *Devash*, usually rendered as "honey," refers more broadly to the sticky, sweet ichor that drips from any appropriate source, be it fruits like dates or figs, or from actual bees' hives. But the sugary sweetness of *devash*, no matter how delicious, does not exhaust the category of good things to eat. In particular, fruits that are sweet are not fatty or rich, and conversely fatty, rich fruits—like the olive or the modern avocado—are not sweet.[20] If the combination of sweet with fatty-rich cannot be found in creation, it must arise from human artifice. But in other contexts the Torah's law imposes various restrictions on the power to effect novel combinations of either plants or animals, perhaps the most obvious example being the prohibition of cooking a kid in its mother's milk (Exod 23:19, 34:26; Deut 12:21).[21]

The artificial combination of sweet and fatty-rich—still, to this day, all but definitive of desserts such as ice cream—stands out not only for being subject to no restrictions but also for serving as unqualified praise for the land that can produce it. This praise, incidentally, applies not only to Israel, since Egypt too is a land of milk and honey (Num 16:13, on which more below). But put more broadly, milk-and-honey is the paradigm of dessert and so serves as an appropriate figure for the goal of fertility reaching its zenith.

One further remark on the verb *zavat*, often translated as "flowing." This is the usual term for bodily discharges, either specifically menstrual or more generally discharges from the sexual organs of male or female. This verb thus emphasizes the spontaneous, perhaps even undesired, character of the discharge in question. The land of Israel thus receives praise as a land that, in a sense, could not help exuding sweet, creamy desserts. Certainly the need to work, farm, and herd is not to be literally obviated, but the figure implies that the land offers an almost automatic source of luxurious delicacies (cf. TB *Ketubot* 111b).

Starting from the core concern of children, land, and fertility, the next issue is security, as in "May God bless you—and guard you" (Num 6:24). Already the Patriarchs are struggling with their neighbors—such as Egypt and Gerar—and so receive blessings expanded to include success in these confrontations (Gen 15:1, 13–14, 28:15).[22] By the time that Israel has grown into a nation of multitudes in Egypt and been subjected to slavery and Pharaoh's genocidal policies, suffering under hostile domination begins to eclipse even the core issue of prosperity and fertility. At the Burning Bush, God commissions Moses for the leadership role in a plan that will dominate the entire Pentateuch: "I will descend to save [my people] from the hands of Egypt and to raise them from that land to a wide, good land, a land that oozes milk and honey" (Exod 3:8). Eventually, the blessings at Sinai and Moab will gloss this secondary goal as military victory over enemies, supremacy, and peace (Lev 26:3–13; Deut 28:1–14).

This Burning Bush pair—leaving the house of bondage to inherit a land of milk and honey—has become a cliché, but really requires highlighting and analysis. The first and more urgent goal presents a negative character: escape from, release from, salvation from. But from what? Leaving Egypt means more than just leaving slavery. After all, slavery will be permitted in the Land of Israel, indeed, even the enslavement of Israelites. Egypt not only allows slavery, but is itself "the house of bondage"—the homepage of slavery, as it were. Egypt houses systematic slavery, even independently of the fate of the Israelites

(Gen 47:18–26). Leaving the "iron furnace" of Egypt (Deut 4:20) thus means escaping this collective, pervasive, and systematic oppression and entering a shared existence that is no longer structured by relations of domination. Other Israelites are "your fellow," "your companion," and "your brother"—which last category must also include Israel's king—while the stranger in one's midst must be loved and not oppressed.[23] The positive goal, of course, is good food—in fact, dessert—serving to symbolize a form of life that affords enjoyment: plenty, prosperity, and leisure. As a pair, these two goals frame communal motion: from negative to positive, from oppression and misery to freedom and plenty. These goals form the structural background to the story of the Exodus and—since the reverse motion always remains possible—to the stories of exile and of redemption as well. In a sense, this pair sets the evaluative background stage-set against which the "plot" of the various large-scale Jewish stories unfolds.

Together with the movement toward freedom and prosperity—or however we gloss the Burning Bush plan—the Torah also holds out a special relationship with God as an aim of the community. Whether in the context of freedom from slavery—"And I will take you to me for a people and I will be your Lord and you will know that I am God your Lord who has brought out from under the oppressions of Egypt" (Exod 6:7)—or of providing food—"At evening you will eat meat and in the morning you will sate yourself with bread and you will know that I am God your Lord" (Exod 16:12)—experience and recognition of God's involvement with the fate of the Jewish people stands as a goal in its own right. This stands out most clearly after Moses has pacified God's anger in the wake of the Golden Calf. God makes clear that he will uphold the terms of his covenant and will bring the people into the land promised to Abraham, Isaac, and Jacob, a land of milk and honey, but "I will not go up in your midst, for you are a stiff-necked people, lest I consume you on the way" (Exod 33:4). This bad news precipitates mourning among the people and generates further rounds of negotiations among Israel, Moses, and God such that, eventually, God relents. Moses urges God to return his relation with Israel from one at a "hands-off" distance to one of direct proximity (cf. Exod 33:13–16 with 34:9–10). The tedious reiteration in Exodus 35–39 of the *Mishkan* [Tabernacle], in all its design and execution details, thus constitutes reaffirmation that the consequences of the Golden Calf have been finally averted and God is willing to take up residence, as it were, in the midst of the camp. God's absence, apparently, constitutes bad news unto itself, even when freedom and prosperity are not at issue.

Even this simplified three-goal Judaism generates many questions and problems. In the first instance, one might wonder about this relationship with God that is not merely described or assumed but also expected, demanded, and indeed commanded: "Love God your Lord with all your mind, all your life and all your power" (Deut 6:5). In some passages, it appears as if God serves merely as the gatekeeper of certain blessings—most obviously rain and progeny. Here, relationship with the divine seems to exercise no independent attraction, but to serve rather as an extrinsic means for getting what one really wants. Indeed, the rhetoric of Deuteronomy returns over and over to something like this extrinsic relation, using locutions such as "in order that" [*le-ma'an*], as if the truly motivating end-goals are leveraged by God to extract some kind of cooperation and submission: "All this commandment which I command you this day shall you take care to perform, in order that you may live and increase and come and inherit the land God promised to your ancestors" (Deut 8:1). "And write them on the doorposts of your house and on your gates. In order that your days and the days of your children on the ground that God your Lord swore to your ancestors to give to them shall be as the days of the sky over the land" (Deut 11:21). "For today I command you to love God your Lord, to walk in his ways and to keep his commandments, statutes and judgments, and you will live and increase and God your Lord will bless you in the land to which you are going to inherit it" (Deut 30:16). In short, "you" should do what God wants in order to get the good things "you" want. As a matter of logic, any role God might take as redeemer, protector, or provider of any good or blessing has lurking within it the potential for such a mercenary, give-and-take approach—though, of course, Deuteronomy clearly insists on the unique and intimate relationship that arises from God and Israel choosing and cleaving to one another (e.g., Deut 26:16–19). Still, the worry that this genuineness might be undermined precisely by God's generosity powers the thought-experiment in the prologue to Job.

THE CENTRAL DILEMMA OF JUDAISM

The ice-cream prosperity implied by the expression *milk and honey* serves not only as the positive moment in the divine plan of redemption, but also as a term of legitimation in disputes over rulership. Though at numerous points in the trials of the wilderness the issue arises as to whether Israel might not prefer to be in Egypt (e.g., Exod 13:17, 14:11–12, 17:3; Num 11:5, 14:3–4, 20:5, 21:5), in none of these cases does the text record an actual confrontation or struggle over leadership and policy. The only case of outright rebellion involves one Korach leading a coalition of the disgruntled against the primacy of Amram's children, Moses and Aaron. Korach, representing the Levitical house next in line after Amram's, conspires together with representatives of the tribe of Reuven (Israel's first born), who presumably nurture resentment against the primacy of the tribe of Judah.[24] Moses initiates separate negotiations with each faction, but the Reuvenites Datan and Aviram reject these overtures:

> Is it so little that you have brought us up from a land that oozes milk and honey to kill us in the wilderness that you should also flaunt your rule over us? But you have not brought us into a land that oozes milk and honey and given us an inheritance of field and vineyard. Will you put out these people's eyes? No, we will not come! (Num 16:13–14)

The first thing to note about this speech is that, on the level of principle, the Reuvenites advance here what could be called the milk-and-honey standard for Jewish leadership: he who can provide the ice cream deserves to rule. "You, Moses," they seem to say, "would have a good claim to rule if you were to give us ice cream—or at least, reliable sources of bread and wine. But you have not done that, now have you?" Not only do they invoke the milk-and-honey standard, but—more important—they expect it to be clear that these are the proper terms for conducting the debate. Their claim is not open to rebuttals like, "But you are no longer slaves, right? That must be worth something?" Indeed, the Reuvenites take their complaint as so irrefutable—and Moses makes no effort to refute it—that it eliminates room for any real negotiations.[25]

A second thing to note is the status of the land of Egypt. Of course Egypt offers flesh-pots and abundant fish and vegetables, and is simply called "the garden of God" (Gen 13:10). But here, the Reuvenites add that Egypt, like the Land of Israel, is also a land of milk and honey. It is not vaguely attractive in some fashion or other but in fact fully satisfies the positive plank in the Exodus plan. Nothing better is to be found in Canaan, at least as far as this matter is concerned. The claim against Moses amounts to a sharpened version of the old "Why did you take us out of Egypt?" complaint: "Even at best, the most you could do is restore to us what we gave up when we left Egypt—and even that you have not done."

Now the deep problems begin to show themselves. Egypt is itself a land of milk and honey, but unfortunately it is also the house of bondage. Even worse, it seems that these two facts are not unrelated. Genesis relates how, after Joseph has stored up the surplus of the seven years of bounty under Pharaoh's control, the ensuing famine eventually brings the Egyptians voluntarily to offer themselves as slaves:

> "We will not hide from our master. Our money and cattle are completely given to our master, and there is nothing to offer our master but our bodies and our land. Why should we die before your eyes, both we and our land? Buy us and our land with bread and we and our land will be slaves to Pharaoh. You give seed, and let us live and not die, that the land may not become desolate." So Joseph bought all the lands of Egypt for Pharaoh, for the Egyptians each sold his field, since the famine was hard on them, and the land become Pharaoh's. . . . They said: "You have revived us. May we find favor in your eyes that we be slaves to Pharaoh." (Gen. 47:18–20, 25)

Systematic slavery, on this account, is not merely accepted but actually chosen. The Egyptians' reasoning here is simple: better to be slaves than to starve—as the Israelites will later agree when contemplating starvation in the wilderness. Since famine is not unique to Egypt—the land of Canaan suffers from it regularly—this specific form of reasoning is made possible, ironically, precisely by Egypt's prosperity; if there were no surplus to be prudently stored up, there would be no choice but to accept the ravages of famine. The survivors might be few, but they would remain free. Indeed, the narrative points silently to the possibility of preferring this outcome. Once Joseph has gathered all the money in Egypt and in Canaan, his next offer is to buy cattle. This, the Canaanites decline to do; they keep their cattle and presumably starve—but remain free. The Egyptians, by contrast, sell their cattle and then, at the next stage, sell themselves. But selling oneself is only possible because, in Egypt, there is something to buy.

This insight raises the harrowing thought that becoming a house of bondage is not a uniquely Egyptian phenomenon. Buying someone's freedom is expensive, which means that prosperity (for some) is a precondition of slavery (for others). But if prosperity contains within it the seeds of oppression, then perhaps Egypt is merely an exemplar of a general tendency. Perhaps lands of milk and honey will always tend to become houses of bondage.[26] If this is so, then the entailed conclusion cannot be emphasized too strongly. The Exodus project of leaving Egypt to enter a prosperous land might turn out, in the end, to be self-undermining and self-defeating. Israel might leave Egypt only to inherit the land of Canaan—and then turn this into a new house of bondage.

This is the central dilemma of Judaism; if prosperity must always lead to systematic oppression, then Judaism as understood in the Pentateuch is impossible. Clearly, this conclusion is intolerable. But precisely for that reason its possibility must be thought through with the utmost care.[27]

The first explicit spokesman for a version of the central dilemma turns out to be none other than the prophet Samuel. In his notorious—and controversial—speech against the establishment of a kingdom, he outlines the oppression that a king can be expected to impose on his subjects:

> Samuel said "This is what you can expect from the king who will rule over you: he will take your sons to appoint them for his chariots and cavalry, that they will run before his chariot, and to appoint captains of thousands and of fifties, and to plow his fields and reap his harvest and to make his tools of war and charioteering. Your daughters he will take for perfumers and cooks and bakers. Your best fields and vineyards and olives he will take and give to his servants. Your seed and vineyards he will tithe and give to his eunuchs and servants. Your male and female slaves and your best youths and your donkeys he will take and use for his labors. Your flocks he will tithe and you will be his slaves. On that day you will cry out because of the king you have chosen for yourselves, but God will not answer you on that day." But the people refused to listen to Samuel's voice and said: "No, but rather we will have a king over us." (1 Sam 8:11–19)

The talmudic sages are already debating whether Samuel outlines here permitted behavior of the king or whether he takes these acts to be wrongful, but nevertheless predictable, outcomes of giving any man such royal authority.[28] But whether the takings in question are legitimate or not, it is hard not to hear in Samuel's warning familiar overtones. Your king will make you slaves—just like you were in Egypt. But when you cry out [*ve-za'aqtem*] in the face of your oppression—as you did in Egypt—now God will not answer your cries—as he did in Egypt. This king, unlike Pharaoh, you have chosen for yourselves.

Samuel's exhortation indicates how systematic subjugation can emerge from prosperity. Only because one already possesses "fields, vineyards, and olives" can these be confiscated. The more productive one's land and flocks, the more these can be taxed. The more children one has, the more who can be conscripted. These takings then have a twofold effect. On the one hand—as in the case of the starving Egyptians—the relationship of exploitation can come into being only in the context of the gifts of prosperity. If a good does not exist, it cannot change hands as a sign of submission. On the other hand, prosperity fuels the mechanism of domination. Though less explicitly, Samuel's warning implies that the more goods become available for confiscation, the more the king's activities and personnel can expand. Presumably the king's horses and men have useful functions to perform, but one of their uses can be to oppress the people and extract more and still more resources—limited, as always, by the available measure of prosperity.

Samuel's warning qualifies as prophecy in the sense of predicting the future. Saul is not a particularly oppressive king—if anything, he is chastised for leading too gently (1 Sam 15:17)—and while David apparently lays the foundations for a royal bureaucracy, his labors are presented as funded not by taxation, but by pillage from foreign wars and as aimed, not at royal aggrandizement, but at building the Temple of God (1 Chr 26–28). The first signs of oppression come in Solomon's reign. The royal bureaucracy can now put endless dainties on the king's table, and while internal taxation clearly receives a substantial boost from foreign tribute, impressed Israeli labor reaches four months a year for each of 30,000 men (1 Kgs 4–5). Eerily, the text pictures the wonderful prosperity of the Israelites hand-in-hand with the growing power of the king and his coercive machinery:

> Judah and Israel were as numerous as the sand by the sea, eating, drinking and merry. Solomon ruled all the kingdoms from the River and the land of the Philistines to the border of Egypt, paying tribute and serving Solomon all the days of his life.
>
> And the bread of Solomon's table for a single day was thirty *kor* fine flour and sixty *kor* of meal. Ten fine cattle and twenty pastured cattle and a hundred sheep, besides deer, gazelles, antelopes and fed fowl. For he held power out to the River Euphrates, over all the kings on this side of the River from Tifsach to Gaza, and he had peace in every direction roundabout. Judah and Israel dwelt securely, each one under his vine and under his fig, from Dan to Beersheva, all the days of Solomon.
>
> And Solomon had forty thousand horse stables for his chariots and twelve thousand cavalry. These officials, each for his month, provisioned King Solomon and whoever was close to King Solomon's table so that nothing was lacking. Each in his turn brought to the proper place barley and hay for the horses and steeds. (1 Kgs 4:20–5:8)

At this point, the role of the governing machinery still appears innocuous, but its capacities lay the foundations for what will come. Eventually,

Solomon will violate enough of the covenant that his kingdom is doomed to division after his death. But his ability to carry out these violations depends on the executive power built into his burgeoning bureaucracy.

At its conclusion, Solomon's reign comes in for public review and scrutiny as his son Rehoboam is about to ascend to the kingship. Rehoboam goes to Shechem for this sensitive occasion, and there the gathered crowd petitions him thus: "Your father made our burden hard, but if you now ease the hard labor [*'avodat 'avikha ha-qashah*] and the heavy burden that your father put upon us, we will serve you" (1 Kgs 12:5). Rehoboam promises a response in three days, during which time he takes counsel. The elders who served during Solomon's lifetime advise Rehoboam to relent and gain the confidence, affection, and obedience of the people, whereas the youths who grew up with him recommend threats and a show of strength. He chooses the latter, answering the people thus: "Now my father loaded you with a heavy burden, and I will add to your burden; my father punished you with whips and I will punish you with scorpions" (1 Kgs 12:14).

The central dilemma begins here to show itself. Obviously, the narrative points to the insolence and imprudence of youth raised in power and prosperity, as opposed to the level-headed sobriety of their elders—who presumably worked to achieve these goods.[29] But greater analytical importance must attach to the retrospective view shared by all parties—the elders, the youth, the populace, and even Rehoboam himself: that Solomon imposed heavy burdens on Israel. No one advises Rehoboam to reply: "Why are you complaining? My father never burdened you at all." All parties agree that Solomon imposed on the people precisely the "hard labor" [*'avodah qashah*] that resounds with the memory of Egyptian slavery (cf. Exod 1:14; Deut 26:6). Perhaps the advice of the elders could have laid the foundations for a better future, but there is little room for doubt that, by the end of his reign—not coincidentally, after marrying Pharaoh's daughter (1 Kgs 11:1)—Solomon had begun to turn the Land of Israel, oozing with milk and honey, into a house of bondage; he had begun to produce an Israeli Egypt. This outcome can hardly be called inevitable, but the course of events that makes it plausible—indeed, likely—exemplifies the central dilemma of Judaism. From the perspective of Moses at the Burning Bush, the question "Who am I, that I should go to Pharaoh and that I should take the Children of Israel out of Egypt?" now seems laden with bitter irony (Exod 3:11). If exodus from Egypt ultimately leads Israel back into bondage—only this time under God's anointed in Canaan—then, indeed, why bother?

CONFRONTING THE CENTRAL DILEMMA

The Torah's laws evince awareness of this central dilemma and include explicit legislation apparently aimed at avoiding the slide of a prosperous Israel into systematic servitude. Clearest of these are the restrictions imposed on the king. On the practical level, he is to limit the number of his wives—presumably, for diplomatic marriage—and of his horses—the core of his military power—as well as the overall extent of his amassed wealth (Deut 17:16–17). On the level of loyalties, he must be an Israelite, committed to the same law and covenant as all his brothers, and he must diligently study the law, "To prevent his heart from being lifted up above his brothers, and to prevent him from turning aside from the commandment right or left" (Deut 17:20).

Solomon violates these restrictions systematically. His annual income in gold is registered as 666 talents, so that "silver was thought of as nothing in Solomon's time" (1 Kgs 10:14, 21). His stables count 1,400 chariots and 12,000 cavalry, the horses of which are sourced—no surprise—from Egypt (cf. Deut 17:16). His wives end up numbering 700—in addition to 300 concubines—so that they "turn aside his mind" (1 Kgs 11:3–4). Solomon also violates the covenant and turns to other gods, and though he is not explicitly described as thinking himself above his brothers, this too seems to belong to overall picture.

Comparison of the Deuteronomy laws and the Solomon narrative suggests how the laws are aimed at evading the central dilemma. If the king can be restrained from certain critical forms of self-aggrandizement, then the Solomonic outcome can, apparently, be prevented. Presumably, for such a law-abiding king, his capacity—and indeed, willingness—to oppress his brothers will be decisively curtailed. In contrast with Solomon's son, who inherits only a fragment of his father's throne and power, the laws justify themselves as "in order that his days of rulership may be lengthened, his and his sons in the midst of Israel" (Deut 17:20).

The Torah's efforts to confront the central dilemma emerge in other contexts as well, since Israel can become a house of bondage even without an oppressive king. While the enslavement of one Jew by another is permitted, it is even more carefully delimited than the powers of the king. Such enslavement must not exceed six years, may not be enforced harshly, must allow midterm redemption, and must conclude with a substantial severance package. Most importantly, the alienation from one's patrimonial land—precisely the concern that led the Egyptians to opt in favor of slavery—must itself be limited by the

Jubilee year. Since slavery is closely related to economic difficulties, the law seeks to inhibit each stage of the slippery slope down to financial ruin—from debt, to interest, to selling land, and finally to selling oneself—by carefully leaving at each stage an opening for return to independence and stability of some sort. Debts are cancelled every seven years; the taking of interest is prohibited; family members can, at will, redeem the enslaved as well as sold land; and every fifty years the land-ownership basis of the economy is reset. Now, the situations regulated by these laws come into being only in a land sufficiently productive that someone has the means to beggar another, buy him out, and then buy him outright. Prosperity thus sets the stage for systematic slavery "from the bottom up," as it were, without the need for an exploitative ruler. The legal framework of which Leviticus 25 is the epicenter makes best sense as a preemptive cure for this "decentralized" version of the central dilemma.

This antislavery regime fails in Judea no less spectacularly than the regulations on the king do in Solomon's case. Jeremiah relates how, in the fading years of the kingdom of Judea, King Zedekiah calls on his people to let their Jewish slaves go free—making a covenant to proclaim liberty [*dror*] in the land. This the Judeans indeed do—for a moment. But having set their slaves free, the people, led by the nobility, promptly turn around and recapture these newly freed individuals and take them back into bondage (Jer 34:8–11). Perhaps Zedekiah embarks here on a last-ditch attempt to turn Judea into something better, into something that does not deserve divine wrath or betray the entire thrust of the Exodus. But it does not work. Even the leadership of the king is not enough to turn what has apparently become an Israelite house of bondage into something that deserves to stand. The response is straightforward. Just as you, says God, have failed the covenant from when I took you out of the house of bondage, to proclaim liberty and to limit slavery, so will I proclaim to you "liberty to the sword, to plague, and to famine, and I will make you a horror to all the kingdoms of the land" (Jer 34:17). *Judea delanda est.*

As law clearly suffers severe limitations in confronting the central dilemma, the Torah also works to do so through its rhetoric. Deuteronomy in particular repeatedly sets out to undermine the confidence, pride, and swagger that prosperity can generate, emphasizing the dependence of Israel's freedom and prosperity on the divine covenant:

> When God your lord brings you into the land that he swore to Abraham, Isaac and Jacob to give to you—large and good cities that you did not build, houses full of all good which you did not fill, carven cisterns that you did not excavate, vineyards and olives that you

> did not plant—and you eat and are satisfied. Beware lest you forget God, who brought you out of the land of Egypt, from the house of bondage. (Deut 6:10–12)
>
> God did not crave you and choose you because you are more numerous than other peoples, for indeed you are the least of all the peoples. Rather, because of God's love for you, and because of his keeping the oath that he swore to your ancestors did God take you out with a strong arm and redeem you from the house of bondage, out of the arms of Pharaoh, king of Egypt. (Deut 7:7–8)
>
> Beware lest you forget God your lord, so that you do not keep his commandments, judgments and ordinances which I command you today. Lest—when you eat and be satisfied, build good homes and settle in them, your cattle and flocks increase, you gain much silver and gold and everything of yours increases—your heart grow high and you forget God your lord who brought you out of the land of Egypt from the house of bondage. . . . Lest you say in your heart "My power and the force of my arm have brought me this success." But remember God your lord, for he gives you the power to succeed in order to fulfill the covenant which he swore to your ancestors as if it were today. (Deut 8:11–13, 17–18)

This near-obsessive rhetoric, like the legal restraints, seems ultimately fruitless. Indeed, both God and Moses announce by the end of the book that they know the Jews well enough to predict that they will fail so that the central dilemma overcomes them (Deut 31:16, 29).

One can imagine a spiritual-minded complainer who finds a bitter satisfaction in this whole picture. "Of course the pursuit of prosperity and freedom from oppression, unto themselves, must ultimately fail," such a one might insist. "We must relate to God directly, intimately, lovingly, or the whole business is pointless. Was not establishing that sort of special relationship precisely one of the three central goals of Judaism? If only Israel had remained committed to the covenant, she would have enjoyed all the freedom and prosperity that God continually promised—and that offer still stands." This complaint certainly captures a main thrust of the Pentateuch and seems to summarize the analysis of the central dilemma so far. Combining the goals of leaving slavery and inheriting milk and honey seems impossible, since insisting on freedom leads to poverty while gaining prosperity opens the way to oppression.[30] So the spiritualist offers a way out: if only one can remember the divine origins of both freedom and well-being and perform the covenantal obligations that follow from this recognition, then all will be well.

The king will not become oppressive, bound as he must be by the law, and so too the laws of debt, land, and manumission will prevent society from splitting apart into slave-drivers and slaves. Israel will not forget, glory in its own power, or allow its heart to become "high." Pursuing justice, loving kindness, and walking humbly with her God, Israel will fulfill Micah's prophetic vision, and more besides.

This approach, despite its admittedly solid textual and analytic foundations, nevertheless generates problems in the ends-means relations analogous to those noted above, if higher level and more refined. The covenant-centric view points to the critical position of devotion to the divine, since without it the central dilemma will remain unsolvable. But even if this is completely correct—precisely if it is correct—it leaves the worry that God will enter Israel's consciousness as merely a means to solving these collective contradictions. Such a relationship to God need not be as crass as searching for some divine ATM to dish out rain and fecundity and beat up one's enemies. The problems embodied in the central dilemma cut much deeper into the collective life and soul of the nation, and invoking devotion to God as the only solution to these is hardly so reductive. But on such a view, relationship with God remains a means—the highest means—that is only extrinsically related to one's real goals. If Israel could just enjoy the fruits of freedom and prosperity without worry about the consequences of her own future behavior, there would be no need for all this law, exhortation, and covenant. Confronted with the central dilemma, Israel might choose God—as the least bad option.[31] This, God does not want—though he may be willing to tolerate it. Such grudging devotion may prevent national disaster, but, ultimately, God does not want Israel to conclude that it is simply prudent long-term policy to love and obey him. This would not constitute a true relationship.

Determining whether a collective's relation to God is genuine or mercenary may require a reversal of the test that opens Job. There, the accuser submits for divine consideration the thought that Job's piety is founded on quid pro quo, that as long as the divine goodies keep coming, Job will remain solicitous and obedient. Conversely, should this alleged payment cease, so too will Job's piety. This suspicion turns out to be ill founded: Job retains his devotion even when his blessings—goods, family, health—are systematically revoked. In a sense, one can say that the experience of the Exile proves that Israel can pass a collective version of this test. Even deprived of land, wealth, security, and the Temple as a clear symbol of God's presence and favor, Israel retained a fundamental devotion to her covenant and her God.

But the reverse test applies to the central dilemma. In the hopes of retrieving—and retaining—her land and the blessings of prosperity, security, and freedom that come with independence, Israel might very well turn to God for help, support, and blessing. The question then arises whether this call is fundamentally utilitarian in intent, and the test for this turns on what happens after these hopes are fulfilled. Will leaving bondage and inheriting a land of milk and honey give Israel the opportunity to forget her God, her covenant, and eventually fall prey to the central dilemma? Will the threat of the central dilemma keep Israel in line, while caring for her provider and protector in precisely those terms, and no more? Put differently, if the freedom and prosperity were reliable or even guaranteed, would Israel still feel that something is lacking, something missing? Who would then say, with the sons of Korach: "Like a buck panting for streams of water, so does my life pant for you, Lord. My life thirsts for the Lord, for the living Power. When will I come and see the face of the Lord?" (Ps 42:2–4)

This issue remains, at the present time, open.

HISTORY'S "END" AND TWO CHEERS FOR LIBERAL DEMOCRACY

The Bible assigns to each of the kings of Judah and Israel an overall assessment regarding his impact on the people and the divine covenant. Of Amaziah, for example: "He did what was right in God's eyes, but not like his ancestor David; everything that his father Joash did, so he did" (2 Kgs 14:3), or, more briefly: "He did what was right in God's eyes, but not with a whole heart" (2 Chr 25:2). Some kings are praised—Josiah outstanding among them—while many others are reviled as doing "what was bad in the eyes of God." Kings, the Bible makes clear, rule for a purpose and can therefore be judged as to how well or poorly they further that purpose. The logic of goals enjoys priority over the logic of regimes.

Presumably, the same is true of melekh. Was Prime Minister Levi Eshkol good for the Jews? Independent of the answer—probably a big "yes"—the analytic emphasis needs to fall on the question. The institutions of Jewish communities from Cairo and Poland to Cape Town and Kansas City have always acted through some unstable, often ill-defined combination of oligarchic *gevirim*, rabbinical leadership, and rank-and-file populism. The mixture in this mixed regime form remained fluid, changing with time, place, and circumstance. But this flexibility was possible because there was rarely serious doubt as to the aims of these institutions, the standards by which their success or failure could be judged. For example, R' Meir of Rothenburg concluded a complex thirteenth century legal ruling with this warning and exhortation: "And this would lead to grievous feuds without end. May God bless us that we become one nation and a unified brotherhood. I pray that we manage to survive amidst our enemies."[32]

In short, Judaism takes the goals of collective life—with all their complexities and contradictions—as logically prior to the various political regime forms; these latter can and must be judged and adjusted according to their value for and contribution to the former. The *politeia* is a means, not an end.

In present circumstances, the most urgent such judgment concerns the value, from the Jewish point of view, of contemporary liberal democracy. Is liberal democracy, as Francis Fukuyama famously suggested, the "final form of human government"? Does the combination of liberal capitalism with egalitarian democracy produce a form of political organization in which humanity can be "completely satisfied"?[33] The prima facie case in favor of this judgment enjoys considerable strength, indeed, precisely with reference to the Jewish criteria outlined above. Liberal capitalism has produced in the past two or three centuries fabulously more prosperity—more milk and honey, more ice cream—than mankind has ever before experienced. Billions have been lifted out of starvation, while hundreds of millions live in a comfort and luxury previously unimagined for any but the wealthiest and most powerful of men. What could qualify as a better fulfillment of the imperative to "fill the earth and subdue it" (Gen 1:28)? At the same time, egalitarian democracy, founding the legitimacy of government in the consent of its citizens, grants to every one of them some share, however small, in the decision-making process. There are thus built-in limitations on the enslavement of the citizens of a democracy (though, of course, these limitations have been at times effectively circumvented). More importantly, however, such democracies see themselves as committed to solidifying and improving these limitations over time. In general, citizens of democracies are freer from oppression than any others and can expect to become even more so. What to make of all this, from a Jewish perspective, is probably both the most urgent and important question. But first it is useful to examine an account of liberal democracy arising from the Greek perspective.

Fukuyama's sophisticated case for liberal democracy as the stable point—indeed, end-state—of human social change consists of two branches, one seemingly economic but ultimately scientific-technological, the other based on the what is termed "the desire for recognition." The first branch begins from the accumulative character of modern natural science as it constantly progresses to new understanding and research based on its earlier stages. The application of such rational inquiry—to productive or military technology, to rationalized social practices like accounting and bureaucracy—thus also develops a progressive character. Next, in order to benefit from these ever-renewed practical fruits of rationality, society must acquire flexibility of various kinds: in its markets for goods, services, and labor, in the social structures that support these, and so forth. One of the central lessons of the twentieth century experience with communism is that central planning of the Soviet style simply cannot set and adjust the myriads of prices that represent these ever-changing needs and their interrelations.[34] The core of the flexibility that can handle the dynamism that follows from rationalization is summed up in the classic slogan "*Laissez-faire*!" Only liberal capitalism reliably turns scientific-technological innovation into social benefits. Furthermore, once some countries have adopted this kind of flexible, progressive liberalism, others—through the desire to imitate the benefits of a prosperous lifestyle or merely through the pressure of military competition—have little choice but, sooner or later, to come into line. The market-oriented reform movements of the 1980s in China and the then-Soviet Union stand as the outstanding examples of this tendency toward rational convergence. In short, science and technology lead to liberal capitalism.

The other branch of Fukuyama's case for liberal democracy appeals to the deep human need for recognition. On Alexandre Kojève's influential interpretation of Hegel, which Fukuyama largely follows, human self-consciousness arises when the basic animal power to change the world into something it previously was not comes to focus, not on things in the world, but precisely on this capacity for innovation. Such a creature is no longer an animal that desires this or that object, but a human who desires desire, who wishes to be the object of another's desire. "Thus, in the relationship between man and woman, for example, Desire is human only if the one desires, not the body, but the Desire of the other. . . . Human history is the history of desired desires."[35] Kojève calls such desired desire the desire for recognition and suggests that, taken to its ultimate form, it leads to competition, to a struggle for prestige, and eventually to a duel to the death. Such a duel will determine who deserves the nonnatural nonthing that is human desire and recognition and who will show oneself bound by animal fear for preservation of one's mere creaturely life.[36]

The relationship of domination and submission established here leads to the so-called master-slave dialectic, for which Hegel's *Phenomenology of Spirit* is famous. Even the winner of such a competition will remain dissatisfied as long as one's worth is affirmed and acknowledged only by one who is, in a decisive sense, unworthy. Only the recognition of equals is satisfying, and this—skipping over intermediate historical stages—eventually underpins the rationality of democracy. Mutual recognition of the equal humanity of all is the resolution of the dissatisfactions and contradictions inherent in any other arrangement of humanity, that is, of the "desiring of desire." Democratic societies recognize the equal dignity of each by grounding rule and power not on domination and violence, but on respect for each one's self-legislating autonomy and fully human desire for desire. In short, egalitarian democracy alone can resolve the paradoxes that Kojève diagnoses as following from the moment human self-consciousness transcends its merely animal state.

These two branches of analysis add up to a theory of capital-H History, that is, not of events but of humanity's sequential search for self-understanding. If rationality applied to desire and the nonnatural struggle for recognition leads to democracy and rationality applied to nature and the satisfaction of natural wants leads to liberal capitalism, then the fully rational and self-conscious outcome for humanity seems to be liberal democracy. Democratic capitalism is thus the endpoint of History—that is, it brings the human search for fulfillment and self-understanding to its conclusion—and therefore exerts a powerful pressure on events, history in the ordinary sense. As it becomes increasingly clear that monarchy, theocracy, communism, fascism, and all other regime types create intolerable dissatisfactions of various kinds, dissatisfactions that only liberal democracy can alleviate, the long arc of political actions and historical events will be more and more pressured in the direction of what Kojève calls the "universal and homogenous state." This cosmopolitan but classless and egalitarian world society extends the principles of liberal democracy to all of humanity. Whether the EU or the UN or some other institution forms the kernel of this future universal state, the core issue is not how long it will take to get there—perhaps millennia—since if the analysis is correct, ultimately nothing else will satisfy. The real question, rather, is whether this understanding correctly describes how the institutions of the future really ought to look.

Having argued for liberal democracy, Fukuyama then registers some doubts—from both Right and Left—regarding the ultimate desirability of Kojève's universal and homogeneous state. The Left suspects that any market free enough to count as capitalist will not only inevitably determine economic winners and losers but also thereby decide who will be important and who will be a nobody. If economic liberty thus undermines equal and mutual recognition, liberal democracy cannot be the "fully satisfying" arrangement it purports to be. The Right, on the other hand, suspects that, since some humans will always exhibit more daring, innovation, and plain old success than others, their inevitable desire to be recognized for this—in essence, to be recognized as superior—can neither be fulfilled nor eliminated in the envisioned liberal democratic order. This already shows that liberal democracy cannot be called "fully satisfying" without qualification and will moreover give such individuals the incentive—quite possibly coupled with the ability—to undermine and perhaps overthrow such a liberal democratic order.

Fukuyama's assessment of liberal democracy, both in its general outlines and in many significant details, looks uncannily familiar when viewed through the Judaic lenses of analysis outlined above. Liberal capitalism attracts due to its promise of prosperity, of comfort and luxury. Many lands—from Spain and Canada to Japan and Singapore—have become lands of milk and honey. Crucially, the land of Israel too has once again become a home where one can sit "under one's vine and under one's fig." At the same time, the promise of democracy has lessened the bondage of nation after nation, from Korea and Thailand to Czechia and (perhaps) Kurdistan. Both prosperity and freedom can, in principle, spread to other lands as well.

Judaism cannot see all this as anything but a shower of blessings from God. Indeed, the blessings accruing at the present time to Jewry in particular are utterly unprecedented. It is difficult to overemphasize the degree to which the Jewish people, both in the Land of Israel and in the Diaspora, enjoy greater material prosperity—whether measured in GDP, in charitable giving, or in ice cream consumption—and suffers less enslavement—be it systematic oppression such as in medieval Europe or the USSR, endemic discrimination such as persecuted Alfred Dreyfus, or military menace such as Egypt posed to the State of Israel until 1977—than at any time before in history. One might say that the plan announced at the Burning Bush is coming to fulfillment.

But one might also say that the Jews are reentering the grip of the central dilemma. Humans crave both freedom and prosperity, but over the long term, these two aims can undermine one another; lands oozing milk and honey tend to become houses of bondage. This may be due to the overweening pride and ambition of a ruler, as in the case of Solomon and Rehoboam, or it may come from below, as more and more of the privileged dispose highhandedly of the livelihoods and persons of their servitors, as with the recapturing of the slaves briefly freed under Zedekiah. These two scenarios—which certainly do not exhaust the possibilities—roughly correspond to the complaints against liberal democracy that Fukuyama attributes to the Right and the Left respectively. While some supporters of liberal democracy assume that economic success and political liberty inevitably go together—even reinforcing one another, as in some cases they clearly do—Judaism focuses on longer term trends that suggest deep tensions between them. Once alert to the thought that it may not be possible indefinitely to continue pursuing prosperity while avoiding oppression, one becomes alert to such trends and can find signs of them in many a contemporary news item.

Mosaic rhetoric has already suggested how to confront the central dilemma. One must remember that blessings come from God, that success springs from power that is not fully one's own, and that one must not bow down to the works of one's hands. At a minimum, this requires cultivating virtues like gratitude, modesty, and piety. Better yet, if Israel will keep to its covenantal obligations—especially the systematic brakes on the slippery slope to oppression—then God promises to play rainmaker, both literally and figuratively. The latter-day prophets exhorting on opinion pages and in social media in defense of the poor, the widow, and the stranger and exposing the wrongdoing of the connected and protected—in short, guarding justice and doing righteousness—shoulder their share of Judaism's central burden. But the liberal democrat's central tools—"more rational productivity" and "more egalitarian recognition"—cannot be counted on to bear this burden (useful as they may be in many circumstances). There is no formulaic solution to what depends on the choice of goodness, justice, and life over evil, sin, and death. Even if humanity's capacity for moral choice can become the subject of some sort of history, imagining an end to that history seems meaningless.[37]

Without in any way denigrating such moral diligence and rectitude, it must be admitted that they aim at a resolution that—as crucial and difficult as it may be—is from God's perspective tolerable, but still not ideal. The threat of social dissolution might constrain Israel to the terms of the covenant as she refrains from trampling divine decrees. Israel would thus become comparable to a middling king like Amaziah, doing what was right [*yashar*] in God's eyes, but no more. This would surely be better than setting the stage for corruption, oppression, and eventually exile. Such a roughly stable outcome might be tolerable, but in Israel's eyes would it be ideal? Would freedom from oppression and inheriting a land of milk and honey, unto themselves, genuinely satisfy—with obedience to the Torah accepted as a least bad concession to the inevitable corruptions of the human heart? Or is it possible, precisely because prosperity and freedom are no longer rarities to be craved but commonplaces to be offhandedly appreciated, that other demands will come to the fore? Might life—however wealthy and secure—come to seem limited and unsatisfying without experiencing the indwelling of the divine presence?

Just because God wants Israel—indeed, all of humanity—to want him, does not mean that we in fact do. Determining for ourselves whether we really want a relationship with the Creator that transcends pragmatic obedience remains the biggest challenge raised by the indisputable successes of liberal democracy.

EPILOGUE

How much of the goal-discourse discussed above applies to nations other than Israel? As in so many other fields, also regarding the relation of the Gentiles to the covenant and the central dilemma, the prophets of Israel agree on important basics while disagreeing on specifics. This is not the place for detailed examination, but it seems that the following summary points enjoy broad support. (1) The central dilemma applies to the Gentiles just as much as to the Jews. Egypt is a land of milk and honey, as well as a house of bondage, without reference to the fate of the Jewish people. Other nations can be "vomited out" of their lands in punishment—the Canaanites as the foremost example—and they can also be restored to these homes. Liberal democracy can thus win only two cheers across the board, and not only in the special case of the children of Israel. (2) The Gentiles are not given the Torah, but they can—and should—fulfill a divine covenant. On one version, the covenant in question is the Noahite covenant that includes all humanity and demands of them the minimal regimen of basic justice and piety. On another approach, the experience of the nations—very much including their understanding of Israel's own experiences—will bring the nations to recognize that they must learn from the God of Jacob, and they voluntarily come up to do so: "For out of Zion shall go forth instruction and the word of God from Jerusalem." (3) Ultimately, all will "know God"—as waters cover the sea—but what exactly that means is a matter of disagreement. Surprisingly, the resolution of these disputes may no longer be relegated merely to some obscure, far-off future.

NOTES

1. F. Fukuyama, "The End of History?" *The National Interest* 16 (1989): 3–18; F. Fukuyama, *The End of History and the Last Man* (New York: Free Press, 1992).

2. On the relation of the American Constitution to the classical tradition, especially Polybius, see: G. Chinard, "Polybius and the American Constitution," *Journal of the History of Ideas* 1:1 (1940): 38–58; B. Bailyn, *The Ideological Origins of the American Revolution* (Cambridge: Harvard University Press, 1992), 70–77, especially nn. 15–16; and G. Wood, *The Creation of the American Republic: 1776–1787* (Chapel Hill: University of North Carolina Press, 1998), 197–206.

3. On this lack, see J. Weinstein, "*Yishuv Medinah* and a Rabbinic Alternative to Greek Political Philosophy," *Journal of Jewish Thought & Philosophy* 23 (2015): 165.

4. Exceptions to the general disinterest in *politeia* analysis among Jewish thinkers display the validity of the generalization. Those Jewish thinkers who take up Greek philosophy as a whole—most importantly Maimonides—include also its political aspects; but this is no surprise. Abravanel, in a context apparently independent of such philosophical concerns, objects to kingship while praising a structure explicitly inspired by the then-current constitution of Venice (*Commentary* to Exod 18 and Deut 1). Though his critique flows from a well-rooted biblical and rabbinic debate, the appeal to republican forms and traditions arises from avowedly external influences and experience. Abravanel's engagement with republicanism and the roots of this engagement are addressed in greater depth in R. Kimelman, "Abravanel and the Jewish Republican Ethos," in *Commandment and Community: New Essays in Jewish Legal and Political Philosophy*, (ed. D. Frank; Albany: SUNY Press, 1995), 195–216. Much earlier than these examples, Josephus already declares it among his aims in the *Antiquities* to outline for the Greek-reading public the special characteristics of the Judaic *politeuma* (1.5). For the name of this form of government he elsewhere offers the—admittedly forced—locution *theokratia* (*Against Apion*, 2.165). Josephus's audience, Maimonides' philosophical commitments, and Abravanel's practical experience do not derive their inspiration from biblical or rabbinic texts.

5. Some scholars have claimed to identify a Jewish political tradition. For references and discussion, see Weinstein, "*Yishuv Medinah*," 162.

6. *Politics* 1253a2–3.

7. An important caveat complicates the analytic framework here. Early modern Europe, while reengaging with the political thought and experience of the ancient world, very much included Hebraic thinking together with the Greek and the Latin. Consequently, it can be very difficult to tease out how much contemporary political discourse and terminology owes in its origins and conceptualization—often in a subterranean fashion—to the very Hebrew sources to which it might happen to be applied. Nevertheless, the essentially Greek contribution of searching for—or claiming to have identified—the right, just, or best political order continues to dominate political thought and discourse. It thus remains methodologically prudent to suspend the presumption in favor of political discourse as such when dealing with Jewish materials. Hebraism in early modern political thought—very much including such rabbinic sources as the Babylonian Talmud and Maimonides' Code—is discussed, both in its general outlines and in some particularly salient exemplars, by E. Nelson, *The Hebrew Republic: Jewish Sources and the Transformation of European Political Thought* (Cambridge: Harvard University Press, 2010); G. Schochet,

et al., eds, *Political Hebraism: Judaic Sources in Early Modern Political Thought* (Jerusalem: Shalem Press, 2008); and O. Haivry, *John Selden and the Western Political Tradition* (Cambridge: Cambridge University Press, 2017).

8. TB *Makkot* 23b–24a, discussed further in Weinstein, "*Yishuv Medinah*," 168–74.

9. Ideally, even Greek-origin terms such as "logic," "method," and "ideally" would be suspended as well. The closest Judaic term to "logic" might be "measures by which to infer"—*middot derash* (cf. T *San.* 7.11; *Sifra, Baraita de-R' Ishmael*).

10. The general command to avoid the ways of Egypt appears at Leviticus 18:3.

11. The triptych freedom-prosperity-divinity shows its importance most clearly in the blessings promised for fulfillment of the covenant at Leviticus 26:3–13 and Deuteronomy 28:1–14. For analytic purposes, military success and preeminence are here included under freedom from oppression, while prosperity includes fertility overall, but most especially progeny.

12. A useful overview of the main issues raised by this passage is provided by D. Asheri, et al., *A Commentary on Herodotus Books I–IV* (Oxford: Oxford University Press, 2007), 471–73.

13. Plato, *Republic* book 8. On democracy, see especially 561a–e.

14. The *Republic* details several examples of the psychological stresses that youths experience when their education sends mixed messages: 549c–550b; 553a–554e; 559d–561a; 572c–573b.

15. Aristotle, *Politics* 1279a22–1280a6.

16. *Politics* 1291b30–1293a34.

17. *Politics* 1293b22–1294b35. The earliest reference to such a mixture seems to be in Thucydides' *History* (8.97.2), on which see D. Hahm, "The Mixed Constitution in Greek Thought," in *A Companion to Greek and Roman Political Thought* (ed. R. Balot; Malden: Blackwell, 2009), 178–80.

18. J. Blythe, *Ideal Government and the Mixed Constitution in the Middle Ages* (Princeton: Princeton University Press, 1992), 5.

19. On this Atlantic tradition of republicanism and its limits, as well as its relation to republicanism in Dutch, Swiss, and other continental contexts, see the contributions of J. Pocock and of J. Soll in *Limits of the Atlantic Republican Tradition* (ed. J. Soll), *Republics of Letters* 2:1 (2010).

20. Perhaps there exist tropical exotics—such as the durian or the cupuaçu—that can be both sweet and fatty-rich. Such fruits were, of course, unknown in the ancient and classical Near East and Mediterranean.

21. The mixing of plant and animal species in planting, plowing, weaving, and breeding is prohibited at Leviticus 19:19 and Deuteronomy 22:9–11.

22. Note that "the blessing of Abraham" that Isaac gives Jacob intentionally (Gen 28:3–4) concerns only land and progeny, not power, while the stolen blessing intended for Esau includes prosperity as well as dominion—but not the Land (27:28–29).

23. *'amitekha* (Lev 19:15, 17), *re'akha* (Exod 20:14; Lev 19:18), *'ahikha* (Lev 19:17; Deut 17:15). Many passages demand concern for and protection of the stranger, e.g., Exodus 22:20, Leviticus 19:33–34, and Deuteronomy 10:19.

24. The importance of priest-warrior coalitions in the Bible's depiction of Jewish rulership is deserving of separate study. In particular, it is no coincidence that Aaron's wife, Elisheva bat Aminadav, is sister to the prince of the tribe of Judah.

25. Of course Moses takes their refusal to negotiate as unjustified by their complaint, invoking instead a different—perhaps procedural—standard. Perhaps the claim against Moses's leadership is well taken, but that is not, unto itself, grounds for refusing to meet with him—given that the Reuvenites have no claim of personal harm or misconduct.

26. Among the Greeks, Plato, Aristotle, and a Hippocratic author all associated Asia—especially Egypt and Phoenicia—with a preference for prosperity and easy living over the rigors of military struggle and fighting for one's independence. To the degree that they sought to explain this, they fingered the mostly stable climate of this region, in comparison with unpredictable Europe: *Republic* 436a; *Politics* 1327b23–32; *Airs, Waters, and Places*, 16.

27. The Greeks offer analyses that might turn out to be logically equivalent to the central dilemma, but the terms in which they would need to be couched are far less direct than those of the Jewish tradition.

28. TB *Sanhedrin* 20b.

29. Hubris in a technical, Aristotelian sense—displaying one's superiority for the pleasure of so doing and humiliating others—is seen as especially the flaw of privileged youth. See Aristotle, *Rhetoric* 1387b23–29, and the discussion in N. Fisher, *Hybris* (Warminster: Aris and Philips, 1992), 493–98. A broader sense for the term—one which raises intriguing parallels to the present study—is defended by D. Cairns, "Hybris, Dishonour, and Thinking Big," *Journal of Hellenic Studies* 116 (1996): 1–32.

30. An example of accepting poverty as the price of freedom might be found in the Rechavites discussed in Jeremiah 35. Of course the figure of drinking wine here functions as more than just a symbol of wealth. The behavior of the Canaanites silently implied in Genesis 47 shows the same dynamic.

31. Plato raises a similar worry in the *Republic*: Is justice something we desire only for its consequences, or do we want it because it is good in its own right (357b–358a)?

32. *Maharam Reponsa* 108, quoted in J. Lifshitz, *Rabbi Meir of Rothenburg and the Foundation of Jewish Political Thought* (Cambridge: Cambridge University Press, 2016), 95n28.

33. Fukuyama, *End of History*, xi, xxi.

34. Fukuyama, *End of History*, 93–94.

35. A. Kojève, *Introduction to the Reading of Hegel* (New York: Basic, 1969), 6.

36. Kojève's view here seems to conjoin both Greek and Jewish conceptions, but a fuller assessment of this matter is beyond the present scope.

37. Even Nietzsche, who pioneered the possibility of moral history and genealogy, never imagined that such choice could come to an end without thereby constituting the end of humanity.

The "Will of the People" in Antimonarchic Biblical Texts

Baruch Alster

Many biblical texts deal with the Israelite monarchy, but only a few present any sort of theoretical discussion of it. Of these theoretical passages, Deuteronomy 17:14–20 and I Samuel 8 stand out as legal or quasi-legal texts that contain lists of the king's rights and responsibilities. However, both texts are widely interpreted as antimonarchic, critical of kingly excesses. Therefore, many use them to show biblical support for basic democratic values. In this essay, I show that while both texts are indeed critical of the monarchy, they differ on a crucial issue: whether the will of the people is a positive or negative factor.[1]

THE LAW OF THE KING: DEUTERONOMY 17:14–20

The Deuteronomic Code is the only one in the Torah that deals with the distribution of authority among the various political institutions:[2] the judiciary (16:18–20; 17:8–13),[3] kingship (17:14–20), priesthood (18:1–8), and prophethood (18:9–22). The law of the king begins with the establishment of the office:[4]

> 14 When thou art come unto the land which the LORD thy God giveth thee, and shalt possess it, and shalt dwell therein; and shalt say: "I will set a king over me, like all the nations that are round about me"; 15 thou mayest[5] set a king[6] over thee, whom the LORD thy God shall choose; one from among thy brethren shalt thou set king over thee; thou mayest not put a foreigner over thee, one[7] who is not thy brother.

The monarchy is to be established at the people's demand. It is not a requirement, and the Israelites would be within their rights not to demand a king at all.[8] Once they do request one, though, there are limits as to who may be appointed: only "one from among thy brethren"—presumably a male[9] member of the Israelite community—may be chosen. Possibly, God himself must also be consulted: "a king . . . whom the LORD thy God shall choose."[10]

The people's demand for a king is explained by their wish to be "like all the nations that are round about me." In Deuteronomy, this expression carries an extremely negative connotation, as these same nations worship other gods (cf. 6:14 and 13:8). This expression seems to cast a negative light on the entire monarchic endeavor. Not only is a king not required, but it seems that according to Deuteronomy, Israel would be better off without one.

Reading on to the next two verses, we see the legal limitations imposed on the king, which may also be taken as a warning against kingship itself:

> 16 Only he shall not keep many horses,[11] nor cause the people to return to Egypt, to the end that he should add to his horses;[12] forasmuch as the LORD hath said unto you: "Ye shall henceforth return no more that way." 17 Neither shall he take many wives,[13] that his heart turn not away; neither shall he amass silver and gold to excess.[14]

While these interdictions possibly only somewhat limit the king's attainment of wealth,[15] I find it more likely, especially after the negative connotation of v. 14, that they cut directly into his political power. Multiple royal marriages are meant for political and diplomatic alliances,[16] horses for the military,[17] and silver and gold for the kingdom's finances. A king limited in these is one without much power.

Moreover, the only comments positing any specific duty for the king see him as mainly a role model for all Israelites, without even mentioning any political power:

> 18 And it shall be, when he sitteth upon the throne of his kingdom, that he shall write for himself[18] a copy of this law in a book, by[19] the priests the Levites. 19 And it shall be with him, and he shall read therein all the days of his life; that he may learn to fear the LORD his God, to keep all the words of this law and these statutes, to do them; 20 that his heart be not lifted up above his brethren, and that he turn not aside from the commandment, to the right hand, or to the left; to the end that he may prolong his days in his kingdom, he and his children, in the midst of Israel.

The king must copy down the law and obey it, just as every citizen must obey the law. He may not lord it over the citizens because he himself is just that—"one from among thy brethren," duty bound to obey the Torah, the law, just like everyone else. Thus, the conditionality of the law on the one hand and the limitations on the king's power on the other hand show that Deuteronomic law can come to terms with a limited form of monarchy, but would prefer there to be no king at all.[20]

This impression is only strengthened by looking at what is missing from the passage. No stipulations regarding the king's political duties or rights are mentioned in our chapter. This stands in stark contrast to other Ancient Near Eastern monarchies, in which the king had a prominent role in judgment, legislation, warfare, and the cult.[21] In the Deuteronomic law of the king, on the other hand, the king has none of these powers.

THE "MANNER" OF THE KING: I SAMUEL 8

While the law of the king in Deuteronomy is implicitly critical of the monarchy, the parallel passage in Samuel—the so-called manner of the king—is explicitly so. On the one hand, contrary to Deuteronomic law, the rules governing the monarchy in Samuel give the king much power vis-à-vis his subjects. But on the other hand, these rules are imbedded in a narrative that is strikingly clear about its opposition to kingly rule.

When Samuel, prophet and judge, reaches old age, his sons being unworthy to succeed him,[22] the people ask him to appoint a king. The prophet objects, presumably considering the people's request as a personal affront to him, and refers the decision to God.[23] This the answer he receives:

> 7 And the LORD said unto Samuel: "Hearken unto the voice of the people in all that they say unto thee; for they have not rejected thee, but they have rejected me, that I should not be king over them. 8 According to all the works which they have done since the day that I brought them up out of Egypt even unto this day, in that they have forsaken me, and served other gods, so do they also unto thee. 9 Now therefore hearken unto their voice; howbeit thou shalt earnestly forewarn them, and shalt declare unto them the manner of the king that shall reign over them."

God sees this as a rebellion against himself, not against the current leader. Although He goes along with the people's request, he proceeds to command Samuel to warn them of "the manner of the king"—how most kings behave—with the hope that the Israelites rescind their request. Samuel then carries out God's command:

> 10 And Samuel told all the words of the LORD unto the people that asked of him a king. 11 And he said: "This will be the manner of the king that shall reign over you: he will take your sons, and appoint them unto him, for his chariots, and to be his horsemen; and they

> shall run before his chariots. 12 And he will appoint them unto him for captains of thousands, and captains of fifties; and to plow his ground, and to reap his harvest, and to make his instruments of war, and the instruments of his chariots. 13 And he will take your daughters to be perfumers, and to be cooks, and to be bakers. 14 And he will take your fields, and your vineyards, and your oliveyards, even the best of them, and give them to his servants. 15 And he will take the tenth of your seed, and of your vineyards, and give to his officers, and to his servants. 16 And he will take your men-servants, and your maid-servants, and your goodliest young men, and your asses, and put them to his work. 17 He will take the tenth of your flocks; and ye shall be his servants. 18 And ye shall cry out in that day because of your king whom ye shall have chosen you; and the LORD will not answer you in that day."

Taken unto itself, this can be read as the legal rights of the king.[24] Such a ruler may recruit his subjects for military or civilian duty, even for his own personal benefit. He may confiscate their land and bestow it as gifts to whomever he favors. Slaves and animals may be seized for his own use. But even if we consider the king's rights as presented by Samuel as legal, it is obvious in the narrative context that such a king is not God's idea of His chosen ruler.[25] God seems to agree to appoint a monarch mostly as a means to punish the people for their rebellion against him, if they actually go through with their plan of choosing a king. All the more so if the passage is not understood as legal at all, but merely an exaggerated threat—this is what the king will do if you actually make the mistake of anointing one. No law can actually control a corrupt king. And a corrupt king is what the people deserve for forsaking the almost direct rule of God, with the prophet-judge Samuel as more intermediary than ruler, for fallible human rule.[26]

THE WILL OF THE PEOPLE

As both Deuteronomy 17 and I Samuel 8 accept kingship only grudgingly, it stands to reason that these texts would be used as proof of the Bible's support for modern democracy. In Protestant Christianity, according to Eric Nelson, this interpretation of the biblical texts may be seen as accompanying the development of democracy since the late sixteenth century.[27] In Judaism, it may even be older, as the best-known such interpretation may be found in Don Isaac Abravanel's commentary on Samuel, written in 1484,[28] using contemporary Italian models of democracy.[29]

However, I contend that when comparing each biblical passage on its own to the modern notion of democracy, we may discern a stark difference between Deuteronomy and Samuel. While much of the modern concept is based on the people being free to decide on their own how to govern themselves, to set their own policy in matters of state, this is not necessarily the case in the Bible, where monarchy may be frowned upon because it is considered dangerous to the covenant between God and Israel.

That said, Deuteronomy 17 may still be seen as a precursor to modern democracy, but I Samuel 8, a passage that served as a religious basis for early modern republican thinkers, implies a very different worldview. Deuteronomy 17 shows a basic trust in the people, placing the responsibility to uphold the covenant directly on the public's shoulders. It is the people who are responsible for appointing the king, while the monarch is just "one from among thy brethren," enjoined to remain that way and not lord it over his subjects, as he is no more and no less than one of their compatriots.

On the other hand, I Samuel 8 stresses how the people's will directly conflicts with God's and should therefore not be trusted. It is they who ask for the king, and God Himself says that they do so in defiance of Him. They do not appoint the king themselves, but rather turn to their current prophet-leader to do so.[30] Once a king is appointed, he is not expected to take their will into account, and the fact that God accedes to the people's demand is more a punishment than an indication that their request is justified or that their opinion should be taken into account.[31]

This distinction between the two texts holds up even when we look at each of them in its own literary context. Deuteronomy as a whole sees the public as responsible for its leadership, while the book of Samuel sees the leadership as responsible for the people's deeds, as I will now show.[32]

THE CONTEXT OF DEUTERONOMY

The king in Deuteronomy—not only in the passage we have already seen—does not engage in the standard spheres of action common among his Ancient Near Eastern colleagues, namely, judgment, legislation, warfare, and the cult.[33] While the cult is left to the Levite priests[34] and legislation to God Himself,[35] we can see in judgment and warfare that the responsibility falls again on the people.

The Deuteronomic laws governing the judicial system come at the end of chapter 16 and the beginning of chapter 17, right before the law of the king.[36] The people are commanded there to appoint local judges (16:18),[37] just as they are responsible for appointing the king: "Judges and officers shalt thou make thee in all thy gates."[38] The king is not mentioned at all in that passage, nor in any other passage dealing with judges throughout Deuteronomy. In much of the rest of Deuteronomy, justice is carried out by the local "elders."[39]

Regarding warfare, Joshua Berman has shown convincingly that not only is the king restricted in the size of his army through the prohibition on amassing horses (17:16; see above, "The Law of the King"), but he is also totally absent from the Deuteronomic laws governing the military (found mainly in ch. 20).[40] It is the people who go to war, referred to—as in most of Deuteronomy—with a second-person pronoun: "When thou goest forth to battle against thine enemies, and seest horses, and chariots, and a people more than thou, thou shalt not be afraid of them (20:1)."

The functionaries in charge of the actual warfare are the "officers" [*shoterim*].[41] They announce exemptions from battle (vv. 5–8) and appoint the actual commanders [*sarei tseva'ot*; v. 9]. But in Deuteronomy, *shoterim* are mentioned with judges as to be appointed by the people (16:18).[42] So it is the public who is ultimately responsible for going to war, just as it is the public who is referred to as going to war.

This is the case as well in the passages relating to the conquest of Canaan. Take for example Deuteronomy 7:1–5:

> 1 When the LORD thy God shall bring thee into the land whither thou goest to possess it, and shall cast out many nations before thee . . . 2 and when the LORD thy God shall deliver them up before thee, and thou shalt smite them; then thou shalt utterly destroy them; thou shalt make no covenant with them, nor show mercy unto them; 3 neither shalt thou make marriages with them: thy daughter thou shalt not give unto his son, nor his daughter shalt thou take unto thy son. 4 For he will turn away thy son from following me, that they may serve other gods; so will the anger of the LORD be kindled against you, and He will destroy thee quickly.

Note especially vv. 3–4: the referent is the average Israelite man; the responsibility for upholding the covenant is on his proverbial shoulders, so the prohibition on intermarriage with Canaanites is relevant to him. But the same "average Israelite" is referred to throughout the passage, even in the verses dealing with warfare. The nation as a whole must conquer Canaan and uphold the covenant; it is their responsibility, not the king's.

According to Berman, Deuteronomy should be understood from a political perspective as a shift from an exclusionary power strategy to a collective one,[43] a shift he rightly regards as no less than revolutionary. The real power in the regime envisioned by Deuteronomy lies not with any one institution, but in the balance of power between the different positions of leadership (judges, king, priests, and prophets) and ultimately with the divine laws and the entire nation's responsibility in upholding them. It is the entire citizenry—the collective "thou"—who is mandated to appoint both judges and kings. No leader is inherently superior to the average citizen. Although Berman sees the priests as a partial exception to this rule, a case can be made that even they are marginalized in the book.[44] Thus Berman correctly presents the requirement of the king to be "one from among thy brethren" (17:15) as implying "that any Israelite male may be appointed for the task. Lineage is of no concern here, because the only lineage that counts is that the candidate be one who stands in covenant with the Almighty—that is to say, everybody. He need only be a 'brother,' that is, a citizen like everyone else, a term mentioned twice in this verse. Potentially, any citizen may serve as king."[45]

Thus Deuteronomy empowers the general male populace, rather than the king, and places on their shoulders the responsibility for upholding the covenant, including the mandate to appoint leaders—judges and kings—who will help them in their task. This may indeed be seen as a precursor to some ideas pertaining to the modern notion of democracy, even while taking into account the differences between ancient and modern values.

THE CONTEXT OF SAMUEL

The book of Samuel, on the other hand, has a very different attitude toward the people, just as we have already seen in the "manner of the king" in I Samuel 8.[46] That chapter begins the Saul cycle, describing the rise and fall of King Saul, Israel's first king. Saul begins as an unassuming young man who had no desire for power. As he hailed from the relatively insignificant tribe of Benjamin[47] and had no political or military record to speak of, it took time for him to be accepted by the people. He is depicted as being first and foremost God's choice, and only secondarily the people's.[48] After his kingship was fully accepted in chapter 12, he began his fall with two sins, both of which entailed succumbing to public pressure.

Chapters 13–14 discuss the battle of Mikhmas, in which Saul and his son Jonathan rebelled against their Philistine overlords and banished them from the nascent Israelite kingdom. Saul had previously been commanded by the prophet Samuel that when he reaches Gilgal, he must wait seven days for the prophet to come and offer sacrifices before proceeding. In the run-up to the actual fighting in chapter 13, Saul reaches Gilgal, but finds that with each passing day, more and more conscripts desert him:

> 7 Now some of the Hebrews had gone over the Jordan to the land of Gad and Gilead; but as for Saul, he was yet in Gilgal, and all the people followed him trembling. 8 And he tarried seven days, according to the set time that Samuel had appointed; but Samuel came not to Gilgal; and the people were scattered from him.

Feeling the popular pressure to either fight or surrender immediately, Saul buckles and offers the sacrifice himself in preparation for battle, disobeying the prophet's command to wait for him. Samuel arrives immediately afterward, and Saul explains himself by invoking the people:

> 9 And Saul said: "Bring hither to me the burnt-offering and the peace-offerings." And he offered the burnt-offering. 10 And it came to pass that, as soon as he had made an end of offering the burnt-offering, behold, Samuel came; and Saul went out to meet him, that he might salute him. 11 And Samuel said: "What hast thou done?" And Saul said: "Because I saw that the people were scattered from me, and that thou camest not within the days appointed, and that the Philistines assembled themselves together against Michmas; 12 therefore said I: Now will the Philistines come down upon me to Gilgal, and I have not entreated the favour of the LORD; I forced myself therefore, and offered the burnt-offering." 13 And Samuel said to Saul: "Thou hast done foolishly; thou hast not kept the commandment of the LORD thy God, which He commanded thee; for now would the LORD have established thy kingdom upon Israel for ever. 14 But now thy kingdom shall not continue; the LORD hath sought him a man after his own heart, and the LORD hath appointed him to be prince over his people, because thou hast not kept that which the LORD commanded thee."

It is due to his soldiers scattering that Saul disobeys the prophet. Their actions warrant, in the eyes of the narrator, a strong leader who will not be influenced by public pressure.[49]

In the following narrative, Saul's battle against the Amalekites in I Samuel 15, we find Saul again bowing to public pressure. Despite an explicit divine command to destroy not only the Amalekites themselves but also their livestock, Saul killed all except King Agag,[50] but kept the choice animals for sacrifices. The narrator presents this as a mutual deed of Saul and the people:[51]

> 7 And Saul smote the Amalekites, from Havilah as thou goest to Shur, that is over against[52] Egypt. 8 And he took Agag the king of the Amalekites alive, and utterly destroyed all the people with the edge of the sword. 9 But Saul and the people spared Agag, and the best of the sheep, and of the oxen, even the young of the second birth, and the lambs, and all that was good, and would not utterly destroy them; but every thing that was of no account and feeble, that they destroyed utterly.

Saul, too, explains himself to Samuel in this manner:

> 13 And Samuel came to Saul; and Saul said unto him: "Blessed be thou of the LORD; I have performed the commandment of the LORD." 14 And Samuel said: "What meaneth then this bleating of the sheep in mine ears, and the lowing of the oxen which I hear?" 15 And Saul said: "They have brought them from the Amalekites; for the people spared the best of the sheep and of the oxen, to sacrifice unto the LORD thy God; and the rest we have utterly destroyed."

Samuel's subsequent criticism of Saul underscores this point in particular:

> 16 Then Samuel said unto Saul: "Stay, and I will tell thee what the LORD hath said to me this night." And he said unto him: "Say on." 17 And Samuel said: "Though thou be little in thine own sight, art thou not head of the tribes of Israel? And the LORD anointed thee king over Israel; 18 and the LORD sent thee on a journey, and said: Go and utterly destroy the sinners the Amalekites, and fight against them until they be consumed. 19 Wherefore then didst thou not hearken to the voice of the LORD, but didst fly upon the spoil, and didst that which was evil in the sight of the LORD?"

Verse 17 is the key here: "Though thou be little in thine own sight, art thou not head of the tribes of Israel? And the LORD anointed thee king over Israel." You were appointed by God to lead the people and are therefore responsible to him, not to them. They must obey your command to implement God's law, you must not obey their wish to defy it.

Even beyond the Saul cycle, the book of Samuel seems to disregard the will of the people as a force of its own. Although the appointment of King David may be seen as involving the people more than that of Saul,[53] there are other instances where the author or editor shows his disdain for popular opinion. The strongest examples of these are in the story of Absalom's rebellion (II Samuel 15–20).

The story begins with what may look to us moderns as a parody on candidates' campaign promises:

> 1 And it came to pass after this, that Absalom prepared[54] a chariot and horses, and fifty men to run before him. 2 And Absalom used to rise up early, and stand beside the way of the gate; and it was so, that when any man had a suit which should come to the king for judgment, then Absalom called unto him, and said: "Of what city art thou?" And he said: "Thy servant is of one of the tribes of Israel." 3 And Absalom said unto him: "See, thy matters are good and right; but there is no man deputed of the king to hear thee." 4 Absalom said moreover: "Oh that I were made judge in the land, that every man who hath any suit or cause might come unto me, and I would acquit him!"[55] 5 And it was so, that when any man came nigh to prostrate himself before him, he put forth his hand, and took hold of him, and kissed him. 6 And on this manner did Absalom to all Israel that came to the king for judgment; so Absalom stole the hearts of the men of Israel.

Absalom promises to acquit all Israel. The absurdity of such a promise portrays the people as easy prey, believing in the impossible, as long as the aspiring leader pledges to do something in their interest.[56]

Throughout the Absalom story as well—each leader in turn sways public opinion in his own favor: from David to Absalom (15:12–13), back to David (19:10–18), on to Sheba son of Bichri (19:41–20:2), and back to David again (implied at the end of chapter 20). Each leader in turn succeeds in persuading the public that he should lead.[57]

Sometimes it is unclear where the public stands—compare these two verses from the beginning of the rebellion:

> II Sam 15:13: And there came a messenger to David, saying: "The hearts of the men of Israel are after Absalom."

> II Sam 15:23: And all the country wept with a loud voice, as all the people passed over; and as the king passed over the brook Kidron, all the people passed over, toward the way of the wilderness.

In the first verse, "the men of Israel" follow Absalom; in the second, "all the country" follows David.[58] And this is at the same time! Public opinion is so capricious that it cannot be trusted to decide anything on its own, let alone to appoint its own leaders. To turn Winston Churchill on his head, so to speak:[59]

Indeed it may be said that according to Samuel, strong monarchy is the worst form of government, except for all those other forms that have been tried from time to time.[60]

CONCLUSIONS

In conclusion, the claim that Deuteronomy 17 may be understood as proto-democratic may be upheld, in line with the outlook of the book as a whole. I Samuel 8, as much of the rest of that book, on the other hand, while being antimonarchic in principle, still deems kingship preferable to allowing the people to actually participate in decision making.[61]

NOTES

Acknowledgements: I would like to thank Leonard Greenspoon for inviting me to speak at the symposium; and my father, Lewis Alster, for reading a draft of this article and pointing out some necessary corrections.

1. Again, this article focuses on the ways the Bible dealt with this issue from a theoretical perspective. For a historical viewpoint on the people as a political force in Ancient Israel, see Hayim Tadmor, "'The People' and the Kingship in Ancient Israel, With My Many Chariots I Have Gone up the Heights of the Mountains," in *Historical and Literary Studies on Ancient Mesopotamia and Israel* (Jerusalem: Israel Exploration Society, 2011 [article originally published 1968]), 759–84.

2. For basic references, see lists brought by Joshua A. Berman, *Created Equal: How the Bible Broke with Ancient Political Thought* (Oxford: Oxford University Press, 2008), 189n6; Mark O'Brien, "Deuteronomy 16.18–18.22: Meeting the Challenge of Towns and Nations," *Journal for the Study of the Old Testament* 33 (2008): 155–58. In addition, see Amnon Shapira, "'And He Set Judges in the Land Throughout All the . . . Cities of Judah' (II Chr. 19:5): An Expression of the Tendency toward Separation of Powers in Israel," in *Reflections on Jewish Democracy* (ed. B. Porat and A. Ravitzky; Jerusalem: Israel Democracy Institute, 2010), 475–83 [Hebrew]. Shapira deals with the concept of separation of powers, not only with the specific text.

3. Between the law of local judges (Deut 16:18–20) and the law of the higher court (17:8–13), we find a pericope dealing with forbidden worship practices (16:21–17:1) and the judicial procedure for prosecuting idolaters (17:2–7). Although the latter is related to the constitutional law discussed here, the former looks very much out of place, causing many scholars to propose that it originated elsewhere; see discussion by O'Brien, "Deuteronomy 16," 162–64, who himself prefers a synchronic solution.

4. Biblical translations in this article are based on the old JPS edition (1917). My deviations from that translation are noted here in the footnotes.

5. JPS: "thou shalt in any wise set," as KJV. "Mayst" may be found in Koren. Translation here is a matter of interpretation. In my opinion, it is extremely unlikely that appointing a king is considered here a requirement. See below. For sources supporting the JPS-KJV option, see below, n8.

6. JPS: "set him king," as KJV and others. Translation here according to NJPS and Koren.

7. JPS does not have the word "one." Added according to NJPS to parallel the emphatic הוא at the end of the verse.

8. Here I present a reading of Deuteronomy in which I show the monarchy as optional. Cf. sources listed below, n20, and also Christophe Nihan, "Rewriting Kingship in Samuel: 1 Samuel 8 and 12 and the Law of the King (Deuteronomy 17)," *Hebrew Bible and Ancient Israel* 2 (2013): 328–29. Other readings, of course, exist as well. For the opposite approach among academic Bible scholars, see, e.g., Moshe Weinfeld, *Deuteronomy and the Deuteronomic School* (Oxford: Clarendon, 1972), 168–71; Marvin A. Sweeney, *King Josiah of Judah: The Lost Messiah of Israel* (Oxford: Oxford University Press, 2001), esp. 160–63. Both Weinfeld and Sweeney see Deuteronomy as strengthening royal authority without burdening it with any serious limitations. Annabel Herzog brings an interesting twist to this dispute, with her equating the biblical idea of "kingship" with the Greek concept of politics, rather than with a specific, monarchic form of government. If she is correct, that would render much of this debate moot. See her "'A King Like All the Nations': The Building of Politics in the Hebrew Bible," *Trumah* 19 (2009): 15–25. For a history of this dispute in Jewish law, see Gershon German, "Kingship in Israel: Sovereignty for All Generations in Light of the Halakha and the Halakhic Status of the Laws of the Knesset," in *Reflections on Jewish Democracy* (ed. B. Porat and A. Ravitzky; Jerusalem: Israel Democracy Institute, 2010), 65–98. Specifically regarding Talmudic literature, see Yair Lorberbaum, *Subordinated King: Kingship in Classical Jewish Literature* (Ramat-Gan: Bar-Ilan University Press, 2008), 50–56 [Hebrew].

9. As the rabbis (*Sifre* Deuteronomy, *piska* 157 [Hammer trans., 192]) say, commenting on v. 15, "*a king*—but not a queen." Indeed, the only queen in the Bible to rule on her own is Athaliah (2 Kgs 11), described in the text as a usurper in every way possible. See Omer Sergi, "Queenship in Judah Revisited: Athaliah and the Davidic Dynasty in Historical Perspective," in *Tabou et transgressions* (ed. J-M Durand, et al.; Fribourg: Academic, and Göttingen: Vandenhoek & Ruprecht, 2015), 111. On the rarity of queens in the Ancient Near East in general and in Israel in particular, see Sergi, "Queenship," 106–7. For a more accepting view of the possibility of queenship in Ancient Israel, see Carol Smith, "'Queenship' in Israel?: The Cases of Bathsheba, Jezebel, and Athaliah," in *King and Messiah in Israel and the Ancient Near East* (ed. J. Day; Sheffield: Sheffield Academic, 1998), 142–62.

10. God's "choice" here seems to contradict the idea that the appointment of a king is the people's responsibility, to the point where some (e.g., A.D.H. Mayes, *Deuteronomy* [New Century Bible Commentary; London: Marshall, Morgan & Scott, 1979], 271) suggest that the idea is a later interpolation. However, synchronic options to solve this problem definitely exist. The most popular approach in both traditional and modern commentaries is that God really appoints the king, with the people playing a relatively minor role

in the process. This seems to also be the opinion of the author of Samuel, who has God appointing both Saul and David directly, with the people merely ratifying His decision. As I show below in "The Context of Samuel," this makes sense in the antidemocratic context of Samuel. However, other possibilities exist, giving the people more of a say in the matter. According to Nahmanides and Abravanel in their respective commentaries on Deuteronomy, God's "choice" is not a specific king at a specific moment, but rather the general rule at the end of the verse, namely, that God chooses only an Israelite, but not a foreign, king. Another option would be that the people may appoint someone and only then ask God if he is worthy, with God ratifying their decision. See also Herzog ("A King," 19–20), who understands the people as having a pivotal role in the coronations of Saul and David, contra to what I write here and below (The Will of the People).

11. JPS: "multiply horses to himself," as most other translations. Amended here according to NJPS for grammatical considerations. Note the *yiqtol*+inflected *lamed* construct here in all three interdictions, using what Takamitsu Muraoka calls "centripetal *lamedh,*" which has "reflexive nuance." But as this is only nuance, conveyed by an idiom, I prefer translating it as such, and not literally as "to him[self]." See Takamitsu Muraoka, "On the So-Called *Dativus Ethicus* in Hebrew," *Journal of Theological Studies* 29 (1978): 495–98; Paul Joon and Takamitsu Muraoka, *A Grammar of Biblical Hebrew* (Rome: Pontifical Biblical Institute, 2006), 133d, 459. See also Bruce K. Waltke and Michael O'Connor, *An Introduction to Biblical Hebrew Syntax* (Winona Lake: Eisenbrauns, 1990), 11.2.10d, 208–9.

12. JPS: "multiply horses."

13. JPS: "multiply wives to himself." See above, n11.

14. JPS: "greatly multiply to himself silver and gold." Amended here according to NJPS. See above, n11.

15. See Sweeney, *King Josiah,* 159–63.

16. See Patricia Dutcher-Walls, "The Circumscription of the King: Deuteronomy 17:16–17 in Its Ancient Social Context," *Journal of Biblical Literature* 121 (2002): 601–16.

17. See Berman, *Created Equal,* 58.

18. Following the distinction made by Muraoka in "On the So-Called" (see above, n. 11), this specific term does not seem idiomatic, as one may write for someone else as well, not just for oneself.

19. JPS (following KJV): "out of that which is before." Most scholars thus understand the preposition מלפני [*millifnei*] as referring to the book—from the book which is before the priests. However, I follow many others here who understand the preposition as referring to the act of writing. See discussion in Duane L. Christensen, *Word Biblical Commentary: Deuteronomy 1:1–21:9, Revised* (Nashville: Nelson, 2001), 386.

20. See e.g., Jeffrey Tigay, *The JPS Torah Commentary: Deuteronomy* (Philadelphia: JPS, 1996), 166, who calls the Deuteronomic king "an optional figurehead"; Christensen, *Word Biblical Commentary,* 387–88.

21. Bernard M. Levinson, "Kingship in Deuteronomy," *Vetus Testamentum* 51 (2001): 511–34. Levinson refers to the entire book of Deuteronomy, and not only to the law of the king. See below, "The Context of Deuteronomy."

22. Note that the people have a positive role here in rejecting Samuel's unworthy sons, just as they had such a role in rejecting Eli's sons (see 1 Sam 2:12–24). See also discussion on the people's role in the battle of Mikhmas (1 Sam 13–14) below, n. 49. Compare, however, the people's support for Absalom, discussed below, "The Context of Samuel."

23. 1 Samuel 8:1–6.

24. See Talmudic dispute on this matter in *b. Sanhedrin* 20b, which is explicitly connected there to the question whether establishing a monarchy is obligatory (see above, n8; see also Lorberbaum, *Subordinated King*, 67–75). On the debate in biblical scholarship, see survey in Jonathan Kaplan, "1 Samuel 8:11–18 as 'A Mirror for Princes,'" *Journal of Biblical Literature* 131 (2012): 626–29. Kaplan himself (629ff.) compares this passage with Babylonian literature to show how this is a warning against kingly excesses, not a list of a monarch's legal rights. Other scholars use comparative material from other sources to come to the opposite conclusion. See, based on Hittite texts, David T. Tsumura, *The First Book of Samuel* (NICOT; Grand Rapids: Eerdmans, 2007), 254–55. Elsewhere in this article, see also Herzog, "A King," as well as Ben-Barak and Hazony, both discussed below, n25.

25. See Zafrira Ben-Barak, "'The Manner of the King' and 'The Manner of the Kingdom': Basic Factors in the establishment of the Israelite Monarchy in the Light of Canaanite Kingship" (Ph.D. diss., Hebrew University of Jerusalem, 1972), 241–43. According to Ben-Barak, the authority given the king in "the manner of the king" is accepted Canaanite practice, while the goal of the prophet Samuel is to avoid such negative foreign influence. A similar approach, based more on political theory than on Ancient Near Eastern comparisons, may be found in John Mauchline, *1 and 2 Samuel* (New Century Bible; London: Oliphants, 1971), 89–92; see also Yoram Hazony, "The Jewish Origins of the Western Disobedience Tradition," *Azure* 4 (1998): 35–36. For them, "the manner of the king" is the inevitable outcome of the establishment of any centralized state, although, for Hazony, Samuel's warning was actually partially successful, and despite the establishment of the Israelite monarchy, a tradition of limiting his authority was established in Israel. For Herzog ("A King," n8, 24–25), this is an unavoidable feature of any noncharismatic form of government, as in politics the rulers are inherently a power distinct from the people.

26. On the rule of God as ideal here and its Mesopotamian background, see Dale Launderville, "Anti-Monarchical Ideology in Israel in Light of Mesopotamian Parallels," in *Imagery and Imagination in Biblical Literature: Essays in Honor of Aloysius Fitzgerald, F.S.C.* (ed. L. Boadt and M.S. Smith; Washington, DC: Catholic Biblical Association of America, 2001), 119–28. See also Menachem Ratson, *Theocracy and Humanity: The Political and Social Principles in the Thought of R. Abraham Ibn Ezra* (Tel-Aviv: Resling, 2012), 21–44 [Hebrew], who stressed this theme regarding biblical kingship.

27. See Eric Nelson, *The Hebrew Republic* (Cambridge: Harvard University Press, 2010), esp. 26–56.

28. See Isaac Abravanel, *Commentary on the Prophets*, vol. 2: *Samuel* (Hebrew; ed. Y. Shaviv; Jerusalem: Horev, 579), in the colophon to his commentary on the book. Abravanel's stance on monarchy may be found in his commentary to 1 Samuel 8 (95–104 in the Shaviv edition). For an English discussion of his view, see Benzion Netanyahu, *Don Isaac Abravanel: Statesman and Philosopher* (Ithaca: Cornell University Press, 1998 [5th edition]), 173ff.

29. For the influence of contemporary Italian democracy on Abravanel, see Abraham Melamed, *Wisdom's Little Sister: Studies in Medieval and Renaissance Jewish Political Thought* (Boston: Academic Studies Press, 2012), 137–39, 230–33, 274.

30. The idea of God directly appointing the king may actually be based on Deuteronomy. See discussion above, n10.

31. Cf. Lorberbaum, *Subordinated King*, esp. 14 (regarding 1 Sam 8) and 39–44 (regarding Deut 17).

32. This is true especially if one of the texts was written as a response to the other. See Nihan, "Rewriting Kingship," 322–39 (esp. sources cited 326, nn32–35).

33. See for example the reference to Levinson, "Kingship."

34. The king is never mentioned in a cultic function, and the closest thing to such an idea is at the end of the "law of the king," where the monarch must copy "this law . . . before the priests the Levites." In my opinion, this just emphasizes the lack of monarchic authority over the cult—in the mandated interaction between the king and the priests, it is they who are responsible for him to fulfill his duty.

35. As for legislation, Deuteronomy posits that God himself creates the laws, delivering them to the people through Moses. On the significance of the concept of divine legislation vis-à-vis the positions of political power in Deuteronomy 16:18–18:22, see Peter T. Vogt, *Deuteronomic Theology and the Significance of* Torah*: A Reappraisal* (Winona Lake: Eisenbrauns, 2006), 225–26. New laws, if any are to be added at all, are to be similarly handed down from God through later prophets (Deut 18:15–18). In the context of this passage, the comparison with Moses seems to imply that later prophets may convey new laws as directed by God, Deuteronomy 4:2 and 13:1 notwithstanding. See Peter C. Craigie, *The Book of Deuteronomy* (Grand Rapids: Eerdmans, 1976), 129–30. However, many scholars, as well as most traditional Jewish exegetes, maintain that the verse here does not refer to actual legislation, but at most to ad hoc instructions. See, for example, Richard D. Nelson, *Deuteronomy: A Commentary* (Old Testament Library; Louisville: Westminster John Knox, 2002), 169–70, 235; compare Tigay, *Deuteronomy*, 43–44. In either case, God is the sole legislator. The king, as I have already shown, is admonished to obey the divine laws, but in no way may he be seen as legislating them. But neither do the people legislate; their sole responsibility, just as the king's, is to obey the laws.

36. See above, n3.

37. On the other hand, judges on the higher, national-level court (17:8–13) are not appointed by the people, nor are they responsible to the people. Rather, their appointment

is not mentioned at all in Deuteronomy, and it seems they are part of the Temple hierarchy (as they include Levite priests), while the people are just commanded to obey them. See below, n44.

38. Emphasis here and in all other biblical quotes is mine.

39. See Timothy M. Willis, *The Elders of the City: A Study of the Elders-Laws in Deuteronomy* (Atlanta: SBL, 2001), 308–11. Willis sees the elders-laws as pre-Deuteronomic laws incorporated into Deuteronomy and expanded to convey a national perspective, broader than their supposed original context in a clan-based society.

40. See Berman, *Created Equal,* 57–58, including n22.

41. A priest is also mentioned, in vv. 2–4, but it seems that his role is mainly to give the troops moral and spiritual encouragement. The actual operational issues begin in v. 5, with the introduction of the "officers."

42. Just as when Moses seeks to appoint judges and officers in Deuteronomy 1:9–15, he asks the people to nominate them. Note that elsewhere in the Bible, officers may be subservient to specific rulers, as are the Israelites appointed as enforcers by their Egyptian taskmasters (Exod 5:14) or various officers mentioned in Chronicles (I 27:1; II 19:11; II 26:11; II 34:13).

43. Berman, *Created Equal,* 53–56. He defines an exclusionary power strategy as one that entails monopolization of the sources of power, and a collective power strategy as one where the source of power is a bureaucratic management structure governed by a code of law (54).

44. See my "Deuteronomy: Religious Centralization or Decentralization?" on the TABS website: http://thetorah.com/deuteronomy-religious-centralization-or-decentralization/ (accessed January 9, 2017), in the sections entitled "Limiting the Power of the Levite Priests" and "Secularization or Sacralization?" and sources cited therein. This would entail, of course, marginalizing those aspects of power the priests retain in Deuteronomy, such as sitting on the higher court (see above, n37). Cf. Berman, *Created Equal,* 65–66.

45. Berman, *Created Equal,* 60–61.

46. I should note here that much of critical scholarship sees two literary strands in Samuel, separated by their incompatible attitudes towards kingship. My discussion here shows what I see as a preferable alternative, namely, that Samuel shows a complex view of the monarchy, rather than two simplistic ones. See discussion in V. Philips Long, *The Reign and Rejection of King Saul: The Case for Literary and Theological Coherence* (Atlanta: Scholars, 1989), 176–83.

47. As Saul himself says (1 Sam 9:21), "Am not I a Benjamite, of the smallest of the tribes of Israel? and my family the least of all the families of the tribe of Benjamin?"

48. After Saul's public coronation by Samuel, he still had his opponents (1 Sam 10:27), who were powerful enough to warrant a second such ceremony (1 Sam 11:14–15) after Saul's victory over the Ammonites, in which Samuel reprimands the people for

demanding a king, while reiterating the divine choice of Saul to fill that role (chap. 12). Thus Saul's acceptance by the people is framed by his divine appointment, which is obviously the more significant of the two.

49. In this story, the people have a positive role as well, as they save the hero, Jonathan, from death at the hands of his father King Saul, after the latter had sworn to execute him (1 Sam 14:24ff). See Hezi Cohen, "Jonathan's Lot," in *Studies in Biblical Literature and Jewish Exegesis Presented to Professor Rimon Kasher* (ed. M. Avioz, et al.; Atlanta: SBL, 2013), 110–11 [Hebrew].

50. It is unclear why Saul spared Agag. Obviously, he did not do this for moral or humane reasons, as he did not spare women or children. See Meir Sternberg, *The Poetics of Biblical Narrative* (Bloomington: Indiana University Press, 1985), 490.

51. It is probably more accurate to say that sparing Agag was Saul's initiative and sparing the animals' was the people's. See Yoel Bin-Nun, "'*Masa Agag*': The Sin of Shaul with Amalek," *Megadim* 7 (1989): 61 [Hebrew].

52. JPS: "in front of." Translation here according to KJV, RSV, and Koren.

53. The people's love for David is stressed in and immediately following the Goliath story (1 Sam 18:6–7, 14–16), and his coronations over Judah (2 Sam 2:1–4) and all Israel (2 Sam 5:1–3) were initiated by the people. However, in these cases God's support is taken in the book as a given, and the people's action is seen as an affirmation of the success promised by God (see esp. 1 Sam 18:14–16). Cf. the people's role in the episode of Saul's oath (above, n49).

54. JPS (as most other translations): "prepared him." See grammatical discussion above, n11.

55. JPS, following KJV: "Do him justice." Koren, Douay-Rheims, and RSV all have similar translations. This follows the interpretation common among traditional Jewish exegetes, following the Targum, that Absalom promises to give everyone a fair trial, implying that David does not do so. However, this does not fit with the Hebrew והצדקתיו. Of the eleven appearances of the *hif'il* form of the root צדק in the Bible outside this verse, at least nine definitely mean "to acquit" (Exod 23:7; Deut 25:1; I Kgs 8:32; Isa 5:23, 50:8–9; Ps 82:3; Prov 17:15; Job 27:5; 2 Chr 6:23), the other two (Isa 53:11; Dan 12:3) being ambiguous but not resembling our verse at all. Abravanel explains the verse this way, based on *Avot DeRabbi Natan* (Version B, 45:5), and thus NJPS has "I would see that he got his rights." Most modern scholars interpret the text this way as well. See, e.g., Jan P. Fokkelman, *Narrative Art and Poetry in the Books of Samuel*, volume 1: *King David* (Assen: Van Gorcum, 1981), 167–68.

56. The absurdity here is likely what gave rise to the traditional understanding of the verse, discussed above, n55. However, we of more electionary experience may actually find the parody startlingly true to life.

57. On this story, see Tadmor, "The People," 763–71, who brings a historical perspective on the meaning of "the people" in each situation, but I do not think that this discounts the literary aspect of the term I discuss here.

58. See also the ambivalent and/or contradictory uses of "all the people," "the people of Israel," etc., in 17:3, 18:1–7, 18:16, 19:3–9, 20:15–22.

59. See Richard Langworth, ed., *Churchill by Himself: The Definitive Collection of Quotations* (Philadelphia: Public Affairs, 2008), 574: "Indeed it has been said that democracy is the worst form. . . ."

60. On this point I agree with David Janzen, *The Necessary King: A Postcolonial Reading of the Deuteronomistic Portrait of the Monarchy* (Sheffield: Sheffield Phoenix, 2013). However, Janzen reads Deuteronomy in light of Samuel, as part of the Deuteronomistic History (Deuteronomy-Kings) rather than as two separate entities, and as positive in general towards the monarchy as a means of upholding the covenant in the face of a disobedient nation. In addition, he does not stress enough the idea that in an ideal world, even for the pro-Davidic book of Samuel, monarchy would theoretically detract from the covenant.

61. I deliberately refrain here from discussing above the historical implications of my thesis, as I think that there are many possibilities to understand the relationship between the two biblical books, and determining the correct one is beyond the scope of this article. Nihan, "Rewriting, Kingship," 338–39) sees Samuel as rejecting Deuteronomy as being too utopian. However, one may just as easily claim that it is Deuteronomy that rejects Samuel as dangerously allowing evil tyrants to ascend the throne; or, alternatively, that the two books do not actually refer to each other. Thus, the reconstruction of this part of Israelite intellectual history cannot rely on their political differences alone.

The Democratic Principle Underlying Jewish Law: Moving Beyond Whether It Is So to How and Why It Is So

David Brodsky

INTRODUCTION

This essay will look at several aspects of democracy and Judaism. First, I shall trace some of the political theory that I deem to be native to the Bible, showing that it has much in common with Jean-Jacques Rousseau's theory of the social contract. Second, I shall demonstrate that it is not a modern imposition to read Rousseau into the text. Indeed, Rousseau himself acknowledges that he owes much of this theory to the Bible. Be that as it may, one could argue that the rabbis of the Talmudic period would not have thought to read the Bible in this Rousseauian way. Nevertheless, I shall show that the rabbis very much read the Torah as a social contract a la Rousseau.[1]

Furthermore, we shall see that the rabbis advocated rule by the majority —as is well known by scholars of rabbinic literature. In the second part of the essay, I shall demonstrate that this seemingly rabbinic democratic principle was not a belief that the majority should get to decide what the laws ought to be, but rather a product of their recognition that the oral system of transmission is inherently flawed and therefore we follow the majority since they are most likely to preserve correctly what the law always already was. Having robbed us of the notion of the rabbis as our democratic heroes in terms of their principle of majority rule, I shall replace it with what I believe to be a more profound principle within liberal democracy expressed by Jürgen Habermas, Robert Goodin, and Michael Morrell, that a healthy democracy needs a citizen body who can see matters from outside of their own perspective and take into consideration the needs of other members of society thereby.[2]

Here I shall show that, whether intentional or not, the give-and-take of the Talmudic *sugya* [i.e., the Talmudic passage, which often is a dialectical explanation of opposing legal positions] inculcates in those who study it precisely this ability to see matters from multiple perspectives, to empathize with the needs of others, and to take those needs into account thereby. In this sense, then, whether or not rabbinic Judaism is truly democratic, the study of rabbinic Judaism, and the Talmud in particular, can be seen as developing precisely the kind of citizen body that Habermas, Goodin, and Morrell find so essential for democracy. Here, I am not claiming that everyone who studies Talmud will come out an empathetic, democratic citizen, just as not every parent who practices yoga develops a sense of inner peace and henceforth stops screaming at their children. But I am saying that when studied with the proper guidance, Talmudic study can be used to inculcate these crucial skills, and this inculcation may well have been intended by the authors and redactors of the Talmudic *sugya*.[3]

Jacob Neusner has written a seminal book on the Mishnah as political theory, and I would be remiss to ignore it.[4] Neusner is focused on those aspects of the Mishnah that sanction the use of force: "judicial acts of killing, judicial infliction of injury, confiscation of valued property and services, ostracism and exclusion."[5] Neusner sees these as a rabbinic exercise of political power, and therefore he reads the Mishnah as a book of rabbinic political theory. In this essay, I am interested in a related but separate question: Can rabbinic Judaism be described as democratic or promoting democratic values, and, if so, in what ways (with a special focus on Talmud and discourse ethics)?

Neusner takes to task scholars who treat the politics of rabbinic literature as a whole or, even worse, of Judaism as a whole, arguing that each period and each document needs to be read in its own light. Neusner, of course, is correct that scholars should not conflate the various texts, authors, and periods with one another and that scholars need to hear their separate and distinct voices from one another. That said, his warning should not mean that each scholarly article and book can address only a single document. Scholars can write articles about the changing vicissitudes of rabbinic and Jewish perspectives on political topics without falling into the pitfall of assuming that all of the texts share the same opinion or that any Jewish text from any one period can be used as evidence for the attitudes of other Jewish texts and authors from other periods and cultures. Here I hope not to be conflating the sources and their disparate attitudes as I show how select Israelite/Jewish attitudes related to democracy develop and change over time.

THE TORAH AS SOCIAL CONTRACT

The Bible offers mixed messages as to which form of government to prefer. On the one hand, the book of Judges ends with a cautionary tale of chaos and mayhem, which the author explains by stating, "In those days there was no king in Israel. Everyone did what was right in their own eyes" (Judg 21:25), seeming to privilege a monarchical form of government.[6] On the other hand, when the people request a king not long thereafter in the book of Samuel (1 Sam 8; cf. Deut 17:14–20), God is said to see it as a betrayal of him as king, and he has Samuel warn the people with a scathing rebuke of monarchy that the king will take their sons to be warriors and laborers and their daughters to be servants, tax their produce, and ultimately make the people into his slaves, concluding, "And you will cry out on that day from before your king whom you chose for yourselves, but the Lord will not answer you on that day" (1 Sam 8:18).

Whether or not the Bible as a whole can be classified as pro- or antimonarchy, what is clear is that the Torah is set up as a kind of social contract that the people accept upon themselves.[7] Thus, the central scene of the revelation at Sinai constitutes an important transition from the narrative part of the Torah to the legal section, using the story of both the creation and the exodus from Egypt to justify the validity of the legal section that follows. After freeing the children of Israel from slavery in Egypt, God appears before them on Mount Sinai and gives them a set of laws. The first thing God declares is, "I am the Lord your God who took you out of the land of Egypt from the house of slavery" (Exod 20:2). God then goes on to declare that they may have no other gods before him and then to give them a lengthy set of laws, beginning with the Ten Commandments, but then moving on from there to a larger set of civil law. In other words, Exodus 20 establishes God's bona fides as lawgiver on the basis that God was the one who gave the Israelites their freedom in the first place. If laws are inherently impositions on the pure freedom of citizens, then here Exodus 20 is saying that God has the right to infringe on their freedom because God was the one who gave them that freedom in the first place. In fact, the biblical story began a book earlier with God creating the world and the human population along with it, which Exodus 20 conveniently reminds us when we get to the commandment to keep the Sabbath (Exod 20:9–11). God not only gave the people their freedom but their very lives and the world they live in as well. In that sense, the whole story has been building towards this moment to set God up as ultimate lawgiver (and here I am only slightly modifying Rashi's famous opening question and answer in his commentary on the Torah).[8]

Indeed, in the section on "The Legislator" in his book on *The Social Contract* (2:7), Rousseau acknowledged that the ideal lawgiver would be God and that the "Judaic law" establishes God as such.[9] Not only does the Bible set up God as the ultimate lawgiver in a Rousseauian sense, but it also sets up the event at Mount Sinai as a social contract also in the Rousseauian sense (*The*

Social Contract 1:6 "The Social Compact"). Thus, immediately following the giving of the law in Exodus 20–23 on Mount Sinai, where the entire nation was assembled, we are told that "Moses came and told the people all the words of the Lord and all the laws, and all the nation answered with one voice and they said, 'Everything which the Lord has said, we shall do'" (Exod 24:3; cf. Exod 24:7 and Deut 5:27). That is, Exodus makes sure to note that all the people were present and each and every person ratified the law. As Rousseau explains the social compact:

> This sum of forces can be produced only by the combination of many; but the strength and freedom of each man being the chief instruments of his survival, how can he pledge them without doing harm to himself, and without neglecting the concern he owes to himself? This difficulty, applied to my subject, may be expressed in these terms:—
>
> "To find a form of association that may defend and protect with the whole force of the community the person and property of every associate, and by means of which each, joining together with all, may nevertheless obey only himself, and remain as free as before." Such is the fundamental problem of which the social contract provides the solution. . . . These clauses, rightly understood, can be reduced to a single one, namely, the total alienation to the whole community of each associate with all his rights.[10]

Here, of course, Rousseau is interested in the contract between the members of the community, while the Torah is interested in the compact/covenant between the people of Israel and God, as David Novak has rightfully noted.[11] With that important caveat in mind, Rousseau's theory is quite informative. Indeed, modern scholars are not the first to see a social compact in the giving of the law on Mt. Sinai. Rabbinic literature also recognizes people's acceptance of God's laws on Mt. Sinai as a formal social contract (or covenant) that the people were entering. The Babylonian Talmud (*Šabb.* 88a) preserves a particularly fascinating and revealing analysis of this issue:

> "And they stood at the foot of the mountain" (Exod 19:17). Rav Avdimi bar Ḥama bar Ḥasa said, "This teaches that the Holy One Blessed Be He overturned the mountain upon them like a barrel and said to them 'If you receive the Torah, well and good, and, if not, this will be your grave.'"
>
> Rav Aḥa bar Yaakov said, "But then we have here a strong protest against the Torah!"

> Rava said, "Nevertheless, they accepted it again in the time of Ahasuerus, as it is written, 'the Jews fulfilled [*qiyyemu*] and received [*qibbelu*]' (Est 9:27), they fulfilled what they had already received."

When Rav Avdimi interprets the verse "and they stood at the foot [*taḥtit*] of the mountain" (Exod 19:17) quite literally as they stood under [*taḥtit*] the mountain (thus Rashi on Exod 19:17),[12] weaving a creative midrash from it that God took the mountain and held it over their heads (making them literally under it) and threatened them that either they accept the Torah or he would drop the mountain on top of them, Rav Aḥa bar Yaakov immediately realizes the deeper legal problem underlying this ostensibly cute midrash: if so, that would negate the covenant since it would then have been made under duress! In other words, for Rav Aḥa, if we allow Rav Avdimi's midrash to stand, the Torah would not be binding since the compact between God and Israel was originally made under duress, and contracts made under duress are by definition invalid. Rava fails to find a way to redeem the Sinaitic moment for this midrash and ultimately has to find another moment in time when the Torah was ratified by the entire people, albeit a millennium later in the time of Esther and Mordechai.

I would argue that Rava finds this other moment in which the covenant was ratified through a creative reading of the grammar of Esther 9:27. The verse reads "The Jews fulfilled [*qiyyemu*] and received [*ve-qibbelu*] upon themselves and their seed . . . that they should keep these two days according to their writing." Read in the context of the rest of the verse, these opening words are discussing Mordechai and Esther's new laws regarding the observance of the festival of Purim. In that case, however, it should have stated that the Jews "established [*heqimu*]" this new law (in the *hiph'il*) rather than "fulfilled [*qiyyemu*]" it (using the *pi'el*, as the author did). Following the famous midrash on the order of the words *na'aseh ve-nishma'* [we will do and we will hear] in Exod 24:7, many scholars understand Rava's midrash here as similarly deriving from the order of the words *qiyyemu ve-qibbelu*.[13] I would argue, however, that the ungrammaticality of the use of the *pi'el* in this verse is more conducive of Rava's interpretation than merely the perhaps problematic order of the verbs (although these exegetical devices are not mutually exclusive).

For Rava, I would argue, this verse implies a midrashic fulfillment or ratification (*pi'el*: *qiyyemu*) of a preexisting law (the Torah) in addition to these words as read in context, which formulates the establishment (*hiph'il*: *heqimu*) of a new law (the festival of Purim). In this way, he is able to find a verse that will allow Rav Avdimi to keep his midrash while still maintaining the notion that the Torah is binding for Jews in his own day (and had been for many centuries, even if not going all the way back to Mt. Sinai). Here we see what is really at stake for Rava: not that the Torah always was a binding social contract, but that the Torah is a binding social contract for the Jews of his day (and for some time prior). That is, Rava cares that even for Rav Avdimi, the Torah must be a binding social contract in present actuality. Perhaps, following Rav Avdimi, King David was not bound by the Torah, but Rava's own constituents are bound by the Torah (and by him thereby)! This is in keeping with Rava's attitude elsewhere (*b. Mak.* 22b) in which he complains that people stand for the Torah scroll but not for the sage who interprets it, mediating the Torah's meaning thereby! At stake for Rava in defining the authority of the Torah, then, is the authority of the sages of his own day. Of less concern, then, would be determining whether ancient Israelites who long preceded him were technically bound by the Torah.

Notice that I am not arguing that Rava necessarily himself accepted Rav Avdimi's midrash nor that Rava considered this midrash to be the only way that Sinaitic moment could or should be read. Rather, I am arguing that Rava accepted Rav Aḥa's claim that the Torah is a form of a social contract and therefore that it is binding only if it was freely ratified by all the people, following the laws of contracts. Novak, in contrast, seems to read this Talmudic passage as concluding not just for Rav Avdimi, but as a whole, that the covenant at Sinai was forced upon the Israelites.[14] Indeed, Novak seems to consider this rabbinic position—that the Torah was forced upon them at Sinai and that they did not ratify it willingly until the Second Temple period—to be historically accurate, understanding ancient Israelite society to have changed from the time when the Israelites received the Torah at Sinai to when they were under the rule of Ahasuerus.[15] I, on the other hand, read this passage as merely salvaging Rav Avdimi and his midrash, though in the course of it teaching the larger rabbinic principle that a contract is not binding if it was entered into under duress. This principle, I believe, holds true for both the rabbis and, as we have seen, the authors of the Sinaitic story, though the principle comes into conflict with the Sinaitic covenant only if we follow Rav Avdimi's midrash.

Rav Aha's challenge, therefore, stands as theory: the rabbis recognize that the Torah can be binding only if it was accepted as a social contract by the entire people without coercion. It is not enough for the Bible or the rabbis that God, the omnipotent and omniscient, gave the people the law. Rather, both recognize that the law had to be ratified by the people following the norms of contract law. In this way, while neither the Bible nor the rabbis of the

Talmudic period are exactly democratic, they do fit in certain basic ways with democratic theory. In what follows, I shall explore some of those ways, assessing not just if the rabbis are democratic, but also some of the ways in which they fit with various forms of modern democratic theory.

THE PRINCIPLE OF RULE BY THE MAJORITY IN RABBINIC LITERATURE

The Mishnah states quite clearly that the law follows the majority:

> 1:4 And why do they mention the words of Shammai and Hillel for naught [i.e., even when the tradition does not follow them]? To teach future generations that a person should not stand on his words [i.e., be uncompromising], for the fathers of the world [i.e., Shammai and Hillel] did not stand on their words [i.e., they compromised].
>
> 1:5 *And why do they mention the words of the individual along with the majority when the* halakhah *follows only the majority? So that if a court will see the words of the minority, they will [be able to] rely on it.* For a court cannot nullify the words of its fellow court unless it is greater than it in wisdom and number. If it was greater than it in wisdom but not in number, in number but not in wisdom, it cannot nullify its words until it is greater than it in wisdom and number.
>
> 1:6 R. Judah said, "If so, why do they mention the words of the individual along with the majority for naught? So that if a person should say, '*thus I received it* [*kakh ani mequbbal*],' he will say to him 'like the words of So-and-So you heard.'"[16]

Strangely, the Mishnah never tells us *why* it advocates following the majority, mentioning it only in passing to go on to discuss why the minority position is recorded if the law is to follow the majority. It offers two answers to that question: the majority opinion, that the minority opinion is preserved so that a later court of equal or greater number and wisdom can revive the minority position,[17] and a minority opinion, that the minority position is recorded should someone claim that they received this position as the tradition [*kakh ani mequbbal*], we can tell them that it is the minority position and therefore not to be followed (*m. 'Ed.* 1:6). Of course, this latter position is somewhat ironic, since it itself is recorded as the minority position, and therefore by its own rules may not be followed! Nevertheless, in answering "Thus I received it [*kakh ani mequbbal*]," it points to an important aspect of the democratic principle in rabbinic literature (that of oral transmission) to which we shall return shortly when we discuss the story of Akavia b. Mehalalel in Mishnah *ʿEduyyot* 5:6–7.

Following on the notion of majority rule, people often quote the famous story of R. Eliezer and the oven of Akhnai in the Talmud (*B. Meṣiʿa* 59a–b), in which R. Eliezer declares an oven made of pieces that had become impure to be pure if it is taken apart, sand is put in between the parts, and it is put back together again. The majority, in contrast, declare it still impure even after this process. Logic would dictate that R. Eliezer should be correct: destroying and rebuilding a vessel is one way to purify it, as new vessels are automatically clean.[18] Nevertheless, the majority ruled (or recalled the ruling—more on this below) against him. R. Eliezer then offers a series of miraculous proofs to support his position, declaring that if he is correct, may the nearby tree uproot itself, may the water in the canal reverse its path, may the walls of the study hall cave in. Each time, the earthly elements do his bidding to show their support. Each time, however, the rabbis retort that such supernatural phenomena do not constitute legitimate legal evidence, and, indeed, the walls ultimately stop falling, out of respect for R. Joshua, though neither do they right themselves again, out of respect for R. Eliezer.

Finally, R. Eliezer calls on heaven itself to support him, whereupon a voice is heard from heaven declaring that the law is indeed as R. Eliezer had declared. Not to be deterred, however, R. Joshua counters with a verse from the Torah itself, declaring, "It is not in heaven!" In its original biblical context in Deuteronomy 30:11–18, this verse is declaring that the law is not far away, not in heaven or across the sea, that the Israelites should have an excuse should they not follow it. At the hands of R. Joshua, however, the verse is instead brought to declare to heaven itself that the Torah is no longer in heaven for God to determine the law! It is now on earth, and it follows a process: the majority rules. In a later Aramaic addition to the story, God is said to have laughed when he heard R. Joshua's creative use of this verse, declaring: my children have defeated me, my children have defeated me! In fact, in explaining R. Joshua's exegesis of Deuteronomy 30:12 that the Torah is not in heaven anymore, R. Jeremiah offers his own creative exegesis of Exodus 23:2 as the basis for majority rule. Exodus 23:2 states, "You shall not follow the majority in wrongdoing; and you shall not testify concerning a quarrel to take sides, *inclining towards the majority* [alternatively: and you shall not testify concerning a quarrel to incline towards the majority, leading astray]." R. Jeremiah lifts out the last clause of the verse "inclining towards the majority" from its context and completely rereads it thereby as a declaration of the principle of rule by majority, in spite of the fact that, in context, the verse is the continuation of the previous clauses *not* to take sides in a quarrel by inclining towards the majority!

In any case, in popular retellings of the story of the oven of Akhnai, people often end the story there, and, indeed, ended there, the point of the story does seem to be that the rabbinic system is democratic. The story, however, does not end with this declaration. Rather, the Talmud goes on to recount that Rabban Gamaliel, the patriarch, had R. Eliezer excommunicated, which left R. Eliezer's feelings so hurt that one third of the produce of the world was stricken and destroyed by his grief. When Rabban Gamaliel later attempted a voyage across the sea, he was nearly drowned by the raging sea. Later, Rabban Gamaliel's sister, who happened also to be R. Eliezer's wife, would always guard her husband carefully to make sure that he was not afforded the opportunity to fall in supplication to God over his grief from his excommunication. When once, out of piety to give charity, she turned her back on her husband and he fell in supplication to God, she knew instantly that her brother was dead, since she had been taught in her father's home that all the gates of heaven are locked except for the gates of wounded feelings. And with that profound moral lesson, the story comes to an abrupt and final conclusion.[19]

This latter part of the story is intended to show the devastating effects of hurting people's feelings, even when one is in the right, meaning that God will punish even the majority who rule against the minority if they hurt the feelings of that minority. Nevertheless, to make that point, this story does indeed assume that rabbinic law follows the majority, revealing the democratic nature of Rabbinic Judaism. The question for us is, why did the rabbis believe that they should follow the majority? What was their rationale for establishing such a democratic system, and what might that rationale teach us about the nature of their system?

Here the story of Akavia b. Mehalalel in Mishnah *'Eduyyot* 5:6–7 is particularly insightful:

> 5:6 Akavia b. Mehalalel testified about four things.
>
> They said to him, "Akaviah, retract regarding those four things that you used to say and we shall make you the head of the court over all Israel."
>
> He said to them, "Better that I should be called an imbecile all my days than that I should become wicked before the Omnipresent for even one hour, that they should not say, 'he retracted for the sake of the office.'" . . .

> They excommunicated him and he died thus excommunicated, and the court stoned his coffin.
>
> R. Judah said, "God forbid that Akavia was excommunicated! For the [divine] courtyard is not locked before any person among Israel with wisdom and fear of sin such as Akavia b. Mehalalel!" . . .
>
> 5:7 When he was dying, he said to his son, "My son, retract regarding the four things that I used to say."
>
> [His son] said to him, "Then why did you not retract?"
>
> [Akavia] said to him, "I heard it from the majority and they heard it from the majority. I stood [firm] on what I had heard and they stood [firm] on what they had heard. But you heard it from the mouth of an individual and [a different opinion] from the mouths of the majority. It is better to let go of the words of the individual and to embrace the words of the majority."
>
> [His son] said to him, "Father, appoint me as one of your peers."
>
> [Akavia] said to him, "I shall not appoint you."
>
> [His son] said to him, "Have you found a falsehood in me?"
>
> [Akavia] said to him, "No, but your deeds will draw you near and your deeds will draw you away."

Akavia is excommunicated by his colleagues for holding fast to his legal position and refusing to accept the opinion of the majority. Even being offered to be head of the court should he change his position is not enough to sway him, declaring that he would rather be called a fool his entire life than spend even one moment in wickedness. In a surprising and moving deathbed scene, Akavia asks his son not to follow his (Akavia's) ruling, to which his son responds by asking his father why he did not himself follow the law of the majority if that is what he wants his son to do. In one of the more revealing passages of the Mishnah, Akaviah explains, "I heard it from the majority, and they heard it from the majority. I stood by what I heard, and they stood by what they heard. But you have heard it from an individual and [the opposite position] from the majority. It is better to let go of the words of the individual and hold onto the words of the majority." That is, Akavia is not committed to his law so much as to the process.

Indeed, we learn from his statement that the ruling never was his in the first place. It was merely his recollection of what he had received from the previous generation. Here we learn from him the purpose of majority rule: in a culture of oral transmission, where memories can err, the majority is to be trusted to be most likely to remember the tradition correctly. Majority rule in the Mishnah, then, is not democracy in the sense that the majority get to decide the laws that they wish to have. Rather, it is following the majority in having the most likely memory of the law as they inherited it. In this sense, then, the rabbis are far from democratic, or their democratic nature is particular to their self-acknowledged faulty memories.

We should add here, however, that when the rabbis fail to have a received tradition regarding a case, they are then free to use logic to extrapolate from a received tradition to the case at hand, and such an extrapolation would seem to need to be accepted by the majority (see *m. Ker.* 3:7–10 and *m. Yebam.* 8:3). Thus, in the absence of received tradition on a topic, there is a democratic process of sorts that takes place in the rabbinic system. Similarly, we should acknowledge that Mishnah Sanhedrin outlines a system of courts of varying sizes in which the ruling follows the majority of judges.[20]

While these are all definitely very real forms of democratic process within rabbinic Judaism, they are not as prominent in the Mishnah (and even the Talmud) as the oral tradition itself and the democratic system underlying that tradition. The Mishnah in its entirety is an oral tradition transmitted from person to person through the generations. We learn from the story of Akavia b. Mahalalel that that system is democratic primarily if not exclusively because of the problematics of memory. Indeed, the very word *halakhah*, often loosely translated by modern scholars as "Jewish law," literally means a "walking," or, I would argue, a "transmission," and is used in the Mishnah to reference material that has been transmitted orally from teacher to student (e.g., *Ker.* 3:7–10 and *Yebam.* 8:3; although this is the subject of a larger paper I am in the process of writing).

Thus, returning to the story of the oven of Akhnai, we should probably read the conviction in that story to follow the majority as a product of this larger debate around oral transmission and the problematics of memory. Indeed, R. Eliezer is elsewhere said never to have recited any ruling that he had not heard from his predecessors (*t. Yebam.* 3:1), which the authors of the story in the Bavli likely knew and perhaps even had in mind as they crafted the story around this earlier Tannaitic dispute. Thus, if the issue is one of establishing and following systematic rules that address the fallibility of memory in oral transmission, then we can better understand why even though logic dictates that R. Eliezer ought to be right in this particular case (given the laws of purity), and even though God Himself confirmed R. Eliezer to be correct, nevertheless, the rules of oral transmission dictate that the *halakhah*, the official transmission, must follow the majority. Any other rule would be sheer folly in a system so reliant on human memory.

DISCOURSE ETHICS AND THE TALMUDIC *SUGYA*

While I am here disabusing us of our notion of the rabbis as promulgators of democratic values when it comes to their use of the principle of rule by the majority, in other ways rabbinic literature actually comports with democratic theory far more than this might at first imply. In my opinion, the most interesting and fruitful connection between rabbinic literature and democratic theory can be found in deliberative theory, and particularly in Jürgen Habermas's theory of discourse ethics and deliberative democracy, Robert Goodin's theory of the importance of internal-reflective deliberation for democracy, and Michael Morrell's work on the importance of empathy for democracy.[21] In a nutshell, these political theorists argue that democracy works best when people vote and act not just in their own interests but when they do so with the interests of the collective—that is, of other people and other groups, as well. They argue that for democracy to be efficacious, it is helpful if members of the society learn to communicate with one another and to be able to hear and understand the position of the other.

As Goodin explains,

> The democratic aim is to get people to respond empathetically to others in a wide range of differing social situations. Confronting all those diverse others and coming fully to terms with their beliefs and values cannot realistically be done in person in society. But something like that might be done internally, by populating one's imaginary with exemplars rendered vivid by representations into the place of others, and imagining how the choice would look from their perspective, might then reshape our own "overall assessment of the options in turn."[22]

Even as disagreement may continue, democracies are better off when their members can understand one another and even empathize with one another. For Goodin, therefore, this political process begins from within, the ability of the individual members to learn to step out of their own position and internalize the perspective of the other. Thus, for Goodin, "a procedure in which people fail to internalize the perspective of one another qualifies as democratic only in the most mechanical of ways: without properly registering what one another is saying, it will be not an exchange of reasons but merely a count of votes."[23]

Here, I think we can see the Talmudic *sugya* as inculcating precisely these skills. Thus, in a classic type of Talmudic passage, we begin with a dispute in the Mishnah, with the majority holding by one position and a minority holding by the opposite position. The Talmudic *sugya* then begins to flesh out the biblical basis for each position and what each side does with the other's prooftexts. The *sugya* develops essentially as follows:

> Mishnah:
> Rabbi X: Law is A
> Rabbi Y: Law is B (= not A)
> Gemara:
> (1) From where does Rabbi X derive Law A? From Verse 1
> (2) Then what does Rabbi Y do with Verse 1? He uses it to derive Law C.
> (3) From where does Rabbi Y derive Law B? From Verse 2.
> (4) What does Rabbi X do with Verse 2? He uses it for Law D.
> (5) Then from where does Rabbi Y derive Law D? From Verse 3.
> (6) What does Rabbi X do with Verse 3? He needs it for Law E.
> (7) Then from where does Rabbi Y derive Law E? From Verse 4.
> (8) What does Rabbi X do with Verse 4? (He holds that) Verse 4 is not enough to derive Law E on its own, requiring Verse 3 for clarification.[24]

While the uninitiated often expect the *sugya* to proceed until one side has won and the other has lost, that is rarely if ever what this kind of *sugya* sets out to do, nor where it ends. Rather, the goal of this kind of *sugya* is to flesh out the positions of each side, walking the reader/listener through all the same verses and laws back and forth from each of the two perspectives. The end comes not when one side has won and the other lost, but when (in 8 in the sample outline above), one side does not hold by one of the other side's laws or read the other's verse in such a way that each side then makes sense within its own internal system. In other words, the goal of the *sugya* is to inculcate in the adherent the ability to see a complex system of analysis from multiple perspectives and appreciate that each one makes sense within their own system. It trains the person to be able to move in and out of their own perspective and to develop the cognitive skill to be able to do so without fear of losing their own perspective or train of thought. This frees the deliberator to be able to listen fully even as they hold in abeyance their own perspective until their time comes to exposit.

One of the biggest impediments for people in listening to others in debate is that they are so busy holding on to their own perspective to debate effectively that they are unable to listen to the arguments of their opponents. Talmudic study, then, solves this problem by building the cognitive skills to hold multiple positions in mind at the same time, which allows people to listen fully even as they retain their own position in mind.[25] As for the law, especially in a *sugya* that began with a majority and a minority position, the Talmud always already knew that the law followed the majority. Its goal, then, never needed to be to figure out which position won, which in some way frees it to go the next step to helping its reader simply understand all sides in all of their complexity. The conflict of the Talmudic *sugya*, then, is used as a way to sharpen the adherent's cognitive skills. As John Stuart Mill wrote, "Every one who knows history or the human mind is aware, that powerful intellects and strong characters are formed by conflict."[26]

At the same time, the *sugya* is developing the adherent's ability to understand and empathize with the other, for, as Habermas explains, "empathy—the ability to project oneself across cultural distances into alien and at first sight incomprehensible conditions of life, behavioral predispositions, and the interpretive perspectives—is an emotional prerequisite for ideal role-taking, which requires everyone to take the perspective of all others."[27] Or, as Goodin explains, "the process of 'democratic deliberation within' . . . has each of us empathetically projecting ourselves into the place of (ideally) every other. We would then conduct the 'democratic conversation' imaginarily, inside our own heads rather than in any actually discursive forum."[28]

Indeed, the Babylonian Talmud itself posits empathy for the other as Judaism's most essential attribute. Thus, in a famous story, the Talmud teaches that a gentile went before Hillel the Elder with the request that Hillel teach him the entirety of the Torah while standing on one foot (i.e., requesting a brief summary of its most essential points). Hillel responded with the Golden Rule, saying, "That which is hateful to you do not do to your fellow. That is the entire Torah, and the rest is its explanation. Go and learn" (*b. Šabb.* 31a). For Hillel, empathy for the other, an ability to put oneself in the place of the other, is the essence of the Torah, and one must also learn to choose one's actions accordingly (i.e., in a democracy, to vote and to act politically accordingly). Moreover, Hillel declares the rest as its explanation. While this is often incorrectly understood as claiming that the rest is insignificant in comparison (i.e., "the rest is commentary"), I would argue that he is claiming that the rest of the Torah is in service of this main function. In a sense, it is there to train the adherent to practice the empathy that underlies this Golden Rule.

Finally, the last instruction is to "go and learn," to inculcate in oneself this Golden Rule through the practice of that study. In this sense, then, the Talmud may indeed be self-aware of the fact that it is designed to inculcate empathy in those who study it effectively. Indeed, like Hillel in this Talmudic story, even certain late antique nonrabbinic forms of Judaism had already seen the purpose of the commandments to be to develop the moral character of the adherent. Thus, the author of 4 Maccabees has the martyr Eleazar explain the larger philosophical purpose of the commandments to the tyrant Antiochus as the latter was trying to force the former to transgress the law by eating pork:

> Therefore do not suppose that it would be a petty sin if we were to eat defiling food; to transgress the law in matters either small or great is of equal seriousness, for in either case the law is equally despised. You scoff at our philosophy as though living by it were irrational, but it teaches us self-control, so that we master all pleasures and desires, and it also trains us in courage, so that we endure any suffering willingly; it instructs us in justice, so that in all our dealings we act impartially, and it teaches us piety, so that with proper reverence we worship the only living God.[29]

With this late antique Jewish backdrop in which the commandments are seen as serving to develop the moral character of those who keep them, it does not seem a far stretch to imagine that the authors of the Talmud might have similar intentions for their style of inquiry and analysis, though unfortunately they never make this point explicit (at least not to my knowledge).

While the Talmud is not here consciously advocating democracy (though a certain level of democratic practice does underlie it), it is developing precisely the qualities that democracy needs to prosper. As US Supreme Court justice Louis Brandeis argued:

> Those who won our independence believed that the final end of the State was to make men free to develop their faculties, and that, in its government, the deliberative forces should prevail over the arbitrary. They valued liberty both as an end, and as a means. They believed liberty to be the secret of happiness, and courage to be the secret of liberty. They believed that freedom to think as you will and to speak as you think are means indispensable to the discovery and spread of political truth; that, without free speech and assembly, discussion would be futile; that, with them, discussion affords ordinarily adequate protection against the dissemination of noxious doctrine; that the greatest menace to freedom is an inert people; that public discussion is a political duty, and that this should be a fundamental principle of the American government.[30]

To be sure, significant differences exist between these different sources, yet they are all addressing the same basic or related issues from different angles. Fourth Maccabees claims that the commandments train people to control their passion so that they can act more justly toward others in spite of their own personal wants and desires. Hillel in the Talmud claims that the purpose of the commandments is to make one better at treating one's fellow with empathy and thereby appropriately. Goodin is arguing that large democracies require citizen bodies trained to think empathetically, while Brandeis comes at these same issues from the opposite angle, arguing that the goal of democracy is to afford citizens the freedom and the opportunity to develop their character, which in turn reinforces the democracy. While we should not conflate these ancient Jewish sources with these modern thinkers, neither should we ignore how well they situate with one another.

Essential to democracy is healthy deliberation, which in turn requires a population that has been trained in learning how to see matters from more than just their own perspective, how to listen to the other and empathize fully with the perspective(s) of the other even as they may maintain their own perspective. This is essentially the skill set that a complex Talmudic *sugya* like the one above is ingraining in those who study it. As Michael Morrell explains, empathy is essential for healthy deliberation.[31] Goodin and Morrell see poetry, art, and fiction as important modes of teaching people how to imagine themselves in the place of the other. This brings to mind the story of the oven of Akhnai (*b. B. Meṣi'a* 59a–b) described above with its dual themes of democratic process (majority rule) and the paramount importance of not hurting other's feelings. Indeed, in the story of the oven of Akhnai, even democracy, even being in the majority, proves to be no defense for a lack of empathy.

Yet Talmud, I would argue, takes this a step further, beyond Goodin and Morrell, building the cognitive skills that are necessary to be able not just to imagine oneself in someone else's place but also actually to see whole sets of data in someone else's system without losing sight of one's own take on each datum from within one's own system. This allows for a deeper and richer exchange than just the sheer emotional empathy for the other can provide. Of course, as in the story of the oven of Akhnai, empathy is considered a desideratum, but I would argue that at its core, the Babylonian Talmud is attempting to train those who study it to do much more.[32] Thus, while rabbinic Judaism may have embraced the democratic principle for practical rather than idealistic reasons (i.e., as a result of practical concerns regarding the problem of memory in oral transmission), it proves to be committed to developing essential qualities for a healthy democratic citizenship in rather profound ways.

NOTES

Acknowledgements: I would like to thank Sam Brody, Gustavo Hessmann Dalaqua, Lawrence Schiffman, Patricia Tovah Stevens, and Joshua Weinstein for all of their insightful comments and help.

1. David Novak, *The Jewish Social Contract: An Essay in Political Theology* (Princeton: Princeton University Press, 2005), in which he distinguishes between *covenant* and *contract.* Novak explains that Sinai is an eternal covenant, not a finite contract. Novak also underscores the fact that the Sinaitic moment was not a social contract between equals so much as a covenant thrust upon them by God. We shall see, however, that both the Torah and the rabbis underscore the importance of the people's acceptance of this covenant, with the rabbis even accepting that without the uncoerced acceptance of the covenant/contract by the people at some point in history, it would be invalid, as with any other contract. For this reason, while I accept some of Novak's caveats in our ability to use Rousseau to understand the Torah and the rabbinic understanding of the covenant between God and Israel, we shall see that Rousseau's *Social Contract* can still shed much light on how both ancient Israelites and rabbinic Jews understood this covenant.

2. Robert Goodin, *Reflective Democracy* (New York: Oxford University Press, 2003); Robert Goodin, "Democratic Deliberation Within," *Philosophy & Public Affairs* 29 (2000): 81–109; Jürgen Habermas, *Justification and Application: Remarks on Discourse Ethics* (trans. Ciaran Cronin; Cambridge: MIT Press, 1993); Habermas, "Reconciliation Through the Public Use of Reason: Remarks on John Rawls's Political Liberalism," *Journal of Philosophy* 92 (1995): 109–31; Michael Morrell, *Empathy and Democracy: Feeling, Thinking, and Deliberation* (University Park: Penn State University Press, 2010).

3. Here we should acknowledge that many ultra-Orthodox communities today are at times hardly democratic (or particularly empathetic toward the Other), which serves to underscore the point that while the study of Talmud can perhaps be used to develop such empathy and such skills, it need not necessarily do so and that empathy need not necessarily lead to the value of democratic principles. A proper phenomenology of these modern communities and their changing relationship to Late Antique Rabbinic Judaism, however, is beyond the scope of this essay.

4. Jacob Neusner, *Rabbinic Political Theory: Religion and Politics in the Mishnah* (Chicago: University of Chicago Press, 1991).

5. Ibid., 6.

6. Unless otherwise noted, all translations of the Bible are modified from the NRSV.

7. As mentioned in note 1 above, Novak distinguishes the covenant from the social contract. While Novak is correct that the word "contract" is not fully appropriate to the biblical concept, since a contract can be voided at a later date while this covenant is to be

eternal, nonetheless, the concept of Rousseau's "social contract" still applies in too many other ways, as we shall presently see, to warrant abandoning the phrase.

8. Rashi's commentary on Genesis 1:1 begins, "R. Isaac said, 'The Torah ought to have begun with "This month shall be to you . . ." (Exod 12:2), which is the first commandment that Israel were commanded. So why did it begin with "In the beginning"?'" That is, Rashi asks why the Torah begins with nearly a book and a half of stories before it starts to get to the legal section, which he sees as the central purpose of the Torah. In our answers to this question, both Rashi and I see the narrative section as serving the legal section to which it leads. Unless otherwise noted, all translations of rabbinic sources are my own.

9. Rousseau writes:

> In order to discover the rules of association that are most suitable to nations, a superior intelligence would be necessary who could see all the passions of men without experiencing any of them; who would have no affinity with our nature and yet know it thoroughly; whose happiness would not depend on us, and who would nevertheless be quite willing to interest himself in ours; and, lastly, one who, storing up for himself with the progress of time a far-off glory in the future, could labor in one age and enjoy in another. Gods would be necessary to give laws to men. . . . The Jewish law, which still endures, and that of the child of Ishmael, which for ten centuries has ruled half the world, still bear witness today to the great men who dictated them; and while proud philosophy or blind party spirit sees in them nothing but lucky impostors, the true statesman admires in their systems the great and powerful genius which directs durable institutions.

(Jean-Jacques Rousseau, *The Social Contract* 2:7 as translated in Gita May, Robert N. Bellah, David Bromwich, and Conor Cruise O'Brien, *The Social Contract and the First and Second Discourses* [ed. S. Dunn; New Haven: Yale University Press, 2002], 180–83).

10. Rousseau, *The Social Contract* 1:6 (May et al., 163).

11. See notes 1 and 7 above.

12. Alternatively, following the Maharsha and Amram Tropper, Rav Avdimi focused on the preposition (*be-taḥtit*) as literally "in the underside" of the mountain (Maharsha on *b. Šabb.* 88a, s.v. *she-kafah 'aleyhen ha-har ke-gigit*; and Amram Tropper, "A Tale of Two Sinais: On the Reception of the Torah according to bShab 88a," in *Rabbinic Traditions between Palestine and Babylonia* [ed. Ronit Nikolsky and Tal Ilan; Leiden: Brill, 2014], 148).

13. Maharsha on *b. Šabb.* 88a, s.v. *qiyyemu mah she-qibelu kevar*; Tropper, "A Tale of Two Sinais," 149; Novak, *Jewish Social Contract*, 71. Tropper notes that this midrash is found on *b. Šabb.* 88a following our passage. He correctly notes, therefore, that the redactor of this passage likely saw these two exegetical motifs as related. Be that as it may, this does not prove that Rava himself (or whoever was the original author of the statement attributed to him) saw his interpretation as deriving from the order of the words in Esther 9:27.

14. Novak, *Jewish Social Contract*, 65–72.

15. Ibid., 72. In Novak's defense, he bases his position at least in part on Jeremiah (ibid., 65–66, 70–71). Nevertheless, even his reading of Jeremiah seems to me a stretch. Novak reads Jeremiah 31:30–31 as acknowledging that the old covenant was made by force and that God will make a new covenant to replace it. Novak derives this position from the forceful language "my seizing/taking them by the hand [*heḥeziqi be-yadam*]" and "I mastered them [*ve-anokhi ba'alti bam*]" (Jer 31:30–31). I read these verses, however, not as saying that God seized the Israelites and mastered them against their will, but that he took them by the hand, led them out of Egypt, and became their master/lawgiver. In other words, I see no claim here by Jeremiah that this old covenant was made against their will, but merely a claim that the Israelites were not faithful to the God who took them out of Egypt and became their lord. Since they broke that covenant, God will soon make a new one with them. Even if Novak's reading of Jeremiah is correct, Neusner's general methodological critique is applicable: while Novak's position may be true for Jeremiah, that does not make it correct for the authors of the story of the covenant at Sinai nor for the rabbis of the Mishnah and Talmud, including those who produced our passage in *b. Šabb.* 88a.

16. *M. 'Ed.* 1:5.

17. In other words, for the Mishnah, democracy does not require unanimity (I would like to thank Patricia Tovah Stevens for this insight).

18. Mira Balberg, *Purity, Body, and Self in Early Rabbinic Literature* (Berkeley: University of California Press, 2014), 74–95, esp. 80–82.

19. I am here analyzing the full story as found in the Babylonian Talmud with the later Aramaic additions. I am doing so purposely to analyze the story as the Talmud chose to tell it. Embedded within this larger story is an earlier Hebrew story. While that tale does not focus as much on the significance of hurt feelings, it still does not end with the addition of this first Aramaic interpolation into the story, with God exclaiming, "My children have defeated me," as is popular to end the story today, with that conclusion focusing thereby on the triumph of the democratic process over the divine will. Rather, I would argue that the original Hebrew story, as well, is not so much about democracy as about the problematics of oral transmission, although for the sake of time I shall save my analysis of that version of the story for another time. For a longer discussion of this tale and its Hebrew and Aramaic constituent parts, see Jeffrey Rubenstein, *Talmudic Stories: Narrative Art, Composition, and Culture* (Baltimore: Johns Hopkins University Press, 1999), 34–63.

20. On majority rule in rabbinic courts as a central tenet of rabbinic Judaism, see Shimon Shkop, *Sha'arei Yosher, sha'ar* 3.

21. This is not to negate other ways in which the rabbis can be seen as democratic. For some of those, see note 18 above.

22. Goodin, *Reflective Democracy*, 17.

23. Goodin, "Democratic Deliberation Within," 84.

24. Examples of this kind of *sugya* can be found in the Babylonian Talmud in *Ber.* 13a, 50a; *Šabb.* 131b; *b. 'Erub.* 15b; *Pesaḥ.* 28b; *Sukkah* 24b, 43a; *Mo'ed Qaṭ.* 8a; *Yebam.* 8b–9a, 101a–b; *Soṭah* 32b–33a, 44b–45a; *Giṭ.* 21b; *Qidd.* 14b–15a; *Tem.* 7a; and *Nid.* 40a. The passages are too long and complicated to reproduce here. For a detailed analysis of *b. Nid.* 40a and the nature of this kind of passage in the Palestinian and Babylonian Talmuds, see David Brodsky, "From Disagreement to Talmudic Discourse: Progymnasmata and the Evolution of a Rabbinic Genre," in *Rabbinic Traditions between Palestine and Babylonia* (ed. T. Ilan and R. Nikolsky; Leiden: Brill, 2014), 212–26.

25. In a related yet different way, Sarra Lev has also advocated the study of Talmud to promote the development of empathy in the student (Sarra Lev, "Teaching Rabbinics as an Ethical Endeavor and Teaching Ethics as a Rabbinic Endeavor," in *Turn It and Turn It Again: Studies in the Teaching and Learning of Classical Jewish Texts* [ed. Jon A. Levisohn and Susan P. Fendrick; Boston: Academic Studies Press, 2013], 388–414). Her method relies largely on Hans Georg Gadamer's theory of hermeneutics, in which one develops empathy through the encounter with the other in the text. Thus, Lev attempts to teach her students empathy through their encounter with the other that is the Talmudic text. That is, for Lev, it is our distance from the Talmud that makes it useful as a tool for teaching us empathy. While I find this also to be a valid way to use the Talmud to develop empathy, I am here trying to show that the Talmud itself is inherently developing the skills for empathy when it forces the reader to see issues from multiple perspectives in all of their complexity. That is, even for students of the Talmud's own time period, who presumably may not have seen the Talmudic text with its cultural context as foreign, they would still have been forced to develop the skills that underlie empathy through the process of studying Talmud with its complex logical system in which issues are examined from multiple perspectives. While I cannot yet confirm that the redactors of the Talmudic *sugya* intended this effect, it seems inherent to the nature of the study of the text.

26. John Stuart Mill, *The Collected Works of John Stuart Mill, XXV—Newspaper Writings December 1847–July 1873 Part IV* (ed. Ann P. Robson and John M. Robson; Toronto: University of Toronto Press, London: Routledge and Kegan Paul, 1986), 1106.

27. Habermas, *Justification and Application*, 174, as quoted in Morrell, *Empathy and Democracy*, 76–77. See also Habermas, "Reconciliation Through the Public use of Reason," 11, where he states:

> Discourse ethics . . . views the moral point of view as embodied in an intersubjective practice of argumentation which enjoins those involved to an idealizing enlargement of their interpretive perspectives. Discourse ethics rests on the intuition that the application of the principle of universalization, properly understood, calls for a joint process of "ideal role taking." It interprets this idea of G. H. Mead in terms of a pragmatic theory of argumentation. Under the pragmatic presuppositions of an inclusive and noncoercive rational discourse among free and equal participants, everyone is required to take the perspective of everyone else, and thus project herself into the understandings of self

> and world of all others; from this interlocking of perspectives there emerges an ideally extended we-perspective from which all can test in common whether they wish to make a controversial norm the basis of their shared practice; and this should include mutual criticism of the appropriateness of the languages in terms of which situations and needs are interpreted.

28. Goodin, *Reflective Democracy*, 72.

29. 4 Macc 5:19–25 (NRSV).

30. *Whitney v. California*, 274 U.S. 357, 375 (1927).

31. Morrell, *Empathy and Democracy*.

32. On the relationship between the dialectical nature of the composition of the Babylonian Talmud and the importance of not shaming others or hurting their feelings, see Jeffrey Rubenstein, *The Culture of the Babylonian Talmud* (Baltimore: Johns Hopkins University Press, 2003).

Mipnei Darkhei Shalom: The Promotion of Harmonious Relationships in the Mishnah's Social Order

Simcha Fishbane

The Constitution of the United States has a preamble that states that the goal of democracy is to create an environment of tranquility. Judaism is not a democratic religion per se, but includes many aspects that advocate democratic traditions. This paper will examine the principal of *mipnei darkhei shalom* [in the interest of peace] as it manifests itself in the social order of Mishnah. The application of this concept creates an environment of peaceful and mutual respect between all persons irrelevant of their race or religion. This principle was used by the rabbis to modify putative laws sometimes explicitly stated in Mishnaic texts and at other times only implied. The Mishnah presents its reader with ten cases of *mipnei darkhei shalom.* I will first present eight assumptions on which Mishnah is based. These assumptions will be employed to analyze these cases and search out the components that motivate and justify the rabbis' changing of an accepted law. Based upon my conclusions of the analysis of *mipnei darkhei shalom*, I apply the Durkheim school of social theory to our evidence to better understand the social and cultural ideal world of Mishnah and its structure as presented by an early Palestinian rabbinic group.

This essay examines the concept *mipnei darkhei shalom* in Mishnah, which I translate as "in the interest of peace." Although a literal translation would read "because of the paths of peace," the term is popularly understood and used as meaning in the interest of peace. The Mishnah, redacted in the early third century,[1] marks the first appearance in rabbinic literature of the term *mipnei darkhei shalom.*

METHODOLOGICAL CONSIDERATIONS

Scholars such as Jacob Neusner[2] and Jack N. Lightstone[3] as well as myself[4] have written on the nature and the problems of defining the approach to Mishnah in detail. Therefore, I will simply note them here in brief.

1. Mishnah is a highly redacted document. Lightstone[5] describes Mishnah as a "distinct literary oeuvre, authored, not simply compiled, by

some person or persons with their own agenda, outlook, style, purpose, and social provenance." This work, the entire corpus, can be viewed as a self-consistent whole. Thus, Mishnah contains not only authoritative modes of behavior but also its author's message.

2. Mishnah represents the rabbis' view of an ideal Temple-centered society. In this ideal society, the Jerusalem Temple (destroyed in 70 C.E.)[6] and its related institutions stand and occupy the center 130 or so years after the Temple and everything related to it was destroyed.[7] Although there are sections or statements in Mishnah that would be relevant and can be applied to the functioning of a rabbinic post-Temple culture, these appear within the Mishnaic document that represents the Temple society. Therefore it can only be suggested that these statements, even though they are culturally relevant, are focused on the synchronic message of the Mishnah.
3. In a Temple-structured culture, the religious authority is the priest. In the post-Temple era, the rabbis saw themselves as the inheritors of this role, including the authority that it could embrace. The Mishnah often implicitly (and at times explicitly) manifests the importance of the rabbis within an idealized Temple society.[8]
4. The Mishnah, amongst the earliest authoritative rabbinic documents in our possession, offers a synchronic message. It also offers a diachronic view of society, and both these views serve to view its present order as an ideal Temple-focused society. The purpose of this essay is to seek out the message of the redactor concerning *mipnei darkhei shalom* within its constructed Temple society and not to understand or shine light on the actual Palestinian culture and society of the rabbis during the third century.
5. As a rabbinic document with its resolve to create a social structure for the rabbinic Jew, boundaries were created that excluded any outsider, such as gentiles.[9] Thus the focus of Mishnah is on the Jew. The only concern for the outsider is that which affects the life of the Jew but not of the outsider himself. The Mishnah's concern is to protect the rabbinic Jew from various types of threats or dangers, be they economic, religious, or security.
6. Post-Mishnaic, Tannaitic documents, *Tosefta* and *midreshei ha-halakhah* are often considered as statements not utilized by the Mishnah redactor but having parallel authority. This essay takes an alternate view.[10] If we follow the suggestion that Mishnah is a tightly

redacted document, any additional monograph would suggest the redactors had an alternate agenda. An examination of *Tosefta* compiled in the aftermath of Mishnah would suggest a document dependent upon Mishnah but that is not Mishnah. Neusner[11] describes *Tosefta* as a "vine on a trellis. It has no structure of its own but most commonly cites and glosses a passage in Mishnah, not differentiating its forms and wording of sentences from those of the cited passage. . . . The *Tosefta* covers nearly the whole of Mishnah's program but has none of its own." *Tosefta* is not Mishnah and does not necessarily seek to convey the same message as that of the Mishnah's redactor(s). Neusner,[12] in two approaches, offers a greater in-depth understanding of the relationship between Mishnah and *Tosefta*. First, he states:[13] "Pericopae which clearly present a more refined, more subtle, or more complicated picture of the same law as found in Mishnah must be regarded as developments of Mishnah's pericopae and therefore as a commentary generated by Mishnah itself, not by considerations absent in Mishnah." Second, he refers to "autonomous" or "independent" items. He states[14] that "*Tosefta* gives essentially the same principles as Mishnah, but in its own formulation or with its own examples. They are a supplement to Mishnah: The secondary meaning of supplement, i.e., a collection of additional materials relevant to, but not found in, Mishnah will then apply to the autonomous and independent materials." This essay is concerned with Mishnah. Therefore, following Neusner's lead, I will refer to *Tosefta* only when it serves as a commentary or as an exegesis to Mishnah, on individual pericope and not Mishnah as a complete document.[15]

7. The redactor of Mishnah was not always forthcoming regarding clarification of the laws. Laws dependent on Torah passages are conspicuously absent. Statements based on basic principles are ignored, and then subsequently laws that require elucidation are presented. The rabbi-teacher had these answers and had to be petitioned for the explanations. (This will be demonstrated in our discussion below).

MIPNEI DARKHEI SHALOM

The term *shalom* is most commonly translated as "peace." This, however, is only one way it is used, for the term often appears as a way to greet and part from people. It is also explained as meaning completeness, wholeness, health, welfare safety, soundness, tranquility, prosperity, perfection, fullness, rest, harmony or congeniality,[16] the absence of agitation or discord. An additional name for God is Shalom. In Mishnah it is used as peace or something that can be referred to as a harmonious or congenial relationship.

Mipnei darkhei shalom appears in Mishnah fourteen times within five separate *Mishnayot.* In Tractate *M. Shabiit* 4:3 once, *M. Shebit* 5:9 twice, *Tractate Mishnaishnah Gitin* 5:8 eight times, *Mishnah Gitin* 5:9 twice, and in *Tractate Mishnah Sheqalim* 1:3 once. The *Mishanayot* in *Tractate Gitin* presents an overall summary and presentation of the Mishnah's entire occurrences of *Mipnei darkhei shalom*, except for the individual case in *Mishnah Sheqalim.* Therefore we will focus upon tractates *Gitin* and *Sheqalim* but not *Shabiit.*

These *Mishnayot* state:

> *Mishnah Gittin* 5:8[17]
> A. And these rules did they state in the interest of peace:
> I B. A priest reads first, and afterward a Levite, and afterward an Israelite, in the interest of peace.
> II C. They prepare an *erub* [boundary marker] in the house where it was first placed, in the interest of peace.
> III D. A well nearest to the stream is filled first, in the interest of peace.
> IV E. Traps for wild beasts, fowl, and fish are subject to the rules against stealing in the interest of peace.
> F. Yose says, "It is stealing beyond any doubt."
> V G. Something found by a deaf-mute, an idiot, and a minor is subject to the rule against stealing, in the interest of peace.
> H. Yose says, "It is stealing beyond any doubt."
> VI I. A poor man beating the top of an olive tree-
> J. what is under it [the tree] is subject to the rule against stealing, in the interest of peace.
> K. Yose says, "It is stealing beyond any doubt."
> VII L. They do not prevent poor gentiles from collecting produce under the laws of Gleaning [*leket*], the Forgotten Sheaf [*shichikhah*], and the Corner of the Field [*peah*], in the interest of peace.
> 5.9
> VIII A. A women lends a sifter, sieve, handmill, or oven to her neighbor who is suspected of transgressing the law of the Seventh Year,
> B. but she should not winnow or grind wheat with her,
> IX C. The wife of a *haber* lends the wife of an *am haaretz* a sifter and a sieve.

D. She sifts, winnows, grinds, and sifts wheat with her.
E. But once she has poured water into the flour, she may not come near her,
F. for they do not give assistance to transgressors.
G. And all these rules they stated only in the interest of peace.
X H. They give assistance to gentiles in the Seventh year but not Israelite.
XI I. And they inquire after their welfare,
J. in the interest of peace.

Mishnah Sheqalim 1:3

A. On the fifteenth of that same month [*Adar*] they set up money changers' tables in the provinces.
B. On the twenty-fifth [of *Adar*] they set them up in the Temple.
C. Once they were set up in the Temple, they begin to exact pledges [from those who had not paid the tax in specie].
D. From whom do they exact a pledge?
E. Levites, Israelites, proselytes, and freed slaves,
F. But not from women, slaves, and minors.
G. Any minor in whose behalf the father began to pay the shekel does not again cease [to pay].
H. And they do not exact a pledge from priests,
I. For the sake of peace.

As Hebert Basser correctly points out,[18] *mipnei darkhei shalom* refers to the need to establish standards of behavior to avoid conflict in *potentia*. "This rubric offers protocols to avoid undue strife. These protocols override or amend either the intention or the explicit rulings of the Mishnaic rabbis." The issue to be considered is whether the concept of *mipnei darkhei shalom* amends or enhances an existing law. Why, in some cases, does it transform a thing that is permitted into a prohibition, while in others it overrides a rabbinic ruling prohibiting something to then allow it? In my analysis of such cases involving *mipnei darkhei shalom*, I will explore this query.

CASE 1. "A PRIEST READS FIRST, AND AFTERWARD A LEVITE, AND AFTERWARD AN ISRAELITE, IN THE INTEREST OF PEACE."

This ruling is based upon a discussion of reading the *Sefer Torah* discussed in Mishnah Tractate *Megillah* 4:2, 4. These *mishnayot* discuss the number of individuals who are to be invited to read from the Torah (during the prayer service on days that the Torah is read in the synagogue) but no specific category of persons is identified. The *Mishnah Horayot* 3:8, while not specifically referring to *Sefer Torah*, presents the established hierarchy for the Mishnah's world:

A. A priest takes precedence over a Levite, a Levite over an Israelite, an Israelite over a *mamzer* [bastard], a *mamzer* over a *Netin*, a *Netin* over a proselyte, a proselyte over a freed slave.
B. Under what circumstances?
C. When all of them are equivalent.
D. But if the *mamzer* was a disciple of a sage and a high priest was an *am haaretz*, the *mamzer* who is a disciple of a sage takes precedence over a high priest who is an *am haareetz.*

Although not explicitly stated, this division of status discussed in the above Mishnah should also include Torah reading—the educated rabbi would supersede the priest. The rabbis, in this instance, where it is an issue of honor rather than of authority or financial implications, for the sake of harmonious relationships relinquish their prior place of honor.[19] In the Mishnah's perceived ideal Temple society, in which the priest is the religious leader, the priest still enjoyed a place of symbolic honor. The rabbis chose to apply the principle "in the interest of peace" to alter and override an existing ruling. The rabbis, the inheritors of the priests even with this awarded honor, still ruled.

CASE 2. "THEY PREPARE AN *ERUB* IN THE HOUSE WHERE IT WAS FIRST PLACED, IN THE INTEREST OF PEACE."

Tractate Sabbath and *Erubin* both discuss the Torah prohibition against carrying any object from one domain to another on the Sabbath. One scenario regards cases when houses in an urban area were constructed within courtyards (common during late antiquity). In order to permit individuals to carry objects from their houses into the courtyard [*hatzer*] and vice versa, an *erub hatzarot* is created. The rabbinic process requires that all the neighbors place food items in one of the courtyard houses before Shabbat. The *erub hatzarot* thus organizes all these domiciles into a single domain in which carrying is permitted.

There are various options for obtaining these food items. One person from the courtyard can contribute the food, or the other residents can jointly contribute toward the amount of food required to make the *erub hatzarot.* There are instances as discussed in *Mishnah Erubin* 7:11 in which money is donated towards the purchase of food items.

Our paradigm, which discusses *erub hatzarot*, seems to imply that in order to reduce clashes between neighbors, maintain harmonious relationships, and not insult the householder, the *erub hatzarot* should remain in the home of the residence where it was initially placed. I believe there is an additional consideration implied in this instance—the possibility for financial gain on the part of the homeowner where the *erub hatzarot* is assigned. Although the food products belong to everyone in the courtyard, after the Sabbath this individual would have the opportunity to acquire it before the others. As mentioned above, there are also possibilities for the transfer of monies. Although it is no more than a possibility, this consideration would offer greater clarity in understanding why *mipnei darkhei shalom* is a factor in placing the *erub* and amending the law.[20]

CASE 3: "A WELL NEAREST TO THE STREAM IS FILLED FIRST, IN THE INTEREST OF PEACE."

This Mishnah would seem[21] to portray a scenario in which a channel flows from a river alongside a series of fields. The owners of these fields use the channel's water to irrigate their fields. To avoid the possibility of water drying out before the fields are irrigated, the owners dug cisterns at the edge of their fields to collect water from the channel. To avoid conflict between the field owners as to who had first rights to the water from the channel the Mishnah, applying the principle of *mipnei darkhei shalom*, decides who has first entitlement to the water.

The Mishnah chooses to amend a situation that could lead to conflict and strife. There is no halachic ruling that the principle of "in the interest of peace" would be required to override. Rather, this is a financial issue in which the strongest person would win and thereby cause a clash.

CASE 4: "TRAPS FOR WILD BEASTS, FOWL, AND FISH ARE SUBJECT TO THE RULES AGAINST STEALING IN THE INTEREST OF PEACE."

The following three cases (4, 5, and 6) are concerned with the acquisition [*kinyan*] of various objects through different methods. Our case deals with acquisition through one's property or utensils rather than by placing it in one's hand or dragging[22] it with his hand. Mishnah is not explicit in defining the principle of acquisition through the use of an individual's utensil with a receptacle as its base [*beit kibul*].[23] It is implicitly alluded to in *Mishnah Gitin* 8:1, in the sentence "He who threw a writ of divorce to his wife . . . [If he threw it] into her bosom or into her basket she is divorced." The basket makes the acquisition, since it has a *beit kibul* while the trap does not, thus preventing its owner from legally acquiring the catch. The Mishnah employs the principle *of mipnei darkhei shalom* to amend the law of *kinyan* and allow the owner of the trap to keep the prey. The rabbis permit the trap owner to retain his catch and one who takes it is a thief.

CASE 5. "SOMETHING FOUND BY A DEAF-MUTE, AN IDIOT,[24] AND A MINOR IS SUBJECT TO THE RULE AGAINST STEALING, IN THE INTEREST OF PEACE."

Although not stated explicitly in Mishnah, it is based on a principle that anyone identified with these three categories of Jewish persons (deaf-mute, idiot, minor) cannot acquire property. For example, in *Mishnah Baba Metzia* 1:5, discussing an object found by a minor, the Mishnah informs us that such objects are not acquired [*kinyan*] but become the property of the father (after he makes a *kinyan*). These three were unable to own property and to conduct independent business transactions. The reason for this limitation on the deaf-mute [*heresh*], idiot [*shoteh*], and minor [*katan*] is the lack of mental capacity. This understanding was common during the Greco-Roman period by the Jews and gentiles.[25] It is clarified in *Mishnah Arakhin* 1:1 in the discussion of the valuation of different type of individuals, including the use of one's monetary value of his body for determining a pledge amount to the Temple. The Mishnah rules that a *heresh*, *shoteh*, and *katan* may not dedicate such a valuation since they are not mentally competent. The lack of the mental capability for dealing with reality would also exclude the *heresh*, *shoteh*, and *katan* from making a *kinyan* on any object.

The Mishnah amends this law in prohibiting the taking of a found object from these three types of individuals. In this case there is a clear possibility of monetary gain.

CASE 6: "A POOR MAN BEATING THE TOP OF AN OLIVE TREE. WHAT IS UNDER IT [THE TREE] IS SUBJECT TO THE RABBINIC OVERRIDE FORBIDDING OTHERS TO TAKE WHAT HAS FALLEN TO THE GROUND. IN THE INTEREST OF PEACE. YOSE SAYS, IT IS STEALING BEYOND ANY DOUBT."

The Mishnah commentaries explicate this scenario referring to the laws of Gleaning [*leket*], the Forgotten Sheaf [*shikhahah*], and the Corner of the Field [*peah*]—agricultural gifts awarded to a poor[26] person. The second individual claiming the right to the produce is forced to comply with this suggestion, since an individual who is not poor has no right to these products, and if appropriated they would be his if not for the principle of *mipnei darkhei shalom*. Again, this case is an issue of acquisition. The poor person shakes the tree, but since he does not hold the olives in his hand, he does not acquire them. Therefore, if another poor person grasped them first, if not for the case of *mipnei darkhei shalom*, they would belong to him. The Mishnah thus amends a permitted circumstance and prohibits any other individual from acquiring the produce.

I would like to suggest an additional consideration. The gifts offered to the deprived person can be his basic means of sustenance. If guidelines for receiving these assistances are not clearly and well defined, this could lead to brawls and possible damage to property, in our case that of the field's owner. The need for *mipnei darkhei shalom* would therefore go beyond a mere clash between two individuals and could result in financial loss to the owner of the property. The fear of violence from a poor person is implied in *Mishnah Peah* 4:4, which reads, "Peah, they [the poor] do not reap with sickles, and they do not uproot it with spades, lest they strike one another." This violent behavioral pattern found in a destitute individual could also result in physical and material damages.

CASE 7. "THEY DO NOT PREVENT POOR GENTILES FROM COLLECTING PRODUCE UNDER THE LAWS OF GLEANING [*LEKET*], THE FORGOTTEN SHEAF [*SHICHIKHAH*], AND THE CORNER OF THE FIELD [*PEAH*], IN THE INTEREST OF PEACE."

Implied in Mishnah'*s* statement is that a poor gentile is forbidden to receive gifts of produce. As stated above (methodological consideration 5), Mishnah is not interested in the welfare of the gentile but rather in that of the rabbinic Jew and the world of Mishnah.[27] The concern here is not only for the security of the destitute Jew seeking these gifts but also has financial implications. As shown in the above case, the poor can tend toward violence. If the needy gentile could not share in these gifts, that could lead to destruction of property and thus to financial loss both for the poor Jew and for the proprietor of the field. This amended ruling is designed to prevent gentiles from claiming that Jewish law discriminates between Jew and gentile and is thereby intended to reduce conflict. Ultimately, the Jews gain, as it is in their interests to prevent enmity.

CASE 8. "A WOMAN LENDS A SIFTER, SIEVE, HAND MILL, OR OVEN TO HER NEIGHBOR WHO IS SUSPECTED OF TRANSGRESSING THE LAW OF THE SEVENTH [SABBATICAL] YEAR, BUT SHE SHOULD NOT WINNOW OR GRIND WHEAT WITH HER [IN THE INTEREST OF PEACE]."

This statement first appears in *Mishnah Shebiit* 5:9. The Mishnah is discussing a case of a woman who is suspected of not observing the laws of the Sabbatical year and wants to lend an item that can be employed in the transgression of *shebiit* from one who does observes the laws of the Sabbatical year. To clarify: during the seventh year in the Land of Israel, one is prohibited from working the land or enjoying its produce in any fashion, and at a designated time must destroy food in the house from these fields. Our case concerns the cooking utensils, which normally could not be lent, as the receiver, who is suspected of ignoring the laws of the seventh year, might use them with forbidden produce from the Sabbatical year.[28] *Mishnah* 6 and 7 of chapter five state that any utensil employed [during the Sabbatical year] for the purpose of transgression may not be sold. That is permitted only if the item can also be used for a permitted activity. Lending would fall under the same law.

Therefore, our Mishnah would need to override the law as it was considered prohibited to use the utensils. The assistance offered to the suspected woman would benefit her financially. For example, she would not need to buy or rent these items to use them domestically or for her business. In preindustrial rural societies, women played an important economic role in the world of agriculture; they were core economic partners with men. Scott and Tilly[29] correctly argue that women did work and were necessary for the survival of the family unit. Their contribution was primarily in the home but also could include the family fields. This was essential for the family unit whose solidarity provides the basic framework for mutual aid, control, and socialization.[30]

In the ideal world of Mishnah, women were also segregated and assigned specific roles.

One can find in Mishnah at least a partial or limited division of labor between men and women. People resided in close proximity to one another, as demonstrated by the *hatzer*. Closeness gives rise to both great dependencies on each other as well as friction and conflict. Thus, the Mishnah rabbis choose to apply the principle of *mipnei darkhei shalom* to a case that applied to women. They chose to subjugate these tensions by applying the principle of *mipnei darkhei shalom* as a way to override the law that forbade assisting a sinner. Lending a vessel to the suspected woman would be of benefit to her financially since then she did not need to purchase a new one. The point of *mipnei darkhei shalom* here is to avoid conflict caused by the usual strict application of laws.

CASE 9. "THE WIFE OF A *HABER* LENDS THE WIFE OF AN *AM HARES* [SUSPECTED OF NOT KEEPING THE LAWS OF PURITY] A SIFTER AND A SIEVE. SHE MAY SIFT WINNOW, GRIND, AND SIFT WHEAT WITH HER. NEVERTHELESS, ONCE SHE HAS POURED WATER INTO THE FLOUR [ENABLING THE DOUGH TO CONTACT IMPURITY], SHE MAY NOT COME NEAR HER, FOR THEY DO NOT GIVE ASSISTANCE TO TRANSGRESSORS. AND ALL THESE RULES THEY STATED ONLY IN THE "INTEREST OF PEACE."

Since both Mishnah cases discuss women, the consequences of their society's structure and assisting a potential sinner, the rabbi has grouped cases 8 and 9 together. Case 9 works on the same principle as 8 but is concerned with the violation of the laws of tithes and ritual purity [*tuma*] rather than the *haber*.[31] As in 8, there are financial results from the cooperation of both women. In order to permit realization of Mishnah's view, it was necessary to override the law. Mishnah identifies two status levels of individuals, the *haber* who is meticulous in the observance of Sabbatical purity laws, and the *am haaretz* [uneducated in Torah and rabbinical law] who is distrusted. There should be limited interaction between these different classes of women (as specified in *Mishnah Demai* 6:7 and 2:3), since the Mishnah is concerned that the wife of a *haber* would become ritually impure or eat from foods not tithed. Even so, in the interest of peace, the Mishnah overrides the law and offers restricted assistance from the wife of the *haber* to the wife of the *am haaretz* up to the point where the *tuma* becomes an actual danger and not only a concern.[32]

CASE 10: "THEY GIVE ALLOW (REAL) ASSISTANCE TO GENTILES IN THE SEVENTH YEAR BUT NOT ISRAELITES [IN THE INTEREST OF PEACE]."

This Mishnah first appears in *Shebiit* 4:3 then in 5:9. Later it is presented in *Gitin* 5:9. The opening of the *Mishnah* (in *Shebiit* 4:3) reads:

> During the Sabbatical year they [Jews] lease from gentiles fields newly ploughed [during that year for the purpose of cultivating them during the following year,] but [they do not (lease) from an Israelite a field which he has plowed during the Sabbatical year, in violation of the law].

This opening is not repeated in the other two Mishnaic citations. It is clear throughout the entire Mishnah that the focus is upon the Jew and not the gentile. The gentile's role is to assist the Jew to better function in his world of Mishnah.

This case implies that even though the Land of Israel is holy and should not be worked by either Jew or gentile on the Sabbatical year,[33] one cannot prohibit the gentile from working the land. Thus, the Jew, if this were the only consideration, should not encourage the gentile to work the land aside from the principle the rabbis applied of *mipnei darkhei shalom.* By maintaining a harmonious relationship with the gentile, the Jew will receive financial gain, by having a plowed field in the eighth year ready to plant, in addition to the security of friendship.

CASE 11: "AND THEY PERMIT INQUIRING AFTER THEIR [THE GENTILE'S] WELFARE, IN THE INTEREST OF PEACE."

This statement as the case above is first found in *Mishnah Shabiit* 4:3, then copied to 5:9. An examination of Mishnah will demonstrate that there is no discussion concerning a prohibition to greet pagan gentiles even on their festivals, when Mishnah prohibits various kinds of interaction with them. The Mishnah's concern is that any interface with the pagan gentiles during their religious festivals would encourage and enhance their practice of idol worship. There is no reference in Mishnah to any type of prohibition regarding asking after their welfare. To clarify the issue I turn to *Tosefta*[34] in *Abodah Zarah* 1:2 discussing pagan festivals, which reads, "nor should one ask after their welfare. . . . But if one happened to come across him in a routine way, he asks after his welfare with all due respect. They permit inquiring after the welfare of the gentiles on their festivals for the sake of peace."

I choose to view this *Tosefta* under the category of Mishnah clarification or commentary rather than an autonomous *Tosefta.* Two issues are elucidated: first, that Mishnah is concerned with the different occasions when the pagan holiday was celebrated. Other than on these times (when it would be prohibited), it was permitted to greet the gentile in a specific fashion. Second, the *Tosefta* clarifies that if not for the principle "for the sake of peace," it would be prohibited to ask after the well-being of the gentile on their holiday. This is demonstrated in the language of *Tosefta*, identical to that of Mishnah, except that *Tosefta* adds the words "on their festival."

In the above case, the motivation for assisting the gentile is economic. In our case, I suggest that it is primarily a security issue as in case 7 concerning

Peah, although financial loss is also conceivable. Religious holiday gatherings can be a time of incitement to violence and the destruction of property. The Mishnah is interested in the Jew and his welfare, not in the gentiles. Thus, we need to look at these texts with only the rabbinic Jews' concerns in mind. If offering greetings on the pagan festival will offer greater security to the Jewish community, their physical well-being, and the protection of their property, one would seek to override the prohibitions.

Cases 10 and 11 are parallel in structure as are cases 8 and 9. Cases 8 and 10 override a law related to *shabiit*. Cases 9 and 11 are not related to *shabiit* but override a prohibition connected to the status of the person in the previous case, 9, which relates to women, who appear in 8, and 11 relates to the gentile, who appears in 10.

CASE 12: "AND THEY DO NOT EXACT A PLEDGE FROM PRIESTS, FOR THE SAKE OF PEACE."

The Mishnah in *Gitin* omits the case in *Mishna Sheqalim* 1:4. Ancient custom saw in Exodus 30:12–16 a basis for all Israelites during the Temple period to give a tax of a half shekel annually for community sacrifices. If a person could not pay the tax, the rabbis required the giving of a security pledge for the payment of the half-shekel tax. Priest also were required to contribute and if they did not, they too, strictly speaking, were subject to giving a security pledge. The authorities felt it necessary, as Samuel Safrai[35] explains, to maintain the internal solidarity of the community by exempting them from giving security although they were expected to pay. Safrai,[36] based upon *Tosefta Menahot* 13:18–19 and *Zebahim* 11:17, shows that the priests were aggressive when their financial gain was involved. This behavior would explain why the rabbis of the Mishnah needed to employ the *mipnei darkhei shalom* principle, a principle used to avoid bickering and strife, to override the law obligating priests to give security.[37]

This ruling differs from the cases in *Mishnah Gitin*. In the *Gitin* scenarios all were undisputed. *Mishnah Sheqalim* 1:4 demonstrates that not all Tannaim were in agreement as to whether the priests should be exempted from the paying the half shekel. The first opinion in *Mishnah* 1:4 exempted the priest from paying the half shekel, and thus they would also be exempted from giving collateral; therefore, the *mipnei darkhei shalom* principle would not apply.

It is clear that there is financial gain as well as prestige for the priests in having an exemption from this tax security-pledge. I would like to suggest that there is an additional advantage for the rabbis, the inheritors of the priests, through their inclusion in this law. Religious taxes took different forms after the destruction of the Jerusalem temple, when the half-shekel tax was no longer required. If the priests were exempt from a religious tax, that could serve as a basis for the rabbis to expect exemptions from the religious taxes of their time.

Summary of *Mipnei Darkhei Shalom* in Mishnah

	Jew	*Gentile*	*Harmony*	*Security*	*Financial gain*	*Amend law*	*Override law*	*Social status*
Case 1	yes	no	yes	no	no	no	yes	high
Case 2	yes	no	yes	yes	yes	yes	no	middle
Case 3	yes	no	yes	yes	yes	yes	no	middle-low
Case 4	yes	no	yes	yes	yes	yes	no	middle-low
Case 5	yes	no	yes	yes	yes	yes	no	low
Case 6	yes	no	yes	yes	yes	yes	no	low
Case 7	no	yes	no	yes	yes	no	implied	outsider
Case 8	yes	no	yes	no	yes	no	yes	low
Case 9	yes	no	yes	no	yes	no	yes	low
Case 10	no	yes	no	yes	yes	yes	no	outsider
Case 11	no	yes	no	yes	yes	no	yes	outsider
Case 12	yes	no	yes	yes	yes	no	yes	high

SUMMARY AND CONCLUDING REMARKS

It can be concluded from the above cases that Mishnah is concerned with civil and religious laws,[38] primarily those regarding financial concerns, affecting varied strata of society beginning with its leadership and concluding with the gentile outsider. The Mishnah sought social stability and social order. Therefore, to avoid conflict and ensure a secure and stable society, the principle of *mipnei darkhei shalom* was instituted to amend or override rabbinic stringencies that encompassed elements endangering this stability. The rabbis chose cases in which they applied the principle of "in the interest of peace" primarily in scenarios with financial implications. It was the area of economic relationships, interdependence, and cooperation that would most strongly impact the social solidarity of the collective. What was required was the "moralization" of economic relationships.

In order to understand how the above cases play a role in understanding the sociology and culture of the "ideal world" defined by Mishnah, I turn to the Durkheim school of social theory. I do not believe that there is one neatly packaged world of Mishnah, but rather there is what appears as different variables, which are presented in this document. For example, we find that on the one hand Mishnah presents a Temple-based culture and on the other hand a third-century Palestinian social reality. Many pieces make up the puzzle of Mishnah. The topic of *mipnei darkhei shalom* is only one piece in this puzzle, but it may reflect on the others when all the pieces are examined and placed together.

Emile Durkheim in his work, *The Division of Labor in Society*,[39] presents[40] his theory of society, moral consciousness, social order, and stability. I do not believe that this theory in its entirety can be applied to the unpacking of the world of Mishnah. However, there are elements in this theory that, even taken out of context, can be used to understand the Mishnah's topic *mipnei darkhei shalom*, and therefore one segment of the Mishnah's ideal world.

Positive solidarity in society can be considered as playing an essential role in creating the social order; it is an entirely moral phenomenon. To achieve this, a legal system with a complete moral consciousness is necessary. Moral ideals and codes of conduct order the functioning of society, and when this functioning is strong, it unites individuals in their social framework. This could then facilitate the basis of the authority necessary to retain the social order. The solidarity would result in what Mary Douglas[41] terms a *strong grid group*. A strong legal system in a diverse society as manifested in Mishnah brings people together. Solidarity overcomes the diversity and strengthens the collective. Furthermore, based upon our examples of *mipnei darkhei shalom*, I suggest that if we apply the group grid cosmology to the ideal world of Mishnah, we find that "there are visible rules about space and times related to social roles. Individuals do not, as such, transact with each other."[42] In other words, in this world the individual is not the focus of this cosmology, as the individual's recognition would weaken the culture.

It also must be considered that, as in our case of Mishnah, religion and religious law often initiate moral consciousness. Moral bounds were provided by religion. In a religious social structure, morality is permeated with religion. Juridical life protects these moral bounds and is essential for ensuring social harmony. The rabbis' social order was religious in character and articulates moral behavior. Religion provided for all social aspects of their ideal society. The world of Mishnah had the maximum characteristics[43] for the development of a collective consciousness. Durkheim identifies these, which compose the collective consciousness of this religious social order, as the volume, intensity, rigidity, and content of the beliefs and values. For Durkheim,[44] the state was a moral agency. The role of this body was to focus the collective representation on moral consciousness. For Mishnah, it was the rabbis' role to take on the responsibility to implement the moral phenomenon into their ideal world and to either develop or retain the stability required for that world and their authority. One tool they used to achieve these goals was the application of the principle *mipnei darkhei shalom.*

NOTES

1. For a comprehensive discussion of Mishnah, see the numerous volumes published by Jacob Neusner, for example, *Judaism: The Evidence of the Mishnah* (Chicago: University of Chicago Press, 1981), and *Introduction to Rabbinic Literature* (New York: Doubleday, 1994); also Jack N. Lightstone, *Mishnah and the Social Formation of the Early Rabbinic Guild* (Waterloo: Wilfrid University Press, 2002). Lightstone in his introduction also reviews the major texts of scholars offering various other approaches to the study of Mishnah; see also Naftali S. Cohn, *The Memory of the Temple and the Making of the Rabbis* (Philadelphia: University of Pennsylvania Press, 2013).

2. Neusner, *Judaism* and *Introduction.*

3. Lightstone, *Mishnah.*

4. Simcha Fishbane, *Deviancy in Early Rabbinic Judaism* (Leiden: Brill, 2007).

5. Lightstone, *Mishnah*, 7.

6. As Cohn explains (*Memory*, 1–4), there was no one alive to testify or even experience Temple life or ritual, and a new form of Jewish rabbinic ritual life was in the making. The Temple life, ritual, and society were chosen to serve the rabbis' agenda and enhance if not justify their authenticity and authority. As Jewish history has shown time and time again, when the new becomes the old, it acquires legitimacy.

7. See Lightstone, *Mishnah*, 26.

8. Cohn's monograph (*Memory*) focuses primarily on this hypothesis, that the Mishnah places the rabbi in the major role even in the Temple society. I believe that Cohn's maximalist position is overemphasized, but the purpose of this essay is not to take him to task.

9. See Gary G. Porton, *Goyim: Gentiles and Israelites in Mishnah-Tosefta* (Atlanta: Brown University–Scholars Press, 1988).

10. This argument disclaiming the paralleling of Mishnah and Tosefta is developed in Jacob Neusner, *Tosefta: Its Structure and Its Sources* (Atlanta: Scholars Press, 1986).

11. Neusner, *Judaism*, 129.

12. Neusner, *Tosefta.*

13. Ibid., 3.

14. Ibid.

15. Ibid., 4.

16. Herbert W. Basser and Reena L. Basser, "Ideas of Human Social Concord and Discord in Judaism to Research," in *Human Social Conflict* (ed. J. B. Gittler; Bingley: Emerald Group Publishing, 2000), 147, translates *mipnei darkhei shalom* as "for the sake of congeniality." As I will show later in this essay, this translation is correct only in specific instances in Mishnah.

17. All translations of the Mishnah texts are based upon Jacob Neusner, *The Mishnah: A New Translation* (New Haven: Yale University Press, 1988).

18. Basser and Basser, *Ideas*, 147.

19. For a general discussion of honor and the priest including sefer Torah, see *Talmudic Encyclopedia* 27 (2006): 196–214.

20. In his Mishnah commentary to our case, Maimonides suggests that this is related to a financial issue.

21. Talmud 60b describes a scenario in which the last rather than the first cistern in the field receives the priority for the river's water.

22. See *Mishnah Kidushin* 1:4–5 and *Baba Batra* 5:7 for a discussion of *kinyan* by dragging an object.

23. Throughout the tractate *Mishnah Kelim* clarifies that a utensil is an object with a proliferation. Although not relevant to Mishnah, the *Babylonian Talmud Baba Batra* 85a states this principle.

24. See Tzvi C. Marx, *Disability in Jewish Law* (London: Routledge, 2002), 96–127, for a rabbinic discussion and definition of the deaf-mute and idiot.

25. See Catherine Hezser, *Jewish Slavery in Antiquity* (Oxford: Oxford University Press, 2005), 69–104.

26. *Mishnah Pea* 8:7–9 defines who is considered a poor person and may accept these gifts.

27. *Tosefta* in *Gitin* 5 offers an autonomous statement that poor gentiles are supported along with the Jew. I believe this to be a separate statement independent of the agenda of the redactor of Mishnah with its own agenda.

28. Although the commentators intensively discuss this Mishnah, offering varying interpretations, I am looking at the direct implications of the Mishnah.

29. Joan W. Scott and Louise A. Tilly, "Women's Work and the Family in Nineteenth-Century Europe," *Comparative Studies in Society and History* 17:1 (January 1975): 41.

30. Ibid., 43.

31. The prohibitions regarding the interactions between the *haber* and the *am haaretz* are clarified in *Mishnah Demai* chapter 2.

32. For a detailed discussion of the relationship between the *am haaretz* and the *haber*, see Richard S. Sarason, *A History of the Mishnaic Law of Agriculture: A Study of Tractate Demai* (Leiden: E. J. Brill, 1979), 1–21 and the ArtScroll series edition of *Mishnah Shebiit* 181.

33. This is implied in the passage in Leviticus 25:3 that states that the land should rest in the seventh year.

34. Translation of *Tosefta* is adapted from Jacob Neusner, trans., *Toseta*, 6 vols. (New York: Ktav Publishing House, 1979).

35. Safrai, Shmuel, et al., eds., *Mishnat Eretz Israel with Historical and Sociological Commentary. Tractate Shakalim* (Jerusalem: E. M. Liphshitz Publishing House College, 2009), 75.

36. Ibid., 73–74.

37. The Talmud chooses to explain this action by the rabbis because of the honor the priests deserve. The Mishnah implies otherwise.

38. In the case of Mishnah it is difficult to differentiate between them.

39. Emile Durkheim, *The Division of Labor in Society* (New York: Free Press, 1997), 68–148.

40. Anthony Giddens, ed., *Emile Durkheim: Selected Writings* (Cambridge: Cambridge University Press, 1972). Translated with an Introduction by Anthony Giddens.

41. Mary Douglas, *Cultural Bias* (London: Royal Anthropological Institute of Great Britain and Ireland, 1979).

42. Ibid., 8.

43. See Giddens, *Emile Durkheim*, 5, for a discussion of each of these characteristics.

44. Ibid., 18.

Theocracy as Monarchy and Anarchy

Samuel Hayim Brody

INTRODUCTION: THEOCRACY 101

Since the time of Josephus, it has been argued that the only appropriate regime for the people Israel is the one described by the term *theocracy*, the rule of God.[1] The force of this argument is nearly tautological. It starts from the basic definition of "Israel" as that people formed through its election by God to be partner to a covenantal relationship. Until the most recent centuries, it made no sense to speak of a people Israel without reference to this relationship, and so by the same token it seemed to many to make little sense to ask what would constitute the best regime for the people Israel. There could only be one.

All that seems simple enough, and yet it is only true if we consider theocracy, as Josephus did when he coined the term, as an alternative to the traditional list of types of *politeia* [polity] that was passed down from Greek political thought. Aristotle's list is defined by first counting the number of people who hold the sovereign power and then determining whether they are ruling in the public interest. So you have monarchy, the rule of one, and its negative counterpart, tyranny; you have aristocracy, the rule of the excellent (usually rendered as "the few"), and its negative counterpart, oligarchy; and you have polity, the rule of the many, of which the negative counterpart is democracy. (The distinction between polity and democracy seems to depend, in the Aristotelian tradition, primarily on which economic class is in charge. If it's those in the middle, between rich and poor, that has the potential to be a good constitution; if it's the poor, however, the city is in trouble.) Josephus took one look at this list and immediately intuited what they all had in common: the sovereign power is held by human beings, regardless of how many of them there are. So he added "theocracy" to the list, in order to show how his own people, the Jews or Judeans, couldn't be accounted for in the seemingly exhaustive list of Greek types.

It is not easy for most of us, however, who live in a world in which humans rule other humans, to imagine what it might be like not to be ruled by humans, let alone to be ruled by God. As a result, thinkers of theocracy have most frequently imagined it not as an alternative to the typical forms of human rule, but rather as compatible with one or another of those forms. In this view, it is sufficient for the human rulers to declare that it is not indeed they who rule, but rather God; and that they are merely the stewards, interpreters, or representatives of God's will. Once the possibility of this is granted, any regime on the list, in pure form or mixed, can be interpreted as theocratic. And these varying types and forms can be maintained with more or less seriousness. Over the course of Jewish, Christian, and Muslim history alike, for example, monarchic regimes have based themselves on theocratic rationales almost without exception.[2] However, when it was felt that these rationales were adhered to with insufficient honesty, or that theocracy was being abused as a post facto rationalization for naked human power, monarchies have faced challenges from both aristocratic and democratic quarters. In particular, when grievances are rooted in a sense of insufficient adherence to divine will, the aristocracy of religious specialists—whether priests, prophets, or sages—has claimed the right, minimally, to challenge monarchy in the name of God's rule and, maximally, to establish their own rule in the place of the monarch.

Despite this common-sense understanding of theocracy, however, I want to focus here on the original sense of the term, in which it is considered a free-standing, independent alternative to all the types of human *politeia*. In this strong sense, God is not seen as merely the source of authority—an interpretation that, again, could render theocracy compatible with almost any human arrangement, whether monarchic, aristocratic, or democratic—but literally as ruler. God rules now, and not in some distant future; in this reality, and not in some ideal world. God rules us, human beings, and not just the angels or the other heavenly beings; he rules the earth, and not the "cosmos" in some grand, metaphorical sense. This is God as our actual, present political leader, not as "king of the gods," or object of cultic worship, or origin of everything that happens, or metaphysical substrate of Being.

This sense of theocracy might be hard to understand at first. How can God rule, after all, except through the intermediary of some human or group of humans? Doesn't someone have to tell us what God's will is, and doesn't whoever does so automatically become the de facto holder of sovereign power? Aren't we then inevitably led back to either the divine right of kings or the rule of some clerical class? The answer, for defenders of the strong sense of theocracy, has to be no. Monarchy is always and simply mere human rule, and the rule of the clergy would be better called "ecclesiocracy" or "hierocracy." The idea of true theocracy is direct, and not mediated by any human authority permanently enshrined for the purpose. But how can this be any more than an insistence, an assertion of an ideal against all common sense and the evidence of reality?

In order to illuminate some possibilities for understanding theocracy in this way, I turn to a twentieth century Jewish thinker who dealt with it extensively: Martin Buber. Buber is more commonly studied for his philosophical anthropology, conception of dialogue and the interhuman, and his Chasidic writings, but in his many writings on the Bible he showed a consistent and intense concern to develop the potential meanings of theocracy for both the ancient Israelites and the contemporary world. For various reasons, he did not always make these connections explicitly himself. I therefore take on the task of showing how what he says about the biblical authors and editors, and about the ancient Israelite world of faith in which they lived, is intended also for the twentieth century and for the modern Jewish world, including the Zionist movement of which he was a vocal part.

INTERLUDE ON NATIONALISM, STATISM, AND THE NATION-STATE

As noted above, it made no sense to speak of a people Israel separately from the covenant with God until recent centuries. Modern Jewish nationalism takes its starting point from just such a conception. The social, political, and intellectual factors that made this new conception of Jewishness possible are well known, and there is no need to repeat them here.[3] Suffice it to say that by the late nineteenth century, when the various branches of the Zionist movement emerged in Russia and in Central Europe, the premise that Jews constituted a nation, independent of the religious beliefs of the individual members of that nation, was integral to its project. And according to the theory of nationalism, as it was elaborated from the Balkans to Italy and beyond, each nation was entitled to autonomy and self-determination. The vehicle for achieving such self-determination was most frequently imagined to be the state.

This was not universally true, however. Although nationalist groups living within broad, multinational empires such as the Austro-Hungarian Empire, the Russian Empire, the British Empire, and the Ottoman Empire often envisioned the radical destruction of imperial rule and its replacement with an array of individual national states, each sovereign over its own territory within which its own nation would form a numerical majority, this was not the only way of expressing nationalist aims. The experience of cosmopolitan coexistence in cities like Prague, as well as the experience of communal autonomy within the imperial framework, gave rise to many other proposals for securing local and national self-determination without necessarily seeking statehood. As such, it was possible to combine nationalism with ideologies that might seem at first to make odd bedfellows, including communism—supposedly internationalist and class-based rather than ethnic in orientation, although in practice this was heavily contested—and even anarchism, which sought the destruction of all states in addition to the end of capitalism. An anarchist nationalism could be premised on the idealization of the dispersion of power across a plurality of networks, of small-scale, communal mechanisms for conflict resolution, as well as of the warm intimacy of local life (something left-anarchists shared with romantic conservatives).

I mention this rather exotic alignment of orientations because it was precisely this combination that was at work in the thought of Gustav Landauer (1870–1919), Martin Buber's best friend of two decades and a man whom the Kaiser's secret police gave the honor of "most significant agitator of the radical-revolutionary movement in all of Germany."[4] Although he was indeed an anarchist and a revolutionary, and by no means a German nationalist, Landauer also believed that the trends of political thought descending from the Enlightenment and grouped together under the banner of the "left" made a mistake when they placed the brotherhood of all humanity too far above the intimate ties of particular individuals and groups. Even the identity of the working class, to which he swore allegiance and on behalf of which he opposed private property and wage labor, was too abstract to sustain itself and could not hope to replace the bonds formed by common language and culture. Therefore, Landauer thought, it should not aim to do so. Perhaps anticipating late-century multiculturalism, he once wrote an article called, "Do Not Learn Esperanto!"[5]

For all these reasons, Landauer was a more congenial intellectual friend and mentor to Buber than your run-of-the-mill anarchist communist of the turn of the twentieth century. Like Buber, his primary interest was in community: what was conducive to it, what was detrimental to it, and what distinguished "true" community, *Gemeinschaft*, from the artificiality and mechanical impersonality of *Gesellschaft* [society]. My argument is that Buber eventually adopted a Landauer-style anarchism himself—except that what Landauer interpreted as autonomy, or self-rule, Buber reinterpreted as theocracy, divine rule. His name for this type of anarcho-theocratic tendency, which he uses primarily in his biblical writings, is "theopolitics."[6]

The term *theopolitics* is important. In the context of Zionism, Jews tried to innovate new forms of Jewish polity while also rooting these radical novelties in tradition. Because the Zionist movement conceived itself as rebelling against diaspora Judaism, it reached back beyond the rabbis and Talmud, searching for precedents in biblical times. However, while the Bible offered the examples of the glorious reigns of David and Solomon, it seemed to lack anything that could be used as a blueprint for those interested in modern democratic representation.

Secular Zionists, who dominated the movement prior to the 1970s, often reacted to this dilemma by prioritizing liberalism, socialism, or democracy, and demoting the Bible to the status of literary creation, one that could nevertheless serve as useful evidence for Jewish historical connections to Zion. Religious Zionists, however, even non-Orthodox ones like Buber, did not have this option. Thus they had to envision the messianic restoration of the Davidic monarchy—which meant giving up on democracy—or they had to get creative. This is where theopolitics comes in.

THEOPOLITICS AND THE BIBLE

Although Paul Mendes-Flohr's argument for Landauer's influence on Buber has been widely accepted, the sphere of this influence has generally been restricted to its impact on Buber's movement "from mysticism to dialogue" around the end of World War I.[7] In this narrative, Landauer is the spark that snaps Buber out of his youthful, neo-Romantic reverie, leading him to understand the problematic nature of his support for the war and thereby of the whole mystical worldview underlying his early projects, from the first collections of Chasidic tales to the famous Prague lectures, and on to *Daniel* (1913). Spurred by this revelation, Buber sets out to rectify the problem by allotting an increasing place in his thought to encounter and to the position of the Other; this process culminates in the writing of *I and Thou* (1923) and the development of the dialogic philosophy.

I offer two modifications to this narrative. First, we should consider the positive influence of Landauer on Buber, and not merely the negative. That is, Buber doesn't merely take Landauer's criticism as a sign that he needs to probe what he had previously gotten wrong—there is a positive impact as well, as he turns to a deeper examination of his friend's thought in order to understand what resources it contains that enabled Landauer to get World War I right. Second, I extend the narrative of this impact into the 1920s, beyond the publication of *I and Thou*, so that it encompasses Buber's work with Franz Rosenzweig (1886–1929) on a new Bible translation and the adventure of the Frankfurt *Lehrhaus* [adult education school], and Buber's increasing engagement with Religious Socialism and with the burgeoning kibbutz idea.

This approach allows me to consider *Kingship of God* (1932) as a different kind of culmination: one that expresses neither Buber's prewar mystical neo-Romanticism, nor a narrowly construed philosophy of dialogue, but rather a synthetic and idiosyncratic combination of all these interests as Buber worked them out from 1916 to 1932.

In *Kingship of God*, as well as in Buber's later biblical writings, we read of a hierarchical, covenantal relation between a transcendent God enthroned as king and a people who continually struggle to answer his call, to measure up to their sense of being commanded. There is "content" to this call, and not merely "presence" as in Buber's dialogical thought—they are elected to form the first decent society on earth, to become a "kingdom of priests and a holy nation." Although Buber adheres to the most current trends in biblical criticism as he sees them and although he does not enumerate the rabbinic 613 commandments as the nature of the revelational content, nonetheless we find such institutions as the Sabbath and Jubilee sketched out in terms of how they serve the purpose of the divine election. The divine purpose alluded to, in almost every case in which Buber allows for the expression of some content to revelation, can best be understood as "conducive to true community," in a Landauerian sense. In other words, whenever Buber allows "content" to revelation in his biblical writings, this "content" is theopolitical in nature, which means anarchistic.

In line with Leonhard Ragaz and the Religious Socialists, Buber holds that a transcendent vision of a kingly God does not underwrite an authoritarian political theology but rather undermines it, together with all unjustified human hierarchies, instead lending support to a radical vision of human equality—perhaps even more dependably than the *I-Thou* relation, which is powerful but also fleeting. This has implications for his Zionism, since it casts fundamental doubt on the goal of statehood and sovereignty, or to be more precise, it casts fundamental doubt on the idea that a Jewish polity is best constituted according to ordinary ideas about sovereignty and security. In line with this doubt, Buber refrains from having recourse to the great tales about Jewish kingdoms of the past, in the manner of David Ben-Gurion and other Zionist leaders. Instead, he looks to the period before the establishment of the monarchy, resisting the notion that the monarchy represented the glory of Jewish sovereignty and asserting God's kingship against it.

I will give an example of what I mean. In December 1918, Buber seems to have delivered an address in Munich. One month earlier, Kurt Eisner had declared Bavaria an independent republic, effectively ending hundreds of years of monarchy, and he had invited Gustav Landauer to come to Munich to help him in his work. Landauer, in turn, invited Buber to Munich, writing that "collaboration with Eisner functions very well. I am sure you have seen from his proclamations how 'anarchist' his understanding of democracy is: he favors the active participation of the people in all social bodies, not bleak parliamentarism. . . ."[8] The lecture that Buber gave in Munich was originally titled "Judaism and True Community," and was eventually published as "Der Heilige Weg" [The Holy Way].[9] By the time it was published, the revolution was over. Landauer had been martyred, murdered by the counterrevolutionary Freikorps militias hired by the social-democratic government in Berlin (a crime for which no one would ever face charges). And Buber dedicated the essay to his friend.

Of interest in this text is the significant shift that has occurred in Buber's thinking in contrast to his famous Prague "Lectures on Judaism," delivered only seven years earlier but on the other side of the war, the revolution, and the British conquest of Palestine.[10] In those lectures, Buber offered a powerful but also fairly typical cultural-Zionist reading of Jewish history: once, the Jewish people were vital and creative in their land; then, they were exiled and lost their vitality, which appeared only occasionally in subterranean movements outside the mainstream; now, the Jews return to Zion and to the land and so restore their original creative genius. In "The Holy Way," however, the loss of the Jewish commonwealth is no longer the event that "split Judaism's history in two."[11] Rather, "the true turning point in Jewish history" is declared to be the moment of the establishment of the Israelite monarchy.[12] It is the idolatrous turn toward institutional human authority, not the loss of sovereignty over the land, that rends the mundane from the spiritual and creates the very idea of the political sphere as something separate from religion (by restricting God's rule to "spiritual" matters). Over the course of the 1920s, Buber hones and fine-tunes his understanding of the Bible, so that by 1932 when he publishes *Kingship of God*, he has developed his understanding of philology and biblical history much more deeply. But the basic theopolitical claim remains the same as in the 1918 text dedicated to Landauer.

Buber's position is more or less consistent, too, between *Kingship of God* and his other biblical writings published later: the unfinished sequel *Der Gesalbte* [*The Anointed*] (1936), *Moshe* [*Moses*] (1945), and *Torat Hanevi'im* [*The Prophetic Faith*] (1950). Together, these works narrate a theopolitical history of Israel from the moment of the election of the people in the revelation at Sinai down to the Babylonian Exile. The book on *Moses* describes a charismatic leader who denies the role of institutional leadership for himself lest he end up imitating the Pharaoh against whom he rebelled. He passes leadership onto Joshua for a limited task, the conquest of Canaan, and Joshua passes leadership on to no one, not seeing any need to do so. The period of the Judges, according to *Kingship of God*, is one in which the political system vacillates between rule by a specially chosen charismatic leader, who performs only a limited task before fading back into the body of the people or serving as an arbitrator of disputes on the basis of earned authority, and what we might call anarcho-theocracy, when there is no human ruler at all and the people live under the direct kingship of God. Ultimately, however, the people fail here: only some of them, the most faithful, recognize this anarchy as an opportunity to exercise the highest responsibility; others succumb to fear of external military threats and demand the institution of a human monarchy. The aftermath of this, as described in *The Anointed* and *The Prophetic Faith*, is a decline that could have been avoided. God continues, through the prophets, to exhort the people to obedience of the original covenant; the kings suppress and ignore the prophets and the people pivot wildly between obedience and idolatry.

THEOPOLITICS AND ZIONISM

All this is deeply relevant to Buber's Zionism. A survey of the range of Buber's editorials and occasional writing on Zionism, together with a consideration of his major statement in *Ben Am Le-Artzo* [*Between a People and Its Land*, published in English as *On Zion*] (1944), shows that the post–World War I Buber understands the contemporary Zionist project as nothing less than a renewal of the original attempt of the people Israel to fulfill the terms of its election and covenant. As such, it remains subject to the same specific dangers that inhered in this attempt the first time around. Buber thus assumes the role of the contemporary inheritor of the prophetic, anarcho-theocratic tradition, urging his Zionist fellow-travelers not to succumb once again to the monarchic, statist temptation. In this picture, the ancient tribal system with its clans and sheikhs is updated by modern familial and productive associations, while the contemporary equivalent for ancient anarchy would be something like a network of kibbutz councils. The modern equivalent of the ancient monarchy, of course, is the nation-state, which represents the principles of human sovereignty and domination whether or not it includes a parliament and elections.

The fact that these themes, along with the first appearance in his writings of warnings against capitalist exploitation and imperialist domination, show up in 1917 and 1918 is no coincidence. Buber tried many times to enlist Landauer in the defense of Zionism and was rebuffed just as many times.

Landauer saw Germany as the place to realize his dreams of a nonhierarchical, directly democratic society made up of a network of nested workers', peasants', and soldiers' councils. He worried, further, that the growing British interest in Palestine meant that it would become yet another site of colonial oppression and that this agenda would override whatever independent projects small groups of idealistic Zionists might attempt to realize there. Nonetheless, after his death, Buber mourned the man he called Zionism's "hidden leader," the man who should have eventually realized his place at the side of the new Jewish spirit had history not stolen him away.[13] In the early 1920s, Buber was not the only one to think this way—other, more powerful and influential Zionist figures, such as Chaim Arlosoroff and Nahum Goldmann, spoke similarly about Landauer and his ideas.[14]

This brings us to perhaps the most important thing to realize about the Landauerian anarchist position as it realizes itself in Buber's theopolitics: it is at no time a "utopian" project, in the sense of an abstract ideal to be realized only in fiction or in the far future. From the moment Landauer went to work by Eisner's side in Bavaria, through his declaration of the Bavarian Council Republic, to the growth of the kibbutz movement during the years of the Third Aliyah, there were significant groups of people working to actually put these ideas into practice. To be sure, Buber criticizes Landauer's role in the Bavarian Revolution, but not simply because it was political action—rather, Buber fears that Landauer has badly misjudged the forces arrayed against him and thus acts on the basis of an incorrect political diagnosis, which fear turned out to be correct. This fear was perhaps the mirror image of Landauer's own fear, that Buber was signing on to a Zionist project of which he was not in control and in which he was doomed to be little more than a dissenting minority voice. This fear also turned out to be correct, but given the strength of Labor ideology and of the kibbutz movement in the 1920s, it was hardly completely romantic for Buber to see the cells of a new type of society in the kibbutzim. From the anarchist standpoint, in fact, what happened in Palestine was a mirror of what happened in Germany—a labor-oriented but statist party (Ebert and the SPD in Germany, Ben-Gurion and the Achdut Ha'avoda [Labor Unity] party in Palestine) crowds out those committed to nonhierarchical organization, dominates the scene for a while, then in turn succumbs to forces to its own political right.

It is also important to clarify that we are worlds away here from the "religious anarchism" attributed to Buber by Gershom Scholem in his critique of Buber's writings on Chasidism.[15] When Scholem speaks of "religious anarchism," he means anarchism with respect to the category or particular sphere called "religion," which is to say that he means antinomianism. Scholem identifies this, in turn, with messianism, since the chaotic wind of eschatology blows through the orderly house of religion. But Landauerian anarchism, which I am arguing is manifest in Buberian theopolitics, is antimessianic and highly "nomian." To be sure, it does not accept that the demands upon us are equivalent to what the institutions of the state or the rabbinate say that they are, but this hardly leads straight to nihilism. On the contrary, the demands of divine rule are total; Israel is never free from the need to do *teshuva* [repent] and to become what it was always meant to be. Such a realization must also strive to avoid the temptation of adopting an "anarchist constitution"—a specific form of society, however nonhierarchical, that endures from one generation to another in such a way that future generations are prohibited from altering it.[16] But it is nonetheless, despite being theopolitics, an achievable goal in the mundane world.

To return, then, to the context of Palestine, Buber saw clearly that the so-called Arab question posed a threat to the viability of the only kind of Zionism he believed worth the name, not just because it raised general and fuzzy ethical quandaries about the use of power or the ability to live with others, but because the fear of an external threat called Philistines was the very factor that first gave rise to the temptation of idolatrous human authority in Israel, undermining the rule of God and severing the political sphere from a now-impotent realm of the "spiritual," leading eventually to destruction and exile. Buber's binationalism is, as he put it, "only a temporary adaptation of our path to the concrete, historical situation—it is not necessarily the path itself."[17] He does not arrive at it by taking the generally current ideas about liberal self-governance and nation-state structures and then adding one plus one, nor can it really be understood as some kind of extrapolation or generalization of the teachings of *I and Thou* and *Dialogue*. Rather, the task of finding a modus vivendi for living with, not above, and not merely alongside, the Palestinians is a necessary prerequisite for preventing the reemergence of the kind of fear and hyperconsciousness of security that is conducive to the deformation of a Jewish anarchistic theopolitics into a Jewish authoritarian political theology.

CONCLUSION: THEOPOLITICS AND DEMOCRACY

I want to conclude by restating the connection between this type of anarchist theopolitics and theocracy and then asking how democracy fits into the picture. The relationship between God and Israel in Buber's biblical writings is presented as both hierarchical and covenantal, laying insistent demands on the collectivity of Israel even if those demands are not crystallized in the form of the rabbinic commandments. Instead, this demand requires *teshuva*, a turning to God that manifests in the organization of society according to a theopolitical impulse, which tends to map onto a Landauerian vision of anarchism: a society containing only nonhierarchical forms of organization, in which authority is granted only to those who earn it and only to do particular things. It is this theopolitical vision that Buber deploys against traditional notions of political theology and hierocracy, and it is this vision that manifests in Buber's commitment to the kibbutz as the potential core of a new Jewish society in Palestine. In this context, binationalism should be seen as a pragmatic compromise, not with an ideal of full Jewish sovereignty in a homogeneous society, but with any idea of statehood at all. Binationalism, through establishing clear conduits for cooperation between Palestinians and Zionists, counters the fear-security resonance machine that conduces to the idolatrous recourse to an authoritarian human power.

Of course, Buber and his friends did not win the argument about what form the Jewish polity in Palestine should take. And despite his radical idealism, Buber also had a practical side. He thus accepted the existence of the State of Israel as a liberal, representative democratic state that had resulted from the Zionist project, even though it did not embody what he saw as the true goal of Zionism. Nonetheless, because he believed that his version of Zionism was intimately bound up with the divine calling and commandment to the Jewish people to create a holy nation, he could not give up on his ideal. Thus he spent the last decades of his life trying to push the new State of Israel in the direction he thought it needed to go. This meant taking part in the democratic give-and-take that characterizes the politics of that country, in which relevant voices include the religious and secular Jewish publics, the Arab and Palestinian publics, and the arenas of global politics.

Because of this, I think Buber offers contemporary Jews and Israelis an interesting example of a theopolitics that takes it as axiomatic that God's rule is the end goal of Jewish public life, but at the same time does not assume that this means creating a coercive apparatus that will enforce rabbinic halachah, create facts on the ground in the West Bank, emphasize and stand on Jewish rights to the Temple Mount, and so on. From this standpoint, in fact, even the adoption of laws intended to regulate or enforce a Jewish demographic majority appears extremely problematic. As Buber puts it, the Jewish covenant operates as a dialogue between "a world which does not want to be God's, and a God that does not want to compel the world to become His."[18] If God refrains from dominating the world, then imitators of God must themselves so refrain, even if they think they can glorify God through their domination.

NOTES

1. Josephus, *Against Apion* (trans. H. St. J. Thackeray, Cambridge: Harvard University Press, 1976), 358–61.

2. See, e.g., Francis Oakley, *Kingship: The Politics of Enchantment* (Malden: Blackwell, 2006); Ernst Kantorowicz, *The King's Two Bodies: A Study in Mediaeval Political Theology* (Princeton: Princeton University Press, 1997); Aziz al-Azmeh, *Muslim Kingship: Power and the Sacred in Muslim, Christian, and Pagan Polities* (London: I. B. Tauris, 2001). For sacred kingship outside the monotheisms, see Declan Quigley, ed., *The Character of Kingship* (Oxford: Berg, 2005).

3. The literature on the origins of Zionism and Jewish nationalism is vast. Many of the old, classic resources are still valuable, especially those with an emphasis on ideas: Arthur Hertzberg, *The Zionist Idea: A Historical Analysis and Reader* (Philadelphia: Jewish Publication Society, 1997); Walter Laqueur, *A History of Zionism* (New York: MJF Books, 1972); Gideon Shimoni, *The Zionist Ideology* (Hanover: Brandeis University Press, 1995); David Vital, *The Origins of Zionism* (New York: Oxford University Press, 1995).

4. Cited in Ruth Link-Salinger (Hyman), *Gustav Landauer: Philosopher of Utopia* (Indianapolis: Hackett, 1977), 46.

5. Gustav Landauer, "Do Not Learn Esperanto!," in *Revolution and Other Writings* (ed. and trans. Gabriel Kuhn; Oakland: PM Press, 2010), 276–79.

6. I make this argument in more detail in Samuel Hayim Brody, *Martin Buber's Theopolitics* (Bloomington: Indiana University Press, 2018).

7. Paul Mendes-Flohr, *From Mysticism to Dialogue: Martin Buber's Transformation of German Social Thought* (Detroit: Wayne State University Press, 1989).

8. Landauer to Buber, November 22, 1918, in Gustav Landauer, *Sein Lebensgang in Briefen, Zweiter Band* (ed. Martin Buber; Frankfurt A.M.: Rütten & Loening, 1929), 299. Buber annotates this comment to provide evidence for Landauer's claim by directing the reader to certain of Eisner's speeches. Translation from Gabriel Kuhn, ed., *All Power to the Councils! A Documentary History of the German Revolution of 1918–1919* (Oakland: PM Press, 2012), 173.

9. Martin Buber, *Der Heilige Weg: Ein Wort an die Juden und an die Völker* (Frankfurt am Main: Rütten & Loening, 1919).

10. Both texts are available in English in Martin Buber, *On Judaism* (ed. Nahum Glatzer; New York: Schocken Books, 1995).

11. Buber, "The Spirit of the Orient and Judaism," *On Judaism*, 71–73.

12. Buber, "The Holy Way," *On Judaism*, 117.

13. Buber, "Der heimliche Führer," *Die Arbeit*, II/6, vi. 1920, 36–37.

14. For Arlosoroff, see Shalom Ratzabi, *Between Zionism and Judaism: The Radical Circle in Brith Shalom 1925–1933* (Leiden: Brill, 2002), 413; for Goldmann, see "Appendix II: Exchange of Letters: Goldmann-Landauer," in James Horrox, *A Living Revolution: Anarchism in the Kibbutz Movement* (Oakland: AK Press, 2009), 133–37.

15. Gershom Scholem, "Martin Buber's Hasidism, A Critique," *Commentary* 32 (1961): 315.

16. A problem keenly explored in fiction by Ursula K. LeGuin, *The Dispossessed: An Ambiguous Utopia* (New York: Harper & Row, 1974).

17. Martin Buber, "The Bi-National Approach to Zionism," in Martin Buber et al., eds., *Towards Union in Palestine: Essays on Zionism and Jewish-Arab Cooperation* (Westport: Greenwood Press, 1972), 10. Originally published in 1947 by the Ihud Association, Jerusalem.

18. Martin Buber, *Kingship of God* (trans. Richard Scheimann; Amherst: Humanity Books, 1990), 139.

Jewish Democracy: From Medieval Community to Modern State

Joseph Isaac Lifshitz

INTRODUCTION

Like any political theory, Jewish political theory underwent a change of two major perspectives, ethical and theological. It changed from focusing on legal definitions to values as freedom and equality and from perceiving the political body as a reflection or an extension of God to secularization of the political. In the Middle Ages, questions of political theory were concerned with legal definitions of the political body, the authority of the leaders upon its members, and the rights of the members. Jewish scholars defined the political body, which was the Jewish community, as a quasi-corporation or as an association that was largely based on a social contract.

The Jews in the Middle Ages lived in the European and Middle Eastern cities as separate communities, and as I have shown in a previous study, they were organized as a quasi-corporation for external purposes and internal alike.[1] This legal definition played in the field of private law. The public sphere was gaining slowly its upper hand, but was not defined as inherently different from the private domain. Although not completely equal, they were both legal adversaries within the legal domain. In this sense, politics in the Middle Ages was not different from politics in antiquity. Kings were owners of their land and masters of their citizens, even if the latter were not necessarily defined as slaves or serfs. The legal definition was private law.

Medieval political theory was concerned with theology as well. As medieval historians point out, application of theology to politics in the Middle Ages was taking place. That has become even clearer since Ernst Kantorowicz published *The King's Two Bodies*. In this book published in 1957, Kantorowicz set a guide for generations of historians through the arcane mysteries of medieval political theology. Kantorowicz traces the historical problem posed by the "king's two bodies"—the body politic and the body natural—back to the Middle Ages and demonstrates, by placing the concept in its proper setting of medieval thought and political theory, how the early modern Western monarchies gradually began to develop a political theology.[2]

The king's natural body has physical attributes as do all humans, but the king's spiritual body transcends the earthly and serves as a symbol of his office as majesty with the divine right to rule. The notion of the two bodies allowed for the continuity of monarchy even when the monarch died, as summed up in the formulation, "The king is dead; Long live the king."

Politics in the modern era is different. The medieval social contract is not the modern democratic social contract, and modern rights talk is not a medieval demand for rights. As Joseph R. Strayer claimed in *On the Medieval Origin of the Modern State*,[3] besides changes of culture, a major change arose after the Middle Ages, a political change. The rise of the modern state exhibits a change that started at the Renaissance, before the rise of the democratic state; that is, bestowing responsibility on the state for social justice, education, health, and culture. Unlike the legalistic medieval concept of the social contract, modern democracy is not only a legal construct but rather an ethical principle, embedded either in rights talk or as a virtue. Modern democracy is perceived as protecting a bundle of rights, including the rights of minorities, and not only enhancing the rights of the majority. Thus, the modern state is an entity that became a source of moral identity. It is also usually perceived as a secular source of identity. The modern state is a human construct that expresses human values. It is not created by God and it doesn't present God as its foundation. If that is the case, it is a question if a modern Jewish state is possible, a Jewish state with its religious values at its center.

In this essay I contend that religious values do not necessarily infringe upon the possibility of a modern Jewish state. As I show through an analysis of the works of Jewish philosophers like Franz Rosenzweig, Martin Buber, and Emmanuel Levinas, such a possibility of modern Jewish democracy does exist. As I show, their perception of self and community, and of certitude and doubt, enables a sense of liberty that should generate a new idea of dialogue with secularity and therefore a new Jewish democracy.

A SECULAR AGE

As I mentioned before, the modern state, as Strayer explained, inherited God as the founder or the source of existence, and thus it became in charge not only of securing the safety of the citizens, but also of their education, medicine, welfare, and law. Of course, this revolution couldn't arise without a religious change. Throughout the humanistic revolution of the Renaissance, God shifted from being the center of existence, for the sake of man as the center, and became just a personal experience. Thus, together with the centrality of earth, God lost his place as the foundation of human existence for the sake of a man-made creature—the state, which inherited God. Since that era, people have looked for the state to save them, not only from enemies, but also from catastrophes of nature, and even for their sorrows, the root of their well-being.

Strayer's understanding, which continued Friedrich Nietzsche's well-known claim about the death of God, became common knowledge for many. Charles Taylor, in *A Secular Age*, describes the modern Western perception of religion according to what he calls a change of identity.[4] If until the Renaissance a doubt of faith was hardly an option, in modernity faith became obsolete. God is not perceived anymore as the sole source of nature. There are alternatives to understanding reality, and faith became just one choice among many. I should add that if until modernity, God was indeed the scientific source of existence, the source of energy, and the cause of all creation, modern science doesn't believe in causes and is not teleological. Modern science prefers mechanical or mathematical explanations of nature. It is not that modern science created heresy or atheism. It did not prove that God doesn't exist. It just sees God as irrelevant. As for Taylor, he claims that as a result of the change of identity for humanity, which traditionally identified itself with religion, in the modern era faith became a personal choice, and social identification was now with the state. But it wasn't only a change of identity. Replacing God as the source of reality enabled the Western world to use instrumental reasoning in the political sphere. Societies and states are organized now in a way that was impossible in the past.

It is true that perceiving the polity as secular is not accepted by all. Even if we ignore Carl Schmitt, with his *Politische Theologie*,[5] for using God as a mere symbol for power as an antiliberal strategy, Michel Foucault,[6] Giorgio Agamben,[7] and Erik Peterson[8] took political theology much more seriously. Possibly the most important understanding of the weight of theology in political theory arose in a meeting between J*ü*rgen Habermas and Joseph Alois Ratzinger in the Catholic Academy of Munich during 2004. Both of them agreed that the secular society cannot produce values on its own and that it depends on religion, or at least on a dialogue with religion, in order to create a set of values. Yet these opinions present a call for the voice of God, which answers a need, rather than a secular alternative, while I think that we must accept Taylor's claim that we are in a secular age. For religious people, the modern state does have religious values, but they are peripheral. The modern state is perceived largely as a secular institution, even for religious people.[9]

After stating that, I must ask again, what about a Jewish state as a religious state? One must bear in mind that regarding a Jewish state, the question is not only how much the state represents God and his attributes, but since Judaism is a heavily legalized religion, the question is also how much a Jewish state reflects Jewish laws. If for Taylor as a Christian, religion in modernity may belong to the private sphere, as a mere expression of a whim or a personal emotion, for a religious Jew, religion is not only about faith but also about law. In Judaism, religion can't be limited to the private sphere.

JUDAISM

As Leo Strauss claimed, Judaism can't afford separation between state and religion.[10] Secular values are universalistic values, and accepting them causes a change in principle to a Jewish state, which ceases to be Jewish. Judaism is not just a personal religion but a communal and social structure that has political law. It has a narrative and an end. Strauss envisions the solution of the Jewish state as a return to a creative Judaism, a return to religion. In order to describe his point, Strauss presents Rosenzweig and Buber's philosophy as a possible example of an intelligent, up-to-date Judaism.[11] I will follow Strauss by describing their philosophy and continue with Levinas.

For Rosenzweig, there is no room for a nation-state, with the exception of the Jewish state. According to Rosenzweig, the purpose of all humanity is universal, and the values of such a world are to strive for an ethical world, to enhance the good. He thought that nation-states are an obstacle to such purpose, and if they are created as an end to itself, they are not justified. If that is the case, why is a Jewish state justified? Rosenzweig answers that creating a Jewish state is justified only if it helps the universal, if it creates unity between all nations, unity between man and the world, and most important between man and God. A Jewish state must therefore be a light to the nations as fulfilling the goal of creating space for God in order to create this unity. Rosenzweig emphasized that this unity is achieved through revelation and redemption of God. Rosenzweig explained his theory by describing a geometric model, his famous Star of David, which is made of two triangles consisting of six elements—God, world, and man on one triangle, and creation, revelation, redemption on the other triangle. The meeting of all elements is the Jewish goal.[12]

So the purpose of the Jewish state is to have one God who unites man with the world. At the same time, we are to believe in the idea that God did not leave his creation, but is involved with it and reveals himself as loving, and will at the end redeem the world to become one with him. The purpose of the Jewish state is to bring it to its infanthood, where man will love his neighbor, where man will love God. Rosenzweig's theory may bring to mind the Maimonidean's Universalist utopia, as described at the end of the *Mishneh Torah*:

> In that era, there will be neither famine nor war, envy or competition for good will flow in abundance and all the delights will be freely available as dust. The occupation of the entire world will be solely to know God. Therefore, all will be great sages and know the hidden matters, grasping the knowledge of their Creator according to the full extent of human potential, as Isaiah 11:9 states: "The world will be filled with the knowledge of God as the waters cover the ocean bed."[13]

But Maimonides was a rational philosopher, and his utopia is a triumph of philosophy. Rosenzweig's utopia is a call for overcoming philosophy and rationality, for the sake of revelation, to the realization that human existence is relying on God. Not on his wisdom or intellect, but on his being.

Unlike Rosenzweig, Martin Buber did not accept that certitude of faith. Quoting Martin Heidegger, Buber claimed that God's existence and God's truth are not that obvious. As the prophets taught, man is advised to be human and not to look for a shelter in the temple of God:

> Heidegger warns this way against "religion" in general, but in particular against the prophetic principle in the Judeo-Christian tradition. "The 'prophets' of these religions," he says, "do not begin by foretelling the word of the Holy. They announce immediately the God upon whom the certainty of salvation in a supernatural blessedness reckons." Incidentally, I have never in our time encountered on high philosophical plane such a far-reaching misunderstanding of the prophets of Israel. The prophets of Israel have never announced a God upon whom their hearers' striving for security reckoned. They have always aimed to shatter all security and to proclaim in the opened abyss of the final insecurity the unwished-for God who demands that His human creatures become real, they become human, and confounds all who imagine that they can take refuge in the certainty that the temple of God is in their midst. This is the God of the historical demand as the prophets of Israel beheld Him. The primal realty of these prophecies does not allow itself to be tossed into the attic of "religions": it is as living and actual in this historical hour as ever.[14]

By this acceptance of Heidegger, of placing man in the center, man with his doubts and faiths, Buber permits a secular age à la Taylor, regardless of faith. Even the most famous, in a secular age, assumes his self before God. God is an experience of man. He doesn't exist outside human experience. But there is something else in Buber's thought, regarding Judaism; he denies the priority of the law. Indeed, Buber is antinomianist, and Jewish law receives its value only if it reflects human experience. Otherwise the law expresses relationship of *Ich-Es* or I-It. So although Buber believes in a Jewish state, it is rather a secular state with some Godly values. No Jewish laws. Of course, such an opinion doesn't fit Strauss's view. As I mentioned above, Strauss claimed that there is no Judaism without the law. The Jewish state is not Jewish without its attachment to the laws of the Torah. From a Jewish point of view, the question is not only if a person identifies himself with God, as Tailor says, or if he relies on God instead of on the state, as Strayer says, but if he identifies with the Torah and its laws.

I would like to leave the question of the law for a moment and focus on the definition of the polity. Buber shared one more understanding of Heidegger; it has to do with a disagreement he had with Edmund Husserl. As I quoted Karl Jaspers elsewhere, he describes a sociological dichotomy between Husserl and Heidegger, between egological epistemology and social ontology. For Husserl, the world, including the social world, is a world that a person perceives as a spectator. In what Husserl calls "bracketing," he reduces the world that is relevant to a human being into what appears to the subject: "I am no longer a human Ego *in* the universal, existentially posited world, but exclusively a subject for which this world has being, and purely, indeed, as that which appears to me, and of which I am conscious in some way or the other, so that the real being of the world thereby remains unconsidered, unquestioned, and its validity is left out of account."[15]

As Jaspers describes it, "the world is experienced and known by the transcendental subject in isolation-the Ego. . . . The mental becomes the foundation, rather than the external world of objects, as in the objectivistic tradition." As Husserl himself pointed out: "In respect to order, the intrinsically first of the philosophical disciplines would be the 'solipsistically' reduced 'egology,' the egology of the primordially reduced ego. Then only would come intersubjective phenomenology, which is founded on that discipline."[16]

Jaspers continues by claiming that according to Husserl, man is not inherently social, but is capable of being social, an idea that he shares with Max Weber. As Heidegger already criticized René Descartes and Gottfried Leibniz, the detached subject is unable to communicate with others. Husserl tried to solve this problem by imposing empathy between the ego-poles, and it is the assumption of empathy that is the foundation of Husserlian intersubjectivity.

For Heidegger, instead man is a social entity. He is born into society, and his source of perspective of the world is never his subjectivity versus the world but within the world. Any knowledge of the world is grounded in man as living among other men: "On the basis of this *with-bound* (*mithaften*) being-in-the-world, the world is already the one that I share with others. The world of Dasein is a *with-world* (*Mitwelt*). Being-in is *being-with* (*mitsein*) others. The innerwordly being-in-itself of others is *Dasein-with* (*mitdasein*)."[17] Human beings are conditioned by their past, by history. Man is from the very beginning part of a larger whole, of the world of society. He is not only conditioned by his immediate society but also by his culture of which he is surrounded. The effect of society is not merely conversations or theories he encounters, but objects as well, like tools and buildings. What is important to note in Heidegger's thought is that man is never alone. Man can only be with others, which is the special ontological relation that characterizes man.

Buber sides with Heidegger, and for him a political entity is not necessarily created by man, but is done spontaneously. Man is born into society and is part of it. The same is true of course in a Jewish state. Forcing Jewish law will be foreign to the Jewish state, and will not reflect its citizens' natural social interconnections. Levinas had a different approach to man's social being, and therefore his concept of the polity is different as well. I will thus present Levinas's political perception from this idea in mind.

LEVINAS

Levinas's political philosophy is not as explicit as his other writings on phenomenology. Yet it is assumed that his Third Party is synonymous with "humanity." The Third Party is another way of speaking of other people identified as other selves, and is also a perception of me through the eyes of the other. Human life is a social life, or *mitdasein*, as Heidegger called it. Human beings are born into society. In this sense, being in society is being in the world. But for Levinas, the existence of the other doesn't only signify life or being, but also a call for responsibility. What Levinas calls "the epiphany of the face" of the other creates a total responsibility for the life of the other. Thus, with the mere fact of the existence of two human beings, ethics is created, ethics but not yet law or justice. Justice is created only when a third party watches over:

> By essence the prophetic word responds to the epiphany of the face, doubles all the discourse not as a discourse about moral themes, but as an irreducible movement of a discourse which by essence is aroused by the epiphany of the face inasmuch as it attests the presence of the third party, the whole of humanity, in the eyes that look at me. Like a shunt every social relation leads back to the presentation of the other to the same without the intermediary of any image or sign, solely by the expression of the face. When taken to be like a genus that unites like individuals the essence of society is lost sight of.[18]

For Levinas, the third party as an observer is what develops ethics to law. As I described in the beginning of this essay, it is the legal aspect that forms the Jewish philosophical tradition. Indeed, Levinas did not develop a theory of justice, but he did create a philosophical foundation for a political theology. God is found in his thought in the realm of the individual and his meeting with the other; through the other evolves ethics, but only in society this ethics develops to justice, which is a full application of ethics in the world. But what is missing in Levinas's thought is the place of the law as revelation. Unlike a long tradition of Jewish philosophers, for whom it is the revealed law that creates ethics, for Levinas ethics are revealed and the law evolves from ethics, and thus politics is but an effect of ethics as well.

JEWISH STATE AND JEWISH LAW

We come back to Strauss's claim: because Judaism is about law, the Jewish state should be bound by Jewish law, and of course, there shouldn't be separation between state and religion. But such a demand from a modern democratic state raises many questions: Can a Jewish state be a democracy or must it be a theocracy? Who should decide which laws should apply and which not? Is there any room for a public discussion about which of the Jewish laws should be applied? Doesn't the law bestow power on rabbis and remove any authority from the people? And the most difficult question: How can religion be a subject of discussion? Isn't religion absolute? A religious person can't compromise with his religion. The same is true about Jewish law. Jewish law is considered absolute in the eyes of an observant Jew, and he can't compromise it for the sake of secular law. If that is true, how can a democratic state bear Jewish law?

In order to solve these questions, I want to distinguish between subjectivity and doubt. I claim that the fact that Jewish law should define the Jewish state does not necessitate a rejection of public discussion, and the reason for that is the state of certitude of Jewish faith as well as Jewish law in the modern era. As Buber claimed, certitude of faith is impossible in our time. We do confront our faith in God with doubts about his existence and his Torah. Yet that doesn't mean to say that we are not convinced about the two. As opposed to some claims, Jewish religion should not be limited to the subjective sphere, to the private sphere. Conviction may arise in a background of doubt. A similar claim was made by R. Abraham Yeshayahu Karelitz, the Khazon Ish (1878–1953), who said that despite the authority and the obligation that is given by the Jewish law to force law, that shouldn't apply in the modern era. The reason is that the existence of God is not as revealed as it used to be in the past. When the Divine Providence is concealed, man can demand neither faith nor obedience to the law:

> Individual cohesion of the law is only permitted at times when the Divine Providence was revealed, and only then punishing the sinners was the way to enhance observation of the law. But at a time when His face is hidden, and faith ceased from the indigent, cohesion doesn't add observance anymore, but creates the opposite instead, because it will appear as violence, God forbid. Not as cohesion for the sake of observance. And since the idea of individual cohesion was created for the sake of Tikkun Olam, the law does not exist when there is no Tikkun. And we should try to influence them with means of love and to shade as much light as we can.[19]

Perceiving our time as a time of doubt, as time that we can't be certain about his existence because he hid his face, leaves faith to the individual's conviction. He can't demand it from his neighbor. In my opinion, such perception of certitude of faith enables not only acceptance of secular people within society, but also secularity itself. Understanding it has an enormous importance because it enables public discussion instead of force.

Public discussion is enabled when disagreements are managed with respect to both sides. If in the case of disagreement each adversary does not respect the legitimacy of his adverse, the society is doomed for schism. Each side must accept the opinion of the other as a possible truth. It doesn't mean that he is not convinced that he is correct and that his adversary is wrong, but rather that there is a possibility that he is correct. Accepting the possibility of truth from one's adversary is the most important condition of decent democratic life.

I claim that the same thing is true regarding Jewish law in modernity. An observant Jew must be convinced about the law, but the lack of certitude, as R. Karelitz says, enables the possibility of secularity and therefore its legitimacy. It is this legitimacy that enables a decent discussion about Jewish law in the Jewish state. Observant and nonobservant can meet and decide about the laws of the Jewish state and its public sphere, and both can accept the results of their decisions as legitimate.

The sort of decent discussion that I suggest reminds us of the sort of discussion of the public sphere of Habermas. I think that the importance of my idea is not the fact that I suggest a decent discussion but that I enable it even between such a principled subject as religion and religious law. The distinction between certitude and conviction is thus essential to a decent public discussion.

NOTES

1. Joseph Isaac Lifshitz, *Rabbi Meir of Rothenburg and the Foundation of Jewish Political Thought* (New York: Cambridge University Press, 2015), 82–124.

2. Ernst H. Kantorowicz, *The King's Two Bodies* (Princeton: Princeton University Press, 1997), 193–232.

3. Joseph R. Strayer, *On the Medieval Origin of the Modern State* (Princeton: Princeton University Press, 1970).

4. Charles Taylor, *A Secular Age* (Cambridge: Harvard University Press, 2010), 159–211.

5. Carl Schmitt, *The Concept of the Political: Expanded Edition* [*Politische Theologie*], (trans. Georg Schwab; Chicago: University of Chicago Press, 2007).

6. Michel Foucault, *The Order of Things* (London: Routledge, 2002).

7. Giorgio Agamben, *Homo Sacer: Sovereign Power and Bare Life* (trans. Daniel Heller-Roazen; Stanford: Stanford University Press, 1998).

8. Erik Peterson, *Theological Tractates* (trans. Michael J. Hollerich; Stanford: Stanford University Press, 2011).

9. See more in Michael Walzer, *The Paradox of Liberation: Secular Revolutions and Religious Counterrevolutions* (New Haven: Yale University Press, 2015). Regarding the Jewish state see 34–67.

10. Leo Strauss, *Jerusalem and Athens: Selected Writings of Leo Strauss* (Jerusalem: Leo Baeck Institute and Bialik Institute, 2001), 342.

11. Ibid., 344–52.

12. Franz Rosenzweig, *The Star of Redemption* (trans. William W. Hallo; Madison: University of Wisconsin Press, 2005), 351–56.

13. Maimonides, *Mishneh Torah*, "Kings and Their Wars," 12:5.

14. Martin Buber, *Eclipse of God: Studies in the Relation between Religion and Philosophy* (New York: Harper & Brothers, 1952), 97–98.

15. Edmond Husserl, *Ideas, General Introduction to Pure Phenomenology*, Book I (New York: Collier Books, 1962), 8.

16. Edmond Husserl, *Cartesian Meditations: An Introduction to Phenomenology* (The Hague: Martinus Nijhoff, 1960), 155.

17. Martin Heidegger, *Being and Time* (trans. Joan Stambaugh; Albany: State University of New York Press, 2010), 115–16.

18. Emmanuel Levinas, *Totality and Infinity: An Essay on Exteriority* (trans. Alphonso Lingis; Pittsburgh: Duquesne University Press, 1969), 213.

19. R. Abraham Yeshayahu Karelitz, *Khazon Ish, Yore De'a* (Jerusalem, 1951), 2:16.

Linking "Egypt with Texas": Emma Lazarus's Jewish Vision of American Democracy

David J. Peterson and Joan Latchaw

INTRODUCTION

Emma Lazarus was from a mixed Jewish heritage bridging the eighteenth and nineteenth centuries in America. Her mother's Portuguese Sephardic ancestors (Seixas and Nathan) emigrated to British colonial America before the 1750s, and her father's Ashkenazic family left Germany for the United States in the 1790s. It was largely the Sephardic ancestry that conferred near blueblood status on Lazarus's family. Her great-great-uncle Gershom Mendes Seixas, for example, led New York City's Shearith Israel Synagogue, and her great-great-uncle Moses Mendes Seixas presided over the most fabled of all Jewish American places of worship, Newport's Yeshuat Israel (later Touro Synagogue).

The correspondence between Moses Seixas and George Washington stands as a beacon to American liberty and civil rights. The newly elected president, along with a delegation that included Secretary of State Thomas Jefferson, visited Newport in August 1790. Among the citizens who addressed the president was Seixas, who stated, "Deprived as we heretofore have been of the invaluable rights of free Citizens, we now . . . behold a Government, erected by the Majesty of the People—a Government, which to bigotry gives no sanction, to persecution no assistance—but generously affording to all Liberty of conscience, and immunities of Citizenship."[1] In a letter written soon after the visit, Washington famously assured the Newport Congregation that "'the children of the Stock of Abraham shall sit in safety under his own vine and figtree, and there shall be none to make him afraid,'" an image Emma Lazarus would invoke in several of her poems.[2]

When Emma Lazarus was born in New York City in 1849, her immediate family was prominent in both the Jewish community and, due to her father's prosperous sugar business, the upper echelons of New York society. Social connections further linked the family to America's literary elite, enabling an eighteen-year-old Emma to send her first volume of poetry, *Poems and Translations* (1867), to Ralph Waldo Emerson. He enthusiastically offered to became her literary mentor, and he remained an important advocate of her work.[3] With her family's support (and Emerson's mentoring), she developed into a prolific writer, publishing six volumes of poetry and translations. In the early 1880s she became, moreover, a social advocate for the Russian Jews fleeing the pogroms. She wrote impassioned defenses of European Jews, along with proto-Zionist essays that appeared in prominent American periodicals such as *Century Magazine* and *American Hebrew*. She also volunteered for the Hebrew Immigrant Aid Society and in 1883 organized the short-lived Society for the Improvement and Colonization of East European Jews, which promoted the settlement of Palestine.

Eulogizing Lazarus for *American Hebrew* after her untimely death at thirty-eight in 1887, Rabbi Sabato Morais, Orthodox *hazzan* [cantor] of Philadelphia's Mikvah Israel Synagogue, styled her the "poetical Deborah" of the United States, noting she "would have reached a superlative degree as *the* poetess of the Jews in America" had she lived.[4] While Morais's praise for Lazarus asserts an uncomplicated understanding of her Jewish identity, contemporary Lazarus scholars note a sharp contrast between Lazarus's early poetry—seen as more secular—and the later works that attack European Antisemitism or explore Jewish diasporic experiences, a shift they figure as reflecting an assimilated, secularized American who late in life comes to embrace a Jewish identity.

They further observe that Lazarus shared an uneasy, at times ambivalent, relationship with her Jewish heritage that guided her interest in Jewish philosophers and intellectuals (such as Baruch Spinoza, Heinrich Heine, and Benjamin Disraeli) who experienced similar conflicts between their ethnic and religious heritages and their attraction to a broader, more cosmopolitan world. Esther Schor asserts, for example, that Lazarus shared with Heine a strongly divided sense of self: his between Jewish and German-Romantic identities, and hers between "the double life she was trying to live as an American and a Jew."[5] Indeed Lazarus's own comments on Heine are frequently glossed as summing up her own sense of self: "He was [writes Lazarus] a Jew, with the mind and eyes of a Greek. A beauty-loving, myth-creating pagan soul was imprisoned in a Hebrew frame; or rather, it was twinned . . . with another equally powerful soul—proud rebellious, oriental in its love of the vague, the mysterious, the grotesque, and tragic with the two-thousand-year-old passion of the Hebrews."[6]

Though her family was not religious, Lazarus's Jewish heritage serves as an important touchstone in her writing, drawing on major Jewish figures (mostly Sephardic) from the medieval, Enlightenment, and Romantic periods. She celebrates luminaries such as Solomon ibn Gabirol, Maimonides, Abraham ibn Ezra, Rashi, Spinoza, and Heine for their contributions to both Jewish and European intellectual and artistic culture. Moreover, she herself often made statements that reveal her strong identification with her Jewish heritage even as she explicitly disidentified with the religious aspects of Judaism. Writing to Edmund Stedman, for example, she declares that she is "proud of my blood and heritage, but Hebrew ideals [i.e., religious principles] do not appeal to me."[7] Sending Reform Rabbi Gustav Gottheil (Temple Emanu-El, New York City) some requested translations of Gabirol, Judah Ha-Levi, and ibn Ezra, she notes, "I cheerfully offered to help you to the extent of my ability, and was glad to prove to you that my interest and sympathies were loyal to our race, although my religious convictions (if such they can be called) and the circumstances of my life have led me somewhat apart from our people."[8]

The hypothesis that she struggled with Jewish identity has even been used by some to explain the relative obscurity into which her poetry has fallen. Francine Klagsbrun goes so far as to claim that her writings "[reflect] the discomfort of a woman who was not totally at home in the Christian world she inhabited but had not quite found her footing in the Jewish one either. It has the feel of outsiderness, of a writer who held herself too much apart, too much above the people she sought to defend and counsel. The outsiderness has stood in the way of [her work's] survival."[9] Ranen Omer-Sherman even argues that Lazarus's Jewish-focused poetry tends to present Jewish faith traditions as parochial, comprising what Lazarus calls "'the whole rotten machinery of ritualism, feasts and fasts, sacrifices, oblations, and empty prayers.'"[10] Moreover, Omer-Sherman asserts, Lazarus tends to contrast these insular seeming traditions to American democracy's embrace of the "Enlightenment's universalizing discourse of rationalism."[11] According to Omer-Sherman, Lazarus's dedication to such rationalism leads her to "[erase] Jewish difference" in favor of assimilation and to encourage "the consolations of forgetfulness"[12] whereby unenlightened Jews (especially Eastern European Ashkenazim) could move out of their primitive "Oriental" past and into Enlightenment modernity.

Questions about her religious identity, degrees of assimilation, and commitment to Enlightenment universalism obscure, however, her role as both Jewish intellectual and poet of American democracy, roles highlighted in Rabbi Sabato Morais's eulogy. While Lazarus may have lacked strong religious convictions, she never lost her commitment to the intellectual, spiritual, artistic, and political legacies of her people. Indeed, she belongs in the company of other Jewish-American intellectuals, such as Isaac Leeser, Isaac Mayer Wise, Isaac Harby, and Morais, all advocates for a particularly American-inflected approach to the Jewish Enlightenment, an approach that positions the United States as a new homeland where Jews can enjoy religious, economic, and intellectual liberty.[13] As Morais argues in his famous 1851 Thanksgiving sermon,

> A century has nearly elapsed since the scattered children of Judah here found a home of security and peace; here they have thriven and acquired wealth; no internal adversary has ever molested them, nor has the rod of tyranny from without reached these shores; here they have but to prove themselves worthy, and they will rise as high as any free man can aspire; no disabilities, no legal impediments, militate against them; what a felicity is that of which you are made to partake! dear brethren, the boundless field of knowledge is unclosed to you, you may enter it, and freely gather its delightful fruits; you may give scope to your mental energies, for the advancement of your fellow-citizens and of mankind at large:—Unimpeded in the exercise of your religious duties, in accordance with the Jewish doctrine, you are not merely tolerated, but regarded with respect, for you also form a part of that glorious whole that constitutes the American Republic.[14]

Lazarus's work reflects similar themes. In the subsequent sections of this essay we demonstrate how Lazarus draws on the dominant culture's tropes of universal rights to freedom, liberty, and opportunity to argue for and promote Jewish belonging. As we show in our discussion of poems such as "In Exile," she draws on discourses associated with Jeffersonian agrarian democracy to figure America as providing a new promised land for diasporic Jews. Moreover, her model of American democracy does not necessitate assimilation under the aegis of some universalized rationalism that requires Jewish citizens to forget either their ethnic and religious identities or their diasporic experiences. Nor does becoming, in the words of Morais, "a part of the glorious whole that constitutes the American Republic" necessitate the surrendering of differences within the broader Jewish community. Indeed, as our discussion of "By the Waters of Babylon" suggests, Lazarus presents America as the location where all the "outcasts of Judea" (Morais) may gather to reconstitute the "Soul of Israel." Yet this rebirth cannot fully unfold, Lazarus argues, until the already established Jews of America (the Sephardic Portuguese specifically) are prepared to cast aside their antipathy toward Ashkenazic difference.

"IN EXILE," RUSSIAN JEWS, AND FRONTIER AMERICAN DEMOCRACY

"In Exile" (Appendix 1) is a five-stanza poem that depicts idyllic, pastoral scenes wherein "soft breezes bow the grass" and Jewish comrades, unused to agrarian life, labor "beneath the shadowing oak tree" after "the Southern day of heavy toil." The poem opens with an epigraph that situates the poem on the American frontier. In the epigraph, an unidentified Russian correspondent declares that since their arrival in Texas "our life is one unbroken paradise. We live a true brotherly life. Every evening after supper we take a seat under the mighty oak and sing our songs." We never learn with any certainty how these Jewish immigrants came to be in Texas. Perhaps they are pogrom refugees fresh off the boat, as it were, who were recruited by organizations such as the Alliance Israelite Universelle/Am Olam and sent West to become farmers. Or perhaps they are Russian exiles who brought with them plans to form agricultural utopian communities in the American West, yearning, as Herscher puts it, to "strike roots in the American soil," despite having little farming experience. According to Herscher, these Jewish idealists saw America as a democratic utopia, "a great and glorious land of liberty, whose broad and trackless acres offer an asylum and a place for . . . courageous souls, willing to toil."[15] Lazarus's exiles demonstrate similar yearnings. The poem's images of "brotherly life" and "unbroken paradise," a phrase repeated in the second stanza, link to a broader discourse about agrarian democracy and the American Frontier's role in its development, as envisioned by founders such as Thomas Jefferson and extolled by writers and thinkers ranging from Henry David Thoreau, to Walt Whitman, to Frederick Jackson Turner.[16]

Richard Slotkin explores how the discourse of agrarian democracy represented the frontier as a "Garden of Earthly Delights" that held "restorative and regenerative power"[17] for any individual willing to risk the arduous journey West and undertake the hard work of agricultural labor. We see these revitalizing and restorative aspects of the agrarian life in the poem's opening stanzas. Echoing those peaceful moments when God visits Adam and Eve in the "cool of the evening" after their pleasant labors in the Garden of Eden, we find former Russian peddlers and merchants, these "unused tillers of the soil" and their domesticated animal partners, resting after a hard "day of heavy toil."[18] While we do not see them working in the poem, the transformative power of their labor is clear: a sense of "unbroken paradise" for both men and beasts.

The poem also subtly reflects another important aspect of the political ideology of the American frontier, the belief that it would provide an "inexhaustible stimulus for economic growth" (40), securing material rewards for those willing to do the hard work. This aspect of the frontier is reflected subtly in the opening stanza's images that bespeak of the immigrants' material prosperity, which includes land, livestock, and the rich products of their labor. We see "yoke-freed oxen," the donkey at a "deep trough," along with the "frothy pails" full of milk drawn from the "udder-lightened kine." The "rich, black furrows" evoke both the land's fertility and promise of rich bounty and the dedicated labor (both human and animal) that created them. In short, Texas becomes the site of utopian habitation for these formerly oppressed refugees. These transplanted Eastern European Jews have forged "a true brotherly life" through their agrarian efforts, enabling them to escape the degrading urban sweat shops and marginal economics of the large industrializing cities.[19] At the same time and in contrast to their experiences in Czarist Russia, these immigrants are ensured that they never again will suffer from oppressive, coercive political regimes who have always sought to bring "fire and blood" to the Jewish people.

The exiles, the poem suggests, are thus free to create an agrarian democratic community composed of Whitmanian "comrades" and "brothers," who are equally free to engage in Jewish religious and intellectual traditions (as we discuss further below) or just to "drink / The universal air." Importantly, the frontier enables (again echoing Walt Whitman, Henry David Thoreau, and other American Romantics) a world where humans, animals, and nature itself interact in equanimity in both work and rest. The oxen are "yoke freed," and the unburdened "patient ass" freely enjoys a drink "in the cool, deep trough." Even the cattle, who do not labor like the ox or donkey, have been freed of the painful burden of milk. Humans and animals each prepare to rest, "to lie, with limbs relaxed" and enjoy the cool breeze.

While there is nothing in the poem to indicate that these Jews are preparing for Shabbat, the poem evokes the biblical injunction that establishes the day of rest, down to the presence of oxen and asses: "Six days you shall do your work, but on the seventh day you shall rest, so that your ox and your donkey may have relief, and your homeborn slave and the resident alien may be refreshed" (Exod 23:12). Indeed, the subtle Jewish imagery even seems to echo Havdalah [service marking the end of Shabbat]: the fragrant "Fresh smells of earth" emerge as the day draws to a close, as if the earth itself and the "glebe" [cultivated fields] reward the herdsmen and their animals with invigorating scents, much like the spice box rejuvenates the spirit after separation from the joy and holiness of the Sabbath.

While the traditions of Shabbat and Havdalah are only alluded to and compressed into a single moment, together they suggest a closer connection to Jewish traditions than critics have assumed, particularly given their presumptions of Lazarus's complete assimilation. For frontier freedom, the restorative power of labor and resulting economic security, along with the Whitmanian democratic union of humanity and the natural world, do not necessitate that these Jews forget their heritage and assimilate. For example, though in the midst of evening rest, the poem's speaker in the third stanza attenuates the Texas Jews' joy by recalling both their own suffering during the pogroms as well as that of Jews at other times and places:

> The hounded stag that has escaped the pack,
> And pants at ease within a thick-leaved dell;
> The unimprisoned bird that finds the track
> Through sun-bathed space, to where his fellows dwell;
> The martyr, granted respite from the rack,
> The death-doomed victim pardoned from his cell,
> Such only know the joy these exiles gain,
> Life's sharpest rapture is surcease of pain.

In metaphoric sympathy, the stag and bird extend the relationship between humans and animals that we see in the poem's opening stanzas. The hounded stag's experience resembles that of the Ashkenazim who have escaped the Russian wolves. So, too, the bird's escape may recall their flight beyond the Pale of Settlement. Shifting from animal examples, the speaker remembers the suffering of Sephardic conversos during the Spanish Inquisition, particularly focusing on the graphic horror of the tortuous rack, the victim's arms and legs tied and pulled, sometimes torn out of joint or from the body.

The stag, bird, martyr, and victim's joy in release are explicitly linked to those of all Jewish exiles, whose songs are connected by similar experiences. Their singing reflects what the speaker, in the poem's closing couplet, characterizes as "the conquest of the spirit strong, / The soul that wrests the victory from pain."

The fourth stanza abruptly shifts from the exile's escape to their experience of frontier life and freedom in the New World, which draws another connection to the discourses of agrarian democracy. Slotkin notes that the democratic farmer was often figured as "a free individual, living on his own land, independent of others for the necessaries of life yet depending on his fellow citizens (and society in general) for protection, law, and civilized amenities." We see such idealizations in the poem's fourth stanza, when the Jewish farmers gather together after their various individual labors (plowing, herding, etc.) to enjoy the

> Freedom to love the law that Moses brought,
> To sing the songs of David, and to think
> The thoughts Gabirol to Spinoza taught,
> Freedom to dig the common earth, to drink
> The universal air—for this they sought
> Refuge o'er wave and continent, to link
> Egypt with Texas in their mystic chain,
> And truth's perpetual lamp forbid to wane.

The stanza presents a declaration of independence for Jews who immigrate to the American frontier, guaranteeing these Eastern European Jews a proliferation of freedoms. In Texas, the Torah and liturgical traditions ("the law of Moses" and "the songs of David")—which elsewhere Lazarus associates with the newly arrived Ashkenazim—are engaged alongside Jewish poetic and philosophical pursuits ("The thoughts Gabirol to Spinoza taught") that Lazarus grounds in Sephardic tradition. Together these form a "mystic chain" that links Jewish history, traditions, and culture. The Texas frontier becomes a site wherein Jews of both Ashkenazic and Sephardic traditions are relinked. Both strands of Jewish difference are supported by, grounded in, the agrarian democratic universals of life, liberty, and the pursuit of happiness, represented by "the common earth" and "The universal air" to which all have access. Thus, they are further bound, as Morais asserted in his sermon, to "that glorious whole that constitutes the American Republic."

The mystic chain further binds the Russian Jews and their journey to America to the exilic experiences of all Jews, recalling, then, others' experiences of exile and exodus, whether Egyptian bondage, Babylonian exile, the Diasporic exodus, the expulsion from Spain, or the pogroms of Russia, all of which form the chain that links Egypt with Texas. By linking Egypt to Texas, moreover, Lazarus seems to suggest that rather than mere exiled refugees, these Russian Jews have found a new promised land, which is reinforced by their sense of living in "unbroken paradise." In this sense, we can also see the Texas Jews and their coming out of Russia as reenacting the Pesach story.

The freedom stanza further draws our attention to the fact that American democracy, agrarian or otherwise, is rooted in conceptions of democracy that are specifically Jewish. Although not foregrounded in Lazarus's poem, the

Torah and other aspects of Judaism, as others have argued and demonstrated in this volume, are rich sources for the Western democratic tradition. Moreover, Jefferson and the founders of the United States did not invent the central metaphysical tenets of modern democracy. That honor goes to Spinoza.[20] As Lee Ward argues, Spinoza sought to overcome religious sectarianism (which in his time had torn Europe apart) by championing democracy. Influenced by Gabirol, Spinoza draws on neoplatonist conceptions of the Divine as a universal "substance" that appears as the many "modes" of the created universe. As we see in "In Exile," all beings share in this divinity.[21] While space does not allow for a full disquisition on Spinoza's theological-political system, two aspects are important to American democracy: rational-based governance and religious toleration, both of which Jefferson and other founders championed.[22] In Lazarus's poem, Spinozan democratic principles are pointed to as the Russian immigrants find the opportunity to think the "thoughts Gabirol to Spinoza taught." And these political ways of thinking become part of the mystic chain that links these immigrants together as a Texas community, that bind them to America, and that further link them to Jewish history and to "truth's perpetual lamp."

THE GREAT DIVIDE: JEWISH BELONGING AND "BY THE WATERS OF BABLYON"

That the new emigrants are now free "to think / The thoughts" of freedom and democracy suggests that they were previously not free to think, or even to live out, these thoughts, perhaps a reasonable assumption given their situation when in Czarist Russia. Yet it also suggests that these Eastern Ashkenazim may not have even had exposure to the greatness of Sephardic philosophic thinking until coming to America. In a sense, these Jews are just now getting the opportunity to partake of modernity. While "In Exile" does not push this question of Ashkenazic difference, Lazarus, like many long-established American Jewish families, and, before them, Western European Jews more broadly, took at best a dim view of Eastern European Jews. As Laurel Plapp notes in *Zionism and Revolution in European-Jewish Literature*, it was common in German-Jewish literature to provide positive portrayals of Sephardic characters and negative depictions of the Ashkenazic.[23] As a number of Lazarus scholars have documented,[24] Lazarus's own writings demonstrate that she, like many members of America's Jewish establishment, viewed the influx of Eastern European Jews as problematic, and she struggled to work her way through her own and the American Sephardic community's intolerance.

This struggle over the Jewish Sephardic establishment's ability to see the *Ostjuden* [Eastern European and Russian Jews] as more than fallen and degraded, as worthy of full democratic citizenship is demonstrated by the last poem she published a mere eight months before her death at age thirty-eight in 1887: "By the Waters of Babylon." Perhaps her most accomplished poem, "By the Waters" is, as Michael Weingrad notes, the first prose-poem published in English.[25] Lexically, syntactically, and structurally echoing biblical text, the poem, divided into seven short chapters with numbered verses, compresses nearly 400 years of Jewish diasporic experience, beginning with the Sephardim's expulsion from Spain and culminating in the Ashkenazim's arrival in America.

In order to examine and resolve the conflict between America's Sephardic elite and their negative responses to the influx of Ashkenazic "ghetto" Jews, Lazarus must first examine the basis for Sephardic attitudes of sociocultural superiority. She thus begins the poem with several chapters that measure out "the mystic chain" that links American Sephardim to Europe and to ancient Israel. The first chapter, "The Exodus," recounts the Sephardim's grueling expulsion from Spain and their sojourn to the "Continent of freedom," America. Unlike the biblical Exodus, their story is not about the struggle to achieve freedom from bondage. Rather, it is about the recovery of a people after freedom's loss, represented as a sudden rupture through Lazarus's starting the poem in medias res; we are in the middle of the expulsion, watching as "dusty pilgrims crawl" through the sere landscape under the Spanish sun's "blaze of azure fire."

The verses that follow depict a diverse group of people and animals who are on the march. But instead of the genealogical lists often associated with biblical narrative of sojourns, exiles, and exoduses (e.g., Gen 12, Exod 1, Ezra 2), Lazarus opens the second verse with a single "hoary patriarch" who is followed by a woman with a "sleeping babe," nestled in "her large enfolding arms" along with her other "little ones." The image is generalized: the identity of the "patriarch" could refer to any Spanish Jewish male and thus encompasses all lineages of Sephardim, while also conflating the expelled with the storied biblical patriarchs from whom all Jews descend. The image of the woman with her babe and other children memorializes the extent to which the expulsion impacted Jewish families. It further and strategically recalls the story of Mary and Joseph's flight to Egypt with the infant Jesus to escape slaughter by Herod (Matt 2), an association further reinforced by the "youth with Christ-like countenance" in verse 3. The sentimentality of these images, particularly the plight of the "little ones with bruised and bleeding feet," empathetically appeals to both Jewish and Christian readers. Further identification is enabled by a Whitmanesque catalogue of the people, their animals, and their possessions that equally enables Jewish and non-Jewish readers to identify with the experience of the expulsion.

Moreover, verses 12–14 invite readers not only to empathize but to experience the worries and sorrows of the people. As if writing a haggadah suited to remembering the exodus of August 1493, readers are commanded to "Listen to their lamentation" and are invited to share in the sojourners' loss and doubts ("Whither shall they turn?"). Verse 15 provides the answer to the Sephardim's plight, for Columbus, "the world-unveiling Genoese," will "unlock the golden gates of sunset and bequeath" to them "a Continent to Freedom!" That America is their promised destination (given by the "bird of the air" in the chapter's last verse) is important not only from a historical perspective but also in terms of establishing Sephardic preeminence in the New World. Lazarus thus invokes American democratic feelings[26] that enabled Sephardic Jews like the Seixases and Nathans (in concert with Christians like Washington and Jefferson) to rebuild the lost promised land.

Interestingly, the poem does not explicitly present the arrival of the Sephardim in America. Instead, the speaker shifts, in Chapter II ("Treasures"), to the deep Jewish past, in order to recover the "buried" treasures of Israel: "the golden knowledge, Truth" and "the delicate pearl and adamantine jewel of the Law." Knowledge, Truth and Law, already invoked in Chapter I:6 by the image of "the tenderly-carried silken scrolls," are part of the heritage the Sephardim bring to the Continent of Freedom and the refounding of the promised land, what Chapter III ("The Sower") enigmatically refigures as seeds to be resown by Israel. Indeed, Chapter III traces the impact of Jewish knowledge and law on world history. Echoing Jesus's Parable of the Sower (Matt 13:3–19; but also see Hos 10:12), the "seeds" of Judaism are sown by "seed-bearing Israel," giving rise to both Christianity (verses 3 through 7) and Islam (verses 8–11). While these two postdiasporic sowings yield destructive Antisemitism (the "treacherous boughs to strangle the Sower"), the chapter ends with the promise of yet a third planting, whereby Judaism's "golden knowledge" and "adamantine Law" will flourish in the United States. The chapter is a further reminder to Jewish, Christian, and Muslim readers of their shared history, a history that binds them together (as "People of the Book") and should unite them in democratic inclusion, freedom, and brotherhood in America.

Chapter IV ("The Test") continues to trace the diasporic experience, beginning with "the Passion of Israel," a recasting of the Passion of Christ. As with previous verses, Lazarus once again seeks to enable non-Jewish readers to identify with Jewish experience: like Jesus (the "divinely beautiful man" in III:6) and many early Christian martyrs, Israel was persecuted by the Romans, "bound to the wheel, nailed to the cross, cut off by the sword, burned at the stake, tossed into the sea."[27] Despite the persecutions, the speaker draws our attention to the heroic survivance of Israel and the continuing production of knowledge, poetry, and philosophy during the diaspora. The Prophet, Poet, and Sage certainly have biblical resonance (one thinks, for example of Ezekiel's encounter with the four angels, of King David's psalms, or perhaps Solomon's wisdom), and the storied, "monumental dead" and "standard-bearers of the future" foreshadow the catalog of Sephardic greats (Maimonades, Ha-Levi, Gabirol, et al.) that will open Chapter VI.

Yet this celebration of Sephardic triumph is "suddenly" interrupted in verse 8 by "a burst of mocking laughter" as "the shuffling gait, the ignominious features, the sordid mask of the son of the Ghetto" appears, the first of what becomes, in Chapter V ("Currents"), a "vast oceanic movement" of Ashkenazim fleeing the Russian pogroms. The "son of the Ghetto" marks what has been unmarked through most of the poem: the exclusion of Ashkenazim from the Sephardic imagination as well as (by extension) from the American democratic experience. "Israel," after all, includes both Sephardim and Ashkenazim; yet the narrator has largely spoken as though only the Sephardic experience—including the coming to America—is worthy of remembrance and celebration.

As scholars have noted, the speaker's shock of recognition represents an important shift in the poem. Lazarus's own writings demonstrate that she, like many members of America's Jewish establishment, viewed the influx of Eastern European Jews as problematic, and she struggled to work her way through her own and the American Sephardic community's intolerance. This struggle over the Jewish Sephardic establishment's ability to see the *Ostjuden* as worthy of full democratic citizenship has been the subject of much Lazarus scholarship. In a characteristic reading, Weingrad asserts that Lazarus's stereotyped "ghetto" Jew represents the views of "a late-nineteenth-century assimilated American Jew, uncomfortable with the alien qualities of East European brethren."[28] Weingrad correctly notes that the *Ostjuden* present Lazarus with "a formidable psychological challenge both to her understanding of Jewish identity and to her conviction that . . . American opponents of Jewish immigration were wrong."[29] And he acknowledges some of the ways in which the poem deals with the struggle over the extent of ethnic and cultural tolerance on the part of established Jewish-Americans or Americans more broadly: the ability to "transcend . . . prejudice and love the Jew—with understanding that, as a result, the Jew will shed his ignorance, superstition, and abjection."[30] But it is not the Eastern European Jew alone who suffers from "ignorance," and the point of transformation is not merely assimilation as so many Lazarus scholars have figured it. Missing from such analysis is how the poem also struggles with the question of full inclusion in democratic citizenship as part of the work of renewing Israel itself.

At the end of Chapter V, America, "the generous mother of nations," has welcomed the refugees, drawing them "unto her ample breast." Yet at this point in the poem it remains to be seen whether they will become full members of the American democratic landscape. While welcomed, "The herdsman of Canaan and the seed of Jerusalem" have moved, in keeping with the "safety valve" theory of Jeffersonian agrarian democracy,[31] to the frontier where they can "renew their youth amid the pastoral plains of Texas and the golden valleys of the Sierras." This repeats the image of the Russian Jews in frontier Texas from "In Exile," who found their new "life . . . one unbroken paradise" because of both economic independence and religious freedom. Yet, as we noted in our discussion of "In Exile," the Ashkenazim in "By the Waters" enjoy their freedom at a distance from the urban Sephardic elite; these Jews are, after all, safely stowed away in Texas, unlikely to make an appearance within the gloried halls of Shearith Israel or Touro. There seem, as was implicit in "In Exile," to be limits to democratic inclusion, set in part by the intolerance of the Sephardic elite.

Still ambivalent about including the *Ostjuden*, then, Chapter VI ("The Prophet") returns us (as does the start of almost all the other chapters) to celebrating Sephardic experience and tradition. Once again, readers are reminded of "monumental dead and the standard bearers of the [American] future" (IV:7) whose status appears now threatened by "the exiles of Babylon" (V:4). The first eight verses present a diverse catalog of figures whose philosophical, political, and artistic ideas form additional links in the mystic chain that binds America's Jews and American democracy to Jewish history, something all Americans, the poem implicitly argues, should understand. The doctors, scholars, and artists she celebrates were all part of what Lazarus imagines as illustrious cosmopolitan, tolerant societies that prefigure American democracy: Spain, Egypt, and Portugal, along with medieval French and Enlightenment-era German principalities.

Indeed, their influence was vast. Moses ben Maimon's medical learning (among other things), for example, spread beyond the Jewish world to influence Western medicine. Halevi's religious and secular poems are still considered primary examples of Jewish poetry. Gabirol had less effect on Jewish philosophical and intellectual thinking than he did on Christian thinking,[32] though he further influenced, as we've already discussed, Spinoza's understanding of the Divine, which in turn undergirded his thinking about democratic governance. "The Prophet" thus presents these Western European Jewish thinkers as important to the development of European (and hence American) artistic and philosophical thinking.

Lazarus implicitly (and explicitly) juxtaposes these glorified Sephardim and German Ashkenzim,[33] whose fame "resounds like the brazen-throated cornet," with Eastern European Ashkenazim. In contrast to the rationalistic tone of the first seven verses, verses 8–12 admonish readers to accept and even love their culturally and physically impoverished seeming *Ostjuden* brothers. The speaker draws our attention to the "caftaned wretch," "the ignorant, the coarse, and the abject," "the bigot," and "the creature of darkness" who have arrived on America's shores in Chapter V. As commanded by the speaker through a series of "Thou shalts," these new arrivals should be taken by the hand (verse 9) and welcomed by the American Sephardim as "My Brother" and "My Friend."

Such democratic embrace results in the unfolding of the redemption of Israel as forecasted by the final verse of Chapter III. The newly arrived Ashkenazim experience "fountains of love" cast upon them from the hearts of the American Sephardim, who have now laid aside their limited understanding of who is worthy of both Jewish and American citizenship. Granted, Ashkenazic names do not yet appear in Lazarus's list of famous Jewish thinkers, but that is only a matter of "not yet" rather than "never will." The American Sephardim experience is in turn a purification of their sin of exclusion. Their "quivering lips shall be pressed" with "the live coal," and, as the Seraph tells Ezekiel, "'Now that this [coal] has touched your lips, your guilt has departed and your sin is blotted out" (Ezek 6:7).

The redemption of Israel begins to unfold in the poem's final chapter, "The Chrysalis." America will provide the haven for the formerly oppressed Ashkenazim, who have survived Antisemitic oppression by cocooning themselves in the "cunningly enmeshed web of Talmud and Kabbala." Now safe, they can finally flourish, for "when the Sun of Love shines out with cordial fires, lo, the Soul of Israel bursts her cobweb sheath, and flies forth attired in the winged beauty of immortality" (verse 4). American democracy (the "emancipating springtide") and the American Sephardic community (the "Sun of Love") together enable, then, a rebirth for the Ashkenazim, the "Soul of

Israel." Implicit in this rebirth is a reunification of the two strands of Judaism, which must be sutured before "Israel" can be realized and which is possible only under the specific conditions offered by America: rational governance and religious tolerance.

CONCLUSION

"Identity politics" has galvanized the public sphere, cultural criticism, and academic scholarship, becoming what Kenneth Burke calls a "terministic screen,"[34] the lenses through which we interpret—for good or ill—the world based on individual interests, occupations, or ideologies. In the case of Lazarus scholarship, using religious identity as a primary screen tends to reduce Lazarus to a minor figure in American literature and democracy. Widening the scope, however, we find in poems such as "In Exile" and "The Waters of Babylon" speakers embracing a democratic spirit through empathy and acceptance. However, the speaker's struggle to accept the "strange faces" and "dark-bearded chin[s]" of the strangers in "Exile" reveals Lazarus's own struggle to include herself in the "mystic chain" that links all Jews and by extrapolation all Americans.

In the second decade of the twenty-first century, when hate crimes against Jews, Muslims, and other minorities are on the rise, we believe "Exiles" and "Waters of Babylon" can serve as a reminder of the importance to American democracy of welcoming and including the "other" after these "tired and poor" arrive on our shore. Our contemporary culture too often sees immigrants through the imagery of "The New Colossus": "huddled masses" and "wretched refuse." In contrast, the speaker of "Exile" imagines the *Ostjuden* foreigners as studious and purposeful, though anguished because of religious oppression. But on the Texas frontier they can enjoy freedom of "the common earth" and the "universal air." Likewise, our society might consider how to extend a "beacon-hand" to immigrants and minorities, to become a "Mother of Exiles," as Lazarus's most famous poem proposes. We too, like the speaker in "Waters of Babylon," must widen our vision and embrace our multiple ancestries, just as Lazarus herself came to support her *Ostjuden* brothers. These poems teach us that brotherhood is an ethical, cultural, and political imperative and a bedrock of American democracy.

APPENDIX 1: "IN EXILE" (1882)[35]

Twilight is here, soft breezes bow the grass,
Day's sounds of various toil break slowly off.
The yoke-freed oxen low, the patient ass
Dips his dry nostril in the cool, deep trough.
Up from the prairie the tanned herdsmen pass
With frothy pails, guiding with voices rough
Their udder-lightened kine. Fresh smells of earth,
The rich, black furrows of the glebe send forth.

After the Southern day of heavy toil,
How good to lie, with limbs relaxed, brows bare
To evening's fan, and watch the smoke-wreaths coil
Up from one's pipe-stem through the rayless air.
So deem these unused tillers of the soil,
Who stretched beneath the shadowing oak tree, stare
Peacefully on the star-unfolding skies,
And name their life unbroken paradise.

The hounded stag that has escaped the pack,
And pants at ease within a thick-leaved dell;
The unimprisoned bird that finds the track
Through sun-bathed space, to where his fellows dwell;
The martyr, granted respite from the rack,
The death-doomed victim pardoned from his cell,
Such only know the joy these exiles gain,
Life's sharpest rapture is surcease of pain.

Strange faces theirs, wherethrough the Orient sun
Gleams from the eyes and glows athwart the skin.
Grave lines of studious thought and purpose run
From curl-crowned forehead to dark-bearded chin.
And over all the seal is stamped thereon
Of anguish branded by a world of sin,
In fire and blood through ages on their name,
Their seal of glory and the Gentiles' shame.

Freedom to love the law that Moses brought,
To sing the songs of David, and to think
The thoughts Gabirol to Spinoza taught,
Freedom to dig the common earth, to drink
The universal air—for this they sought
Refuge o'er wave and continent, to link
Egypt with Texas in their mystic chain,
And truth's perpetual lamp forbid to wane.

Hark! through the quiet evening air, their song
Floats forth with wild sweet rhythm and glad refrain.
They sing the conquest of the spirit strong,
The soul that wrests the victory from pain;
The noble joys of manhood that belong
To comrades and to brothers. In their strain
Rustle of palms and Eastern streams one hears,
And the broad prairie melts in mist of tears.

APPENDIX 2: "BY THE WATERS OF BABYLON" (1887)[36]

I. THE EXODUS. (AUGUST 3, 1492)

1. The Spanish noon is a blaze of azure fire, and the dusty pilgrims crawl like an endless serpent along treeless plains and bleached highroads, through rock-split ravines and castellated, cathedral-shadowed towns.
2. The hoary patriarch, wrinkled as an almond shell, bows painfully upon his staff. The beautiful young mother, ivory-pale, well-nigh swoons beneath her burden; in her large enfolding arms nestles her sleeping babe, round her knees flock her little ones with bruised and bleeding feet. "Mother, shall we soon be there?"
3. The youth with Christ-like countenance speaks comfortably to father and brother, to maiden and wife. In his breast, his own heart is broken.
4. The halt, the blind, are amid the train. Sturdy pack-horses laboriously drag the tented wagons wherein lie the sick athirst with fever.
5. The panting mules are urged forward with spur and goad; stuffed are the heavy saddlebags with the wreckage of ruined homes.
6. Hark to the tinkling silver bells that adorn the tenderly-carried silken scrolls.
7. In the fierce noon-glare a lad bears a kindled lamp; behind its network of bronze the airs of heaven breathe not upon its faint purple star.
8. Noble and abject, learned and simple, illustrious and obscure, plod side by side, all brothers now, all merged in one routed army of misfortune.
9. Woe to the straggler who falls by the wayside! no friend shall close his eyes.
10. They leave behind, the grape, the olive, and the fig; the vines they planted, the corn they sowed, the garden-cities of Andalusia and Aragon, Estremadura and La Mancha, of Granada and Castile; the altar, the hearth, and the grave of their fathers.
11. The townsman spits at their garments, the shepherd quits his flock, the peasant his plow, to pelt with curses and stones; the villager sets on their trail his yelping cur.
12. Oh the weary march, oh the uptorn roots of home, oh the blankness of the receding goal!

13. Listen to their lamentation: They that ate dainty food are desolate in the streets; they that were reared in scarlet embrace dunghills. They flee away and wander about. Men say among the nations, they shall no more sojourn there; our end is near, our days are full, our doom is come.
14. Whither shall they turn? for the West hath cast them out, and the East refuseth to receive.
15. O bird of the air, whisper to the despairing exiles, that to-day, to-day, from the many-masted, gayly-bannered port of Palos, sails the world-unveiling Genoese, to unlock the golden gates of sunset and bequeath a Continent to Freedom!

II. TREASURES.

1. Through cycles of darkness the diamond sleeps in its coal-black prison.
2. Purely incrusted in its scaly casket, the breath-tarnished pearl slumbers in mud and ooze.
3. Buried in the bowels of earth, rugged and obscure, lies the ingot of gold.
4. Long hast thou been buried, O Israel, in the bowels of earth; long hast thou slumbered beneath the overwhelming waves; long hast thou slept in the rayless house of darkness.
5. Rejoice and sing, for only thus couldst thou rightly guard the golden knowledge, Truth, the delicate pearl and the adamantine jewel of the Law.

III. THE SOWER.

1. Over a boundless plain went a man, carrying seed.
2. His face was blackened by sun and rugged from tempest, scarred and distorted by pain. Naked to the loins, his back was ridged with furrows, his breast was plowed with stripes.
3. From his hand dropped the fecund seed.
4. And behold, instantly started from the prepared soil blade, a sheaf, a springing trunk, a myriad-branching, cloud-aspiring tree. Its arms touched the ends of the horizon, the heavens were darkened with its shadow.

5. It bare blossoms of gold and blossoms of blood, fruitage of health and fruitage of poison; birds sang amid its foliage, and a serpent was coiled about its stem.
6. Under its branches a divinely beautiful man, crowned with thorns, was nailed to a cross.
7. And the tree put forth treacherous boughs to strangle the Sower; his flesh was bruised and torn, but cunningly he disentangled the murderous knot and passed to the eastward.
8. Again there dropped from his hand the fecund seed.
9. And behold, instantly started from the prepared soil a blade, a sheaf, a springing trunk, a myriad-branching, cloud-aspiring tree. Crescent shaped like little emerald moons were the leaves; it bare blossoms of silver and blossoms of blood, fruitage of health and fruitage of poison; birds sang amid its foliage and a serpent was coiled about its stem.
10. Under its branches a turbaned mighty-limbed Prophet brandished a drawn sword.
11. And behold, this tree likewise puts forth perfidious arms to strangle the Sower; but cunningly he disentangles the murderous knot and passes on.
12. Lo, his hands are not empty of grain, the strength of his arm is not spent.
13. What germ hast thou saved for the future, O miraculous Husbandman? Tell me, thou Planter of Christhood and Islam; tell me, thou seed-bearing Israel!

IV. THE TEST.

1. Daylong I brooded upon the Passion of Israel.
2. I saw him bound to the wheel, nailed to the cross, cut off by the sword, burned at the stake, tossed into the seas.
3. And always the patient, resolute, martyr face arose in silent rebuke and defiance.
4. A Prophet with four eyes; wide gazed the orbs of the spirit above the sleeping eyelids of the senses.
5. A Poet, who plucked from his bosom the quivering heart and fashioned it into a lyre.
6. A placid-browed Sage, uplifted from earth in celestial meditation.
7. These I saw, with princes and people in their train; the monumental dead and the standard-bearers of the future.

8. And suddenly I heard a burst of mocking laughter, and turning, I beheld the shuffling gait, the ignominious features, the sordid mask of the son of the Ghetto.

V. CURRENTS.

1. Vast oceanic movements, the flux and reflux of immeasurable tides, oversweep our continent.
2. From the far Caucasian steppes, from the squalid Ghettos of Europe,
3. From Odessa and Bucharest, from Kief and Ekaterinoslav,
4. Hark to the cry of the exiles of Babylon, the voice of Rachel mourning for her children, of Israel lamenting for Zion.
5. And lo, like a turbid stream, the long-pent flood bursts the dykes of oppression and rushes hitherward.
6. Unto her ample breast, the generous mother of nations welcomes them.
7. The herdsman of Canaan and the seed of Jerusalem's royal shepherds renew their youth amid the pastoral plains of Texas and the golden valleys of the Sierras.

VI. THE PROPHET.

1. Moses ben Maimon lifting his perpetual lamp over the path of the perplexed;
2. Hallevi, the honey-tongued poet, wakening amid the silent ruins of Zion the sleeping lyre of David;
3. Moses, the wise son of Mendel, who made the Ghetto illustrious;
4. Abarbanel, the counselor of kings; Aicharisi, the exquisite singer; Ibn Ezra, the perfect old man; Gabirol, the tragic seer;
5. Heine, the enchanted magician, the heart-broken jester;
6. Yea, and the century-crowned patriarch whose bounty engirdles the globe;—
7. These need no wreath and no trumpet; like perennial asphodel blossoms, their fame, their glory resounds like the brazen-throated cornet.
8. But thou—hast thou faith in the fortune of Israel? Wouldst thou lighten the anguish of Jacob?
9. Then shalt thou take the hand of yonder caftaned wretch with flowing curls and gold-pierced ears;

10. Who crawls blinking forth from the loathsome recesses of the Jewry;
11. Nerveless his fingers, puny his frame; haunted by the bat-like phantoms of superstition is his brain.
12. Thou shalt say to the bigot, "My Brother," and to the creature of darkness, "My Friend."
13. And thy heart shall spend itself in fountains of love upon the ignorant, the coarse, and the abject.
14. Then in the obscurity thou shalt hear a rush of wings, thine eyes shall be bitten with pungent smoke.
15. And close against thy quivering lips shall be pressed the live coal wherewith the Seraphim brand the Prophets.

VII. CHRYSALIS.

1. Long, long has the Orient Jew spun around his helplessness the cunningly enmeshed web of Talmud and Kabbala.
2. Imprisoned in dark corners of misery and oppression, closely he drew about him the dust-gray filaments, soft as silk and stubborn as steel, until he lay death-stiffened in mummied seclusion.
3. And the world has named him an ugly worm, shunning the blessed daylight.
4. But when the emancipating springtide breathes wholesome, quickening airs, when the Sun of Love shines out with cordial fires, lo, the Soul of Israel bursts her cobweb sheath, and flies forth attired in the winged beauty of immortality.

NOTES

1. Quoted in Esther Schor, *Emma Lazarus* (New York: Nextbook-Schocken, 2006), 5–6.

2. Emma Lazarus visited the Newport Synagogue in 1867, which led her to famously reply in verse to Longfellow's 1854 poem, "The Jewish Cemetery at Newport" (elegizing what Longfellow figured as a vanished race and culture), with "In the Jewish Synagogue at Newport" (recasting Jews in secular splendor in "this new world of light").

3. For discussion of Lazarus's relationship with Emerson, see Schor, *Emma Lazarus*, 23–33.

4. Sabato Morais, *The Sabato Morais Ledger*, 396–97, http://sceti.library.upenn.edu/morais. Morais was an Italian immigrant, cofounder in 1886 of the Jewish Theological Seminary and a leading figure of what was known as "enlightened Orthodoxy." Morais

was remembered at his own death in 1897 by the New York *Yudisch Gazeten* as "'without doubt the greatest of all orthodox rabbis in America.'" For further exploration of Morais's role in the American *Haskalah* [enlightenment], see Arthur Kiron, "Varieties of Haskalah: Sabato Morais's Program of Sephardi Rabbinic Humanism in Victorian America," in *Renewing the Past, Reconfiguring Jewish Culture: From al-Andalus to the Haskalah* (ed. Ross Brann and Adam Sutcliffe; Philadelphia: University of Pennsylvania Press, 2004), 121–45. Schor, *Emma Lazarus*, 239–45, provides an overview of the many tributes to Lazarus's memory, but does not mention Morais's.

5. Ibid., 210.

6. Ibid., 210–11.

7. Ibid., 107.

8. Ibid., 79.

9. Klagsbrun, "Forward," in Bette Roth Young, *Emma Lazarus in Her World: Life and Letters* (Philadelphia: Jewish Publication Society, 1995), xv. In contrast to Klagsburn's claim that Lazarus's work is largely forgotten because she "held herself too much apart, too much above the people she sought to defend and counsel," we might equally say that Lazarus suffered the same fate of many nineteenth century women writers: outright dismissal in terms of literary, cultural, political, or social importance first and foremost because she was a woman.

10. Ranen Omer-Sherman, *Diaspora and Zionism in Jewish American Literature: Lazarus, Syrkin, Reznikoff, Roth* (Hanover: Brandeis University Press, 2002), 32.

11. Ibid.

12. Ibid., 33–34.

13. See Kiron "Varieties," for discussion of Morais's contributions to the American *Haskalah*. Isaac Leeser (1806–1868) was a major figure in Jewish biblical scholarship and the founder of the Jewish Press of America; both Isaac Mayer Wise (1819–1900) and Isaac Harby (1788–1828) played important roles in the development of Reform Judaism.

14. Morais, *Ledger*, 2; the sermon was published in the December 12, 1851, issue of *The Asmonean*.

15. Uri D. Herscher, *Jewish Agricultural Utopias in America: 1880–1910* (Detroit: Wayne State University Press, 1981), 32. According to Herscher, the Jewish Ararat farm colony in New York State, for example, was the first Jewish utopian agricultural community to be established; it was perceived by some as the potential site of Jewish redemption (29).

16. For Thoreau, see, for example, *Walden* (1854) and its celebration of rural life, and "A Plea for Captain John Brown" (1859), which Richard Slotkin (*The Fatal Environment: The Myth of the Frontier in the Age of Industrialization, 1800–1890* [New York: Atheneum, 1985], 270–71) argues draws on the frontier myth in its representations of Brown. Whitman produced numerous poems extolling the importance of the western frontier to the American experience; see, for example "Song of the Broad-Axe," "Song

of the Redwood Tree," and "Pioneers! O Pioneers!" Frederick Jackson Turner, one of the first historians of the American frontier, outlines the effects of the frontier on the nation's character, values, institutions, and traditions, focusing particularly on the development of American democracy: "the most important effect of the frontier has been in the promotion of democracy here and in Europe. As has been indicated, the frontier is productive of individualism. Complex society is precipitated by the wilderness into a kind of primitive organization based on the family" (*Rereading Frederick Jackson Turner: "The Significance of the Frontier in American History" and Other Essays* [New Haven: Yale University Press, 1998], 30).

17. Slotkin, *Fatal Environment*, 39.

18. Ibid.

19. As historians such as Herscher and Tobias Brinkmann ("Between Vision and Reality: Reassessing Jewish Agricultural Colony Projects in Nineteenth Century America," *Jewish History* 21 [2007]: 305–24) note, although most of the Russian immigrants of the 1880s had been merchants—some relatively successful—many wanted to avoid the crowded urban environment of New York City's Lower East Side.

20. Lee Ward, *Modern Democracy and the Theological-Political Problem in Spinoza, Rousseau, and Jefferson* (New York: Palgrave Macmillan, 2014), 22.

21. In Ward's understanding, Spinoza uses this pantheistic notion to "provide the metaphysical support for the power of the democratic state, itself the most powerful expression of organized social power. Spinoza's democratic state, organized around the twin principles of power and freedom, strives to resolve the theological-political question with a broadly tolerationist policy that would encourage a general intellectual climate of openness to scientific and philosophical inquiry" (ibid., 5).

22. Ibid., 133–86.

23. Laurel Plapp further argues that "German Jews would choose to identify with a Sephardic background in order to dissociate themselves from the Eastern European Jews, or *Ostjuden*, who were stereotyped as Oriental and degenerate. As German Jews strove to assimilate and gain emancipation, they needed to differentiate themselves from this stereotyped of the *Ostjuden*, and a claim of Sephardic heritage was one means of doing so" (*Zionism and Revolution in European-Jewish Literature* [New York: Routledge, 2008], 118).

24. See, for example, Schor, *Emma Lazarus*, 159–60; Omer-Sherman, *Diaspora and Zionism*, 56–60.

25. Michael Weingrad, "Jewish Identity and Poetic Form in 'By the Waters of Babylon,'" *Jewish Social Studies* 9:3 (2003): 107.

26. In so doing, she again reveals a connection to Whitman; useful studies of Whitman and democracy include Christopher Beach, *The Politics of Distinction: Whitman and the Discourses of Nineteenth Century America* (Athens: University of Georgia Press, 1996); Mark Bauerlein, *Whitman and the American Idiom* (Baton Rouge: Louisiana State

University Press, 1991); Betsy Erkkila, *Whitman the Political Poet* (New York: Oxford University Press, 1989); James Dougherty, *Walt Whitman and the Citizen's Eye* (Baton Rouge: Louisiana State University Press, 1993); and David S. Reynolds, *Walt Whitman's America: A Cultural Biography* (New York: Knopf, 1995).

27. Lazarus's lines recall well-known Christian and Jewish martyrs, including St. Catharine, who was tortured during the reign of Maxentius on the wheel; the apostles Peter and Andrew, as well as numerous other early Christians, who were crucified; the apostle Paul, who tradition says was beheaded; Polycarp, Bishop of Smyrna, who was burned; and Basilisa of Corinth and others who were drowned in various bodies of water (the Mediterranean, the Tiber, sewers, and so forth). The line also recalls the fates of the Ten Great Sages executed by the Romans (see http://www.chabad.org/library/article_cdo/aid/2713682/jewish/The-Ten-Martyrs.htm), who are remembered in the Martyrology service [*Eilleh Ezk'rah*] on Yom Kippur.

28. Weingrad, "Jewish Identity," 116.

29. Ibid., 114.

30. Ibid., 115.

31. Slotkin, *Fatal Environment*, 488–89.

32. Gabirol was argued against by Thomas Aquinas, but adopted by influential Franciscans such as Bonaventure and John Duns Scotus; for discussion see T. M. Rudavsky, "Solomon Ibn Gabirol," in *The Columbia History of Western Philosophy* (ed. Richard Popkin; New York: Columbia University Press, 1999), 173–76; see also Dan Cohn-Sherbok, "Solomon Ibn Gabirol," in *Fifty Jewish Thinkers* (New York: Routledge, 1997), 116–19.

33. Plapp, *Zionism and Revolution*, 118.

34. Kenneth Burke, "Terministic Screens," in *Language as Symbolic Action: Essays on Life, Literature, and Method* (Berkeley: University of California Press, 1966), 45–62.

35. Emma Lazarus, *The Poems of Emma Lazarus, Vol. II: Jewish Poems and Translations* (Boston: Houghton, Mifflin, 1889), 5–7.

36. Ibid., 58–67.

Judaism and Democracy

Lenn E. Goodman

In an incisive piece of analysis, Ann Ward distills the thoughts of Herodotus about Athenian democracy. The historical vision of Herodotus opens onto a secularizing vista, comparable, perhaps, to the secularizing outlook in which the medical work of Hippocrates took root. Herodotus, she finds, sets his Athenian narrative against the backdrop he paints of the birth of the Spartan, Median, and archaic Athenian states. In each case, "a notion of divinity behind the law arises that obscures the rational human agency involved."[1] The dissonance between "what people say"—that "the regime is divinely inspired," and the forces at work in its creation, "human reason and will—" leaves these polities vulnerable to tyranny like that of Deioces in Media. Humans are hard to govern, Herodotus reasons, being "jealous of their freedom and equality"—as witness the institution of the *ostrakon* adopted at Athens after the victory at Marathon and used to exile anyone the demos feared was growing too influential and thus potentially becoming a tyrant. Given the jealousies endemic in human nature, governance seemed possible only if "some men became like gods and other men became like beasts." Politics teetered "on a radical inequality and distortion of what is human." The underlying dilemma: "combining freedom and equality with the need for political power and government."

The rise of Athenian democracy offered a resolution of the dilemma, related by Herodotus in Book 5 of his histories: "movement from a divine to a secular foundation of government." In this account, Athenians take ownership of the state, legitimating the regime no longer by the fiction of its divine founding but "because they believe the regime is theirs." The new patriotism fed on nativism and "equality of speech"—for "all share equally in deliberation." Reciprocity was coupled with ostracism of the gods: "Athens managed to combine equality with government by instituting self-government. . . . what people say of the regime, that 'it is ours,' and what it actually is, a product of human agency, come closer together." The Athenians "internalize their regime." They see it as their own, "not the product of something outside of themselves." So they "possess a sense of wholeness rather than alienation."[2]

Athenian intellectual and cultural prowess, Ward argues, rests on Athenian self-determination, "taking account of the whole of human nature, both body and soul, thus making possible a life according to our highest human potential, the life of the mind . . . integration of the desires of the body with the pursuits of the soul." But there's a rub, a darkness at the heart of this Periclean vision. Athens could flourish and draw to itself the greatest minds, the richest produce, the most elegantly wrought works of art and industry, the most eloquent speakers and writers, partly because she was rich and partly because her men were expected to take risks for her and were willing to do so. Each citizen might pursue his private advantage. But, "pursuit of private material gain coincided with the public good only when conquering other cities."[3] Here lay the dynamic that would breed the Peloponnesian War, the tragedy of Athens as empire and destruction of the two great hegemonies, that of Athens and that of Sparta, losing their grip on the nominally independent city-states they dominated and then losing all, first to Macedon, then to Rome, scarring history with the first great correction to the myth that democracies do not wage aggressive wars or establish colonies—let alone, by their own nature, morph into tyrannies.

I doubt that Athens ever was quite so uniformly secular in outlook or quite so egalitarian as Ward paints it, through the scrim Herodotus cast over the cityscape or the scrum of its later history. Nor can we credit the achievements of an Aristotle or the pre-Socratics to Athenian institutions. The pre-Socratic thinkers who set the agenda of Greek rationalism hailed from elsewhere, and Aristotle was never a citizen of Athens. He came from a medical family at the court of Macedon and could not own property at Athens, let alone succeed Plato as head of the Academy, where he had studied and taught for nineteen years. As tutor and later beneficiary of Alexander, he fled into exile on Alexander's death, lest Athens, he said, sin again against philosophy. For the democratic assembly had chosen the death penalty, as Plato bitterly notes, by a greater majority than had voted to find Socrates guilty of impiety and misleading the youth.

Is democracy incompatible with theism—with monotheism in particular? One challenge faced today by the State of Israel (and echoed in challenges to traditional Judaism) is couched in the dual claim that Judaism is alien to democratic values, and that the ideal proclaimed in Israel's Declaration of Independence, of a democratic Jewish state, founders on an inner contradiction: The state born under fire in 1948 cannot be both Jewish and democratic. Against these claims, I'll argue here that many of the roots of democracy and of the institutions that ground its legitimacy, its moral strength and beauty—and, if carefully guarded, its stability—are anchored in the ideals and institutions of the Torah, where Judaism finds its moral and religious core, a book of law and culture neither authoritarian nor dogmatic, although critics and polemicists have often found it so. Some of the Enlightenment and post-Enlightenment thinkers who made the Bible the whipping boy of their personal struggles or political agendas often aimed more at Christian hierarchies than at authentic Jewish values. Ironically, they often retooled the anti-Jewish arguments of Christian predecessors, whose heirs held the reins at which they chafed: Jews and Judaism were safer targets than Christian hierarchies.

The ancient brickbats long hurled in Christian anti-Jewish polemics are still dusted off for secular or secularizing purposes: Jews were—or are—unreceptive, clannish, legalistic. The mythic sin of deicide yields to another ancient canard: Judaism is wedded to empty ceremonial, the letter rather than spirit of the law. Pious Jews cower before a wrathful, jealous God, hypocrisy shrouded in conformity. The Old Testament, as the Torah is often still called, dismissing the Hebrew Bible as outdated and too primitive for a modern mind, pictures a God far too lofty to descend from His high places and mingle with ordinary folk, let alone suffer and die for them; His once chosen people, too stiff necked to embrace the gentler teachings of Jesus and his God of love. Later, in post-Holocaust polemic, the people of the reborn state of Israel have added pride and even prowess to the sins of their ancestors, refusing, when singled out for bombings, stabbings, car and truck rammings, and relentless, indiscriminate rocket attacks, to turn the other cheek.[4]

A Christianity that barred salvation to anyone not saved by Christ was universal; Judaism, which saw God's love reaching all his creatures (Ps 145:9) and held that God reserves a place in eternity for the righteous of all nations (M. Sanhedrin 10, with Tosefta), was particularistic. The Synagogue was the spent crone on the left as religious processions entered the cathedral. The Church was the fresh young woman on the right. Today's secularizers still repeat the canards of their Enlightenment forbears: The Torah is no law but a storybook rife with myth and magic; its norms, if not dismissed as tribal savageries, are far better recast in the Gospels. They are shards and bones of a patriarchal culture jutting from the soil in an age that should have learned to get past them, fiats of a domineering God hungry for the sacrifice of his favorite son as consummate proof of faith and piety.

Today, in a post-postmodern, wishfully postcolonial era, an era that renders every word fraught, even pairing "democracy" with "Judaism" is meant to sound oxymoronic, as if to ask, "How can a race of black-frocked Talmudists, guarded by jackbooted paratroopers, make any claim to democracy in a state whose land is stolen from innocent, indigenous shepherds and olive growers?" So the only democratic state in the Middle East—one of a handful in the world—is regularly tarred with charges of genocide, while the death toll of the regimes in Syria and Iraq, the dynastic state terror machine of North Korea, and the millions slain by the communist regimes of Mao, Pol Pot, and Stalin are pushed toward history's memory hole, and the real neocolonialism of China in Tibet and Russia in Ukraine, the genocidal threats of Iran's leaders, and the rocketry of Hamas and Hizbullah are backgrounded among the global crises of Africa, Asia, and Latin America that *bien pensants* would rather not notice.

Our discussion, then, falls naturally into two parts: first we should consider just what democracy might mean, then show not just the compatibility of Judaic and democratic ideals and institutions but also the historical and conceptual rootedness of those ideals and institutions in Jewish law. There isn't room for more here; but, given the axe that well-financed campaigns of delegitimation have sharpened and fire-hardened to a fiercely antisemitic edge, we'll have a few well-chosen words to say elsewhere about the State of Israel,[5] which is not just the hope of Jews and Judaism but the canary in the coalmine of politics today. For, its future foretells the fate of every modern democracy and the democratic idea itself.

A WORD ABOUT DEMOCRACY

What exactly are we to mean by *democracy*? In simple terms democracy means rule by the people. But simple definitions are made to trip up simple minds. Rule by plebiscite, as history shows, is not democracy, partly because plebiscites leave little room for compromise and deliberation; partly because plebiscite rule can promise no stable regime. Stability, of course, is not everything in statecraft, as the practitioners of Realpolitik in the last century, and indeed the one before it, were too ready to forget. But a popular system fated to devolve into tyranny, as Plato thought they all would, is hardly democracy at its best. Regrettably, it proves untrue that no nation would give up its right to self-governance, once won. Such rights are all too easily surrendered, sold, or fled, for security, or bread, or luxury, or hatred.

Joseph Schumpeter understood democracy in terms of competition for popular support. Robert Dahl, like Harold Lasky, saw the safeguard, if not the essence, of democracy in the jockeying of diverse elites and institutions, pressing the Greek idea of the *agon* [contest] and taking the idea of checks and balances a step or two beyond mere mechanisms of division and separation of powers. For governance to be by the people and not just for the people, there must be means of selecting and, critically, of replacing those who exercise the final say. So there are good reasons for constitutionalism to set limits to the powers of the state and the duration of a regime. If authoritarian regimes are to be excluded and the rights of individuals and minorities—or even majorities—protected, democracies must be constitutional. It's too easy, without guarantees in practice, not just promises, for a party or person to govern in the people's name but not in their common and accountable interest.

Just how common interests are to be defined, served, protected—and conciliated with the interests of the individual and those dear to him—varies from one democracy to the next. The people need to have a say in defining their interests as persons and as communities—one reason why Jefferson and others of America's founders saw an educated electorate as critical in a democracy.[6] One cannot effectively define one's interests if one's notion of an interest or one's purview of the options is narrow or distracted. But, like democracy itself, the ways and means, content and effectiveness, slant and penetration of education vary widely. So there's a need for firm principles safeguarding the core interests of the citizens who constitute a polity. A written constitution may affirm such principles. But it may also prove farcical, as the Soviet constitution was, promising all sorts of goods but delivering few, and hardly fairly. For a constitution to be more than a paper rag, principle as practice is needed.

Consistency, from case to case and from day to day and year to year, is a necessary condition of justice. An unjust constitution—or erratic laws—can be worse than none at all. So it's easy to see how consistency became a cynosure in jurisprudence, anchoring the foundational idea of a written law and the judicial rule of *stare decisis*. Consistency promises fairness because (and insofar as) it rules out invidiousness and favoritism. But undergirding consistency is the fact that governance serves interests—first, perhaps, those of the governed, but also those of others not present or not spoken for—the needs and rights of foreigners and strangers and future generations, the deserts of other species, the demands of the environment, the claims made by monuments of nature and of culture, and the principles of fairness itself.[7]

The constitutions best known to us in our post-Hobbesian age presume that the governed want their interests served. The founding documents of the modern liberal state tend to equate those interests with liberty and property, although modestly clothing the category of property, at least rhetorically, in gentler words like "pursuit of happiness," effectively identifying happiness, self-judged, with fulfillment; and that generic good, in turn, with the means thought necessary to its attainment. Liquidity is critical here, assuring that earned or vested interests can be freely cashed to gratify desires. A tacit premise equates fulfillment with gratification of desire.

A key assumption of the theories on which modern liberal states were built is that when their rights to liberty or property are threatened, the people will stand up on their hind legs and act. That premise gained voice in the words of leaders ready to shoulder grave risk and contumely and to call on others to rise up with them against grievances readily spiked. Those words caught fire when the same men stood ready to fight or die for what they had uttered.

Two things we've learned from the history of modern states: First, the occasions on which "the people" do stand up for their rights are highly unpredictable but vanishingly small if risks or costs are to be borne in behalf of those conceived as "others," since they live elsewhere, or are not yet born, or speak a foreign tongue, or because some other overt or ascriptive difference allows their dismissal as nonpersons or lesser persons.[8] The readiness of democracies to wage wars, including colonial wars like those of modern Britain and France, and expansive wars like those of nineteenth century America and Australia, is an unhappy consequence of the penchant for popular democracies to turn populist, even *vokisch*. The sense of unity that unites a populace readily sours and turns exclusionary. It can be deadly.

Our second unhappy lesson: liberty and material interests prove rather fungible. That wealth can buy privilege has been known since history began. That people will sell their birthright for a mess of pottage is also an old, familiar fact, too easily overlooked by those who stress the primacy of rights over other interests but still hope to ground a theory of justice on the behavior of actual (or virtual!) human beings. Patrick Henry prized liberty above his life. But when he said, "Give me liberty or give me death," he wisely prefaced his words by saying, "I know not what choice others may make. . . ." His choice, rhetorically declared, was hardly empty. But he counted on others to share his commitment to live or die by and for the principles he was confident that many shared. Their united efforts made those principles actionable, transforming them from inchoate presumptions to bastions of a state. Fortunately for the American enterprise, a critical mass of rebels, rightly called patriots, responded by putting their lives at risk for liberty. But without a common vision of common rights and interests, a very different outcome might have followed.

Many today profess that a democratic state must be secular; some presume it must be socialist. Those claims play upon a pair of confusions. A soundly democratic society must be a free society—not because a democratic tyranny is impossible, the oppression of each by all, but because democracy defeats its purpose and belies its pledge to freedom when the people, as rulers, betray the ends for whose sake governance is tolerated. It's tyrannous to impose beliefs and spiritually laden practices that individuals do not freely embrace and love. But it's wrong to confuse a secular with a secularist state. A secular government neither promotes nor persecutes noncoercive forms of spiritual thought and expression and their moral and social appanages. But the same principle calls on government to foster spiritual exploration and expression. A secular state, by the logic of its franchise, has no more business promoting secularism than it has promoting any other sectarian program. Secularity is just one among the life options its citizens may explore or pursue.[9]

As for socialism, it's easily made a rider to democratic ideals: democracy demands equality before the law and equal opportunity, ideals too readily twisted to plead for equal outcomes. Talent and application then become irrelevancies, and publicly promoted norms distinguish only the more and less fortunate, as though all divergence sprang from chance. A democracy must serve the interest of all. That's reason enough to make social and economic safety nets a public responsibility—not on Immanuel Kant's grounds, that anyone might one day need help, but on Baruch Spinoza's: that need outstrips private sympathy and private means.[10] But state ownership of the means of production and the party rule that grasps such ownership undermine the civil rights that are the pride and test of a democracy. Frederick Hayek exposed the democratic pretensions of socialism in *The Road to Serfdom*, and Karl Marx and Friedrich Engels openly disavowed such pretensions in *The Communist Manifesto*. That was long before party rule had exposed itself as thuggery and bred a kleptocracy in China, North Korea, and other states whose people are caught in the socialist fish trap—easier to swim into than to escape.

DEMOCRACY AND JUDAIC NORMS

Biblical law is rooted in the sanctity of the individual. So we should start with that value in seeking the Judaic roots of the democratic idea. Genesis sharply distinguishes the slaughter of an animal from the slaying of a human being. Noah, surviving God's judgmental flood, is humankind's second founder. He and his progeny are permitted to eat meat and will enjoy the wine from the vineyard that Noah was the first to plant (Gen 9:3). But they must be cautious. Wine will compromise Noah and lead to the offense that foreshadows the destinies of his descendants (Gen 9:20–27). The knife presents a greater risk: The blood of an animal, symbol and vehicle of its life, must be neither consumed nor fetishized (Gen 9:4) but simply spilled out like water (Deut 12:16, 12:23–24, 15:23). Human bloodshed is quite another matter: the inestimable value of each human life is safeguarded by God's proclaiming capital punishment for murder. For human beings, male and female, bear God's image (Gen 1:27–28, 9:5–6).

Unlike Hammurabi's code, the Torah deems the relative status of killer and victim immaterial; likewise their age and sex. As Rashi explains, the law forbids striking down any human being [*kol-nefesh adam*, Lev 24:17, 21].[11] Yet intent does matter. The Decalogue commands not "Thou shalt not kill" but "Thou shalt not murder" (Exod 20:13). Intent sets murder apart from manslaughter. The Torah implements the distinction by instituting Cities of Refuge: "Whoever strikes a person fatally must die. But if he did not stalk him and God simply brought him to hand, I'll afford you a place where he may flee" (Exod 21:12–13; see also Deut 4:41; Josh 20:1–6). Making its rule operational, the Torah sets out markers of intent: malice aforethought and use of deadly force, typified by a malicious blow with some iron tool, or a rock or wooden implement capable of mortal injury. A fatal shove can mean an act was murder (Num 35:6, 15–24). In a characteristic vignette, the Torah pictures an accidental homicide: an ax head flies off its helve and fatally strikes a fellow woodcutter (Deut 19:5).

The Cities of Refuge were to be served by good roads (Deut 19:3), open to all and well signposted, the Talmud specifies. Nahmanides, citing the Talmud (B. Makkot 10a), has it that all forty-eight Levitical cities were Cities of Refuge, four for each of the twelve tribes. As Hermann Cohen notes, "the altar's protection for the murderer was abolished."[12] Maimonides contrasts the Torah's law for a fleeing murderer with the refuge accorded the inadvertent homicide:

> A criminal aggressor, however, is not to be pitied and sheltered when seeking our protection. His statutory treatment is by no means to be slighted, even if he appeal to some illustrious grandee: "take him from My altar for execution" (Exod 21:14), it says. This felon sought God's protection, grasping an object linked to his name. Yet God affords him none—let alone one who seeks human shelter. God orders him surrendered to the officer he fled. He must not be pitied and protected. Pity for destructive criminals is cruelty to the rest of the world. The virtuous middle lies here, of course, as prescribed in God's just laws and statutes (Deut 4:8)—not where the morals of the pagan age place it, when heroes were praised for proudly taking just anyone's part, victim or perpetrator, as celebrated in their stories and poems.[13]

The Torah did not dungeon the inadvertent homicide but protected him amongst the Levites (Num 35:6)—to cleanse him, Philo reasons, through a life with those whose sacred duties would sustain an ethos to heal a guilty soul. "Why," Philo writes, "did God open the cities of the Levites to fugitives from vengeance and deem fit that the holiest should live there side by side with men thought unholy, who had committed involuntary homicide?" Philo's first answer: "sinners come to the consecrated for purification." The hope he vests in the Levites is that their ethos might alter those who shelter among them, a hope fed by his reflections on the story of Abraham's plea for the Cities of the Plain: "we should try our best to save even those whose inner evil is bringing them to sure ruin. . . . Should some seed of recovery appear, however slight, it should be cherished. . . . For we may hope the germ might grow and the man lead a better life."[14]

The precious worth of human life is biblically treated as what we now call natural law. The Torah does not contrast the dicta of nature's law with God's commands but treats the two as articulating the same idea: God's prohibition of homicide specifies one demand of his covenant with nature. For God's creativity reached a peak when he created man in his own image. Human life must be cherished. Nature's universal law trumps positive law. So long before Sinai the midwives Shifra and Puah feared God (Exod 1:17) and disobeyed Pharaoh's genocidal decree against newborn Hebrew boys. These women knew right from wrong. Their work and common humanity gave them daily evidence of God's love of life: they let the boys live (Exod 1:18).[15]

The midwives' honest piety allowed them to heed a command as yet unspoken on the banks of the Nile. By choosing life they bowed to a standard beyond social approval or the fiat of a monarch—even one who might claim divinity.[16] Their choice helped make clear what sort of norms a genuine God would issue and helped define the values that would make the Torah welcome when it came. By flouting Pharaoh's order, much to the dismay of early modern apologists for the divine right of kings,[17] Shifra and Pua marked a course of civil disobedience and the sovereignty of conscience, critical to the democratic idea. Their dangerous choice raised a banner for the Torah's great moral theme, the love of life. So their story is told and their names are recorded not just to explain how Moses could escape infanticide but also to celebrate a commitment to conscience and to human life. Their acts resonate when God distinguishes the law Moses will impart from the practices of Egypt and Canaan by calling its rules laws to live by. So when they read the verse, "You shall keep my laws and statutes, which a man shall perform and live by" (Lev 18:5), the rabbis rule that human life takes precedence over every divine command but those forbidding murder, idolatry, and sexual crimes. Shifra and Pua were not jurists. But they staked their lives on the primacy of life.

One feature of the Jewish principles outlined in the Torah and developed in rabbinic rulings is the dynamism of their moral themes, strikingly emergent over the *longue durée*. Thus the Torah's preference for monogamy, reflecting the preciousness of the individual in God's eyes, leads ultimately, despite Patriarchal precedent, to Rabbi Gershom's famous ban on polygamy in the year 1000. Gerald Blidstein gives a sense of the life of the law through centuries of change:

> We are committed to the monogamous ideal. . . . We also realize that the emotional depth of our commitment is not truly generated by the communal *takkanah* [regulation promulgated by rabbinic authority] of Rabbeinu Gershom which banned polygamy . . . monogamy is strikingly coherent with the basic vision of marriage and the human person described in the tradition from First Man and First Woman on. Our commitment to monogamy fulfills that vision, even if it may have been achieved through the impact of patterns found in other cultures.[18]

One can see why Asher ben Yehiel could say in the fourteenth century that Rabbeinu Gershom's rulings might just as well have been handed down at Sinai. The same moral dynamic hems in the institution of Sotah [the biblical prescription for the case of a woman suspected of adultery], making it ultimately a dead letter. For the Talmud exempts from trial by ordeal any woman suspected of adultery whose accusing husband cannot be presumed innocent as well; it then suspends the very institution, arguing that one can no longer (if one ever could) presume such innocence (Mishnah Sotah 1–5).[19] Rabbinic reasoning similarly transforms the Torah's severity toward the incorrigible son into a regulative idea[20] and reverses levirate marriage from an obligation to an option better foregone. The process is well underway in the era of the written Torah, as clearly revealed by the institution and practice of *Halitzah* [ritual shaming of one who waived the sometime obligation].

A similar process is at work regarding slavery. For, alongside life, the Torah treasures liberty. Its ancient law does allow for bonded servitude. But it stipulates that such a state cannot be permanent without the servant's explicit demand. It treats causing death or injury to a servant in identical terms as the same offenses against a free man. And it commands that runaway slaves may not be returned but must be sheltered (Deut 23:16)—a stark contrast not only with Hammurabi's Code (15, 16, 19) and that of Theodosianus (5.17.2) but with the American Fugitive Slave Act of 1793 and its more stringent sequel of 1850. Nahmanides, characteristically, expands the biblical provision by elaborating its moral theme: the fugitive slave, he argues, having fled servitude, is no longer enslaved but free. Rabbi Naftali Tzvi Yehudah Berlin (1817–1893), known as *Ha-'Emek ha-Davar*, reminds his contemporaries that the fugitive, having sought asylum, must be cared for and sheltered by those with whom he has taken refuge.[21]

In the American case, too, the illogic of slavery was not obscure. Samuel Johnson voiced it sternly in his trenchant Tory criticism of America's restive colonists: "How is it that we hear the loudest yelps for liberty among the drivers of negroes."[22] James Madison saw the contradiction clearly between chattel slavery and natural liberty and listed it among the "vices" of the young republic as he sought to replace the Articles of Confederation before the fissures it left in the fabric of American society rent the infant state asunder. "Where slavery exists," he wrote, "the republican theory" must be judged "fallacious."[23]

Madison knew that a radical cure was needed if America's bold experiment were not to die in the birth canal; but even John Quincy Adams, no slave holder and a generation Madison's junior, saw no way of healing the abscess in the American body politic. Property rights in the capital and tools of the plantation economy barred the way. Madison fantasized that moving to New York state might "provide a decent and independent subsistence" and allow him personally "to depend as little as possible on the labor of slaves." But his political base lay in Virginia, and he keenly understood what a South Carolinan contemporary predicted, that slaves in America would not be freed without a civil war. Madison clearly saw that the ideals of liberty he espoused and labored to enshrine in law and principle were inimical to the slavery on which his way of life and that of many others depended. But seeing the contradiction, as he named it candidly, did not lead him to press to abolish slavery or even ban new imports of slaves. Nor did it keep him from holding the slaves he inherited, on whose labors his livelihood, learning, and leadership depended.[24]

The Torah is strikingly more active here than were America's founding figures. Not only does it forbid the return of fugitive slaves and ban involuntary lifelong servitude, it also demands that freed bondmen be given a start in lives of their own (Deut 15:13–14). Perhaps more tellingly, it forbids Israelites' collecting interest on loans to their fellows, bans permanent alienation of ancestral land, and sets out detailed rules for gleaning, charity, and a special tithe to benefit the poor. It opens the fruits of fallow lands to strangers and the poor and renders licit simple taking of foodstuffs from the fields and orchards where they grow. All these laws restrict debt slavery, aiming to prevent the rise of a permanently dispossessed and desperate class. Nehemiah, in this spirit, secured the release of debt slaves and return to them of their sequestered property (Neh 5:9–13).

The rabbis go much further: as the practice of slavery declined among Jews, the slave's gratuity became an employee's severance pay (B. Kiddushin 16b–17b, Sifre, Re'eh 119). For Talmudic law deemed slavery canceled among Israelites once Jubilee years had lapsed (B. Gittin 65a, Kiddushin 69a, Arakhin 29a; Maimonides, *MT H. 'Avadim* 2.10). But even when slaves were still held, their proper treatment, as mandated in the Torah (by a muscular reading of Deut 15:16) required one to share one's food and wine with them, the same as one's own in quantity and quality. A master must provide his servants with beds as good as his own. And if one had but one bed, the rabbis required that the servant be the one to sleep in it: It would be wasteful to leave it unused and would smack of the ethos of Sodom, a dog-in-the-manger sort of trick. An Israelite may not sell his slave abroad. Nor may masters require a slave to perform demeaning chores or make-work tasks, or jobs a tradesman might have done, unless the slave himself were of that trade. Little wonder the saying became current that to have a slave was to acquire a master.[25] One may work one's slave hard, Maimonides maintains, but both fairness and prudence counsel justice and compassion and exclude rigor. One may not shame or berate slaves but must help them advance materially, morally, and intellectually.

Rabbinic proof texts are often pretexts. But the real arguments in sensitive areas like these pivot on moral themes. Here, what the rules reflect is the recognition that even abjection does not erase the dignity that slavery holds in pawn. That theme in Jewish thought and practice long survives the demise of slavery as a recognized Jewish institution; its prescriptive force will survive when slavery is finally abolished worldwide. It's a universal value, part of what is meant when God promises Abraham (Gen 22:18) that his seed will prove a blessing to every family on earth through the precepts and practices his progeny and successors will spread by their thinking and the example God is confident they will represent.

If life and liberty are sacred biblically, property is not. It is, of course, protected. For the Torah recognizes the relevance of things to the quality of life, the exercise of liberty, and the expression of personal and communal identity. But if a culture inscribes its priorities in its penal laws, the Torah's priorities are etched indelibly in the fact that it never prescribes a capital penalty for a violation of property rights.[26]

In any crime, the Torah mandates presumption of innocence. That bias in favor of the accused is almost too familiar to be noticed. Yet by no means is it universal even today. In Japan criminal convictions are reached in 99.92% of cases, and no trial, in effect, gets underway until the basic facts are deemed by the court to be established; 92% of defendants confess themselves guilty as charged. By shame and psychological pressure confessions are extracted from detained suspects, with cultural and communal norms affording powerful leverage.

American norms of criminal law grew up in reaction to the frequent use of torture, deployed in the Renaissance not only by the Inquisition but also by no less authorities than the sainted Thomas More. Coercion, at least of a physical sort, is forbidden in America (although sometimes countenanced offshore, in the face of heated condemnation). Defendants here have a right to counsel from the moment they're arrested. They must be read their rights and may not be long detained unless charged with a specific crime. Even then they must be released unless found judicially to be at risk of flight or serious crime. But in Jewish law no confession is admissible in a criminal case (B. Sanhedrin 9b). The Torah demands two witnesses in such cases (Deut 17:6, 19:15), and interested parties are ineligible.

Maimonides explains the ban on self-incrimination in cases of capital or corporal punishment by observing that the accused may be troubled of mind—depressed or moved by a death wish to confess to crimes he did not commit (*MT* Sanhedrin 18.6; Laws of Witness 12.2).[27] Even earlier, Joseph b. Migash (eleventh to twelfth century) saw a risk of bias in confessions, since they are likely to accrue greater credence than potentially exonerating evidence. Rabbi David ben Zimra (called the Radbaz, sixteenth century) explains that one's life and body are not one's property, to be disposed of as one pleases (commenting on *MT* Sanhedrin 18.6 and citing Jer 18:4)—although in monetary cases acknowledgment of responsibility is not only admissible but desirable. Steven Resnicoff underscores the contrast of Jewish legal principle with the norms familiar to anyone who has seen a television police drama: Secular authorities, he writes:

> routinely question suspects and, when doing so, use lies, tricks and promises of leniency—undermining the reliability of any resultant confession. . . . Perhaps the most remarkable aspect of Jewish law's treatment of confessions is that not only is it impermissible to force someone to testify against himself, but a person is not even allowed to testify against himself. . . . Secular authorities often assert that the

> constitutional right against self-incrimination reflects the basic sanctity of the individual. Nevertheless, by cynically allowing confessions to be elicited by trick and deception, secular law makes a mockery of such pretensions. Under Jewish law, no ruse changes the rule: a criminal confession is not admissible.[28]

The Talmud tells proudly of Simeon ben Sheta who swore he saw one man chase another into a ruined building. Pursuing the pair, he found the aggressor standing over the still quivering corpse of the victim, his sword dripping blood. "Wretch!" he cried, "Who killed this man? Either you or I! But what can I do? Your blood is not given into my hands. For the Torah says, 'On the testimony of two witnesses or three shall a man be put to death'" (Deut 17:6). "May he who knows men's thoughts requite the man who slew his fellow!" (B. Sanhedrin 37b).

Many of us know the words ascribed to Jesus in the Gospel of John (8:7),"Let him who is without sin cast the first stone."[29] The story of the woman taken in adultery is related there pointedly to contrast Christian mercy with Hebraic asperity. Far fewer know that the challenge put into the mouth of Jesus (and so brilliantly realized graphically by Rembrandt) in fact welds a principle of law found textually in the Torah to another laid out by the very Pharisees John condemned: Deuteronomy (17:5–7) requires that those accusing someone of the capital crime of rejecting the Law and pursuing pagan worship must indeed cast the first stone—bringing home to all the enormity of the crime but also, to the accusers themselves, the enormity of their charges.[30]

The Mishnah (Sanhedrin 4.5) speaks vividly to the sanctity of each human life when it relates the cautions given witnesses in a capital case. Such cases, witnesses are warned, are unlike any other. A conspiring witness is liable for any miscarriage of justice (Deut 19:18). But, in a capital case, should one's testimony lead to conviction of an innocent, the witness is guilty not just of one death. For in Genesis God is heard by Cain to say, "the bloods of thy brother cry out to Me from the earth" (4:10)—suggesting, by the use of the plural, that not just Abel's life has been lost but so have the lives of all his potential progeny to the end of time.

The Torah, as the homilist suggests, affirms the inestimable worth of each human life, an inference confirmed by each person's link to God, the ultimate source of life. For the Torah's prohibition of murder is predicated on God's creation of humanity—male and female—in his own image (9:6). "Why was just one man created at the start?" the Mishnah asks. "To teach us that anyone responsible for a single death is seen as though he had caused a world to perish; and whoever saves a life, in effect has saved a world." The text goes on to invoke the uniqueness of each individual. A mortal stamps many coins from a single die, and all are alike. "But the King of kings, the Holy One, blessed be He, stamped every man with the seal of the first, yet not one is the same as another." In Greek thought, as Shmuel Sambursky explained, uniqueness can count as a deficit, amounting to idiosyncrasy. Here uniqueness is precious. For each human being is irreplaceable.

Only after anchoring human worth in personal uniqueness does the Mishnah move on to speak of equality—not as a formal principle but as a consequence of our common roots: Since we share a common ancestry—and are fashioned of the same earth—there is no nobler or gentler lineage. Yet there's still another implication of individual uniqueness: Each one of us may say to himself "For my sake was the world created"—for each of us brings to his life a unique perspective, takes from it a unique experience, and has the potential to make a unique contribution.

The idea of equality is implicit, as I've intimated, in the very idea of a written law. God's commands in the Decalogue were carved in stone (Exod 31:18), emblematic of their permanence. Publicity is a related demand, a corollary of the principle that just rules do not shift and morph from case to case. "No law is binding," Haim Cohn writes, "unless and until publicized"—a principle acknowledged in the Torah's frequent reference to God's instructing Moses to speak unto the entire congregation of Israel and report his commands (Exod 12:3; see also 20:18, 22; 35:1; Deut 5:4, 19). The Law was to be read publicly at regular intervals (Deut 31:11–12), informing all whom it governed of their rights and obligations. Historic instances of such readings are biblically recorded (2 Kgs 23:2; Neh 8:1–3).[31] They were important occasions and indeed democratic affirmations and celebrations of the Law's authority. But they were also instructional, and the ritual aspect of such instruction was integral to the Law's acceptance. For one cannot live by rules one does not know. Explicitness and invariant formulation are critical to the legitimacy but also to the effectiveness of the Mosaic law.

The Torah records Moses and Israel's elders instructing those who are to enter the promised land to inscribe on great, plastered stones set up on Mount Ebal detailed notice of God's law.

These were no phallic stelae like the *hermai* still venerated at Athens in the days of Socrates. They were inscribed with commands banning idolatry and mandating honor of parents and respect for others' property boundaries. No one was to mislead the blind; all must deal justly with strangers, widows, and orphans, honor the parental marriage bed, respect the sexual privacy of a sister, shun bestialism, assault no one, abhor murder for hire—in short, sustain the Mosaic law. The people, in a body, are to pledge allegiance not to some leader but to this law, cursing anyone who breaches it, themselves and their dear ones included (Deut 27).

In the Book of Ezra we read that scrolls of the law were to be deposited in a suitable archive as well as publicly proclaimed (1:1, 6:1).[32] There's quite a contrast here, as David Daube explains, with Roman secrecy about the procedures needed for successful litigation, enshrined in documents "jealously guarded in the archives" of a body "consisting entirely of high aristocrats." It was around 300 B.C.E., Livy reports, that a patrician, Appius Claudius, allowed his scribe, Cnaeus Flavius, to publish his account of these secret procedures and the calendar of dates suitable or unsuitable for litigation and other key transactions. Despite the predictable outcry from Roman nabobs, Flavius escaped punishment. He became a popular hero and was elevated to high office, far beyond what his birth had seemed to promise.[33]

Today when the Torah scroll is to be read in synagogue it is paraded through the congregation; and, once read, raised high for all to see, while the congregation chants: "This is the Torah that Moses set before the children of Israel" (Deut 4:44)—"at God's bidding through Moses" (Num 9:23). When Pauline teachings substituted Christ crucified for the life of the Law (Eph 2:15; Heb 8:13; Gal 2:19–21, 3:10–27), "zo't ha-Torah" [This is the Law] became "Hoc est corpus Meum" [This is my body] (Luke 22:19; Matt 26:26; Mark 14:22; 1 Cor 11:24), a phrase later ridiculed by Protestants who scoffed at the idea of transubstantiation and mocked as "hocus pocus," the sound echoing through cathedral apses at the magical moment when the elevated host became the very flesh of Christ. The law, patent to all, was itself transfigured into a mystery.

Rabbinic law moved in quite the opposite direction, extending the principle that a law must be promulgated before an act is criminalized, to demand that a would-be criminal must be cautioned as to the unlawfulness of the act he is about to commit—otherwise, a human court is deemed unauthorized to order the statutory penalty, and punishment is left to God (B. Sanhedrin 54ab, 60b, 66a; Makkot 5b, 13b; Avodah Zarah 51b; Yevamot 3b; Yoma 53a).

A core element of freedom in democratic theory and practical norms is liberty of thought and the liberties of expression deeply intertwined with it—since expression is at once the fairest fruit and the deepest root of intellectual and spiritual liberty. For thought of any subtlety or complexity needs articulate expression to attain clarity—and needs debate too, if it's to attain cogency. Freedom of thought and expression—of speech and the press—like freedom of association were demands that grew from Europe's bitter schooling in centuries of religious wars and persecutions that barely ended with the rise of the secular republics and constitutional monarchies that gained prominence and credence in good part from popular and learned reaction to those horrors.

The American Constitution and its Bill of Rights in particular were among the more explicit expressions of that reaction. Examining the Torah, we find that intellectual liberty is not promised but presumed. As Cohn writes, "neither the Written nor the Oral Law contains any explicit precept to believe in God or not to believe in other deities."[34] The very idea of framing religious obligations in terms of faith is Christian, an offshoot of the Christian idea, central to the Reformation and its Augustinian roots, that salvation is by faith. Salvation is not the core issue in Judaism, where the goal is sanctification of this life, not escape from it. Faith in the Hebrew Bible means trust. Its locus is communal, not strictly individualistic; its basis is covenantal; its chief expression is practical, not verbal.

Maimonides speaks not of faith but of belief—which, he argues, must be grounded in understanding: "Belief is not what you say but what you think when you hold something to be so. . . . There is no believing without first thinking."[35] The Torah, in fact, does not ask us to rest our hopes on faith. Belief is not a thing to be commanded by some authority or even by one's own sheer will power. Following in the footsteps of Moses Mendelssohn, Cohn puts it well: Only experience can lead one "to have confidence in God" or even, "to be aware of God." That is why the Torah appeals to Israel's experience when it calls on the people to accept God's laws.[36]

Many of the commandments, Maimonides argues, do have a doxastic function. They aim to instill certain beliefs and attitudes. But there's a subtle dialectic in play: attitudes affect actions; and actions, when made customary and habitual, affect character. Rituals and symbols like those of Sabbath observance set a trellis for beliefs; and beliefs, in turn, as Maimonides understands the dialectic, when examined and reflected on, lay foundations for understanding. His celebrated Thirteen Articles[37] are a case in point. Each of them is meant to function as a gateway to understanding, allowing all Israel and the righteous of all nations to be promised "a portion in the World to Come," even though many lack the conceptual prowess that would link their minds with the Divine.

Building on Plato's thesis that for most practical purposes belief is as good as knowledge—it can get one from Piraeus to Larissa even without mastering navigation—Maimonides finds that the ethical practices and the shared beliefs embedded in the Torah's rituals bear implicit reference to higher ideas. By sharing in these, ordinary people gain their "portion" in immortality, even if they cannot articulate their linkage to divinity in conceptual terms. Sabbath observances, being active, are sanctioned biblically; beliefs are not. Ritual practice, then, so prominent in biblical and rabbinic law as to provoke critique in Christian and especially in Protestant and post-Protestant settings, subtly solves a problem that other religions have addressed by futile, often bloody, efforts to enforce dogmas: these institutions of the culture the Torah founds communicate ideas, some rather elevated, without demanding or imposing feats of faith.

COVENANT AND DIGNITY

The Torah ordains no specific mechanism of governance. The legislator, biblically and rabbinically, is God. While Moses lived, it was he who brought God's commands to Israel. For forty days and nights he kept to his mountain to learn God's will. But it was he who conveyed God's expectations to the people in human words, spoken and carved in stone (Exod 20:16, 24:18; Deut 9:9, 10:1–5). Israel accepts God's rule by acclamation. But it is not a leader that the people acclaim, as they would acclaim Saul as king. What they accept are the provisions of God's law (Exod 19:5, 19:8, 24:3, 24:7; Deut 27). They have joined a covenant. Daniel Elazar, a brilliant thinker who devoted much of his far too short but highly productive life to the study and advancement of the covenant idea, defines a covenant in generic terms:

> A covenant is a morally informed agreement or pact based upon voluntary consent and mutual oaths or promises, witnessed by the relevant higher authority, between peoples or parties having independent though not necessarily equal status, that provides for joint action or obligation to achieve defined ends (limited or comprehensive) under conditions of mutual respect which protect the individual integrities of all the parties to it. Every covenant involves consenting, promising and agreeing. Most are meant to be of unlimited duration, if not perpetual. Covenants can bind any number of partners for a variety of purposes, but in their essence they are political in that their bonds are used principally to establish bodies political and social.[38]

A covenant does not presume its parties equal. But the very act of cutting a covenant, as the Hebraism has it—forging, as we might say—does presume one sort of equality since it requires free consent. That's true not only of a pact among the governed formalizing what was, perhaps, a more informal communal unity, but also of a covenant with a ruler, and even Israel's with God. God has chosen and been chosen by Israel as a nation. He has freed the people and called them his own. He has declared himself their God, and they have accepted him—as they sing in their moment of liberation at the Sea of Reeds: "This is my God, and I will exalt him" (Exod 15:2).[39] The need for mutuality seems obvious here in terms of natural law: a law is ineffective unless accepted and cannot remain effective unless lived by. Indeed, the principle of desuetude is integral in rabbinic ideas of law. When ancient rabbis sought to extend to olive oil the stringent rules of purity and sanctity that govern wine, the rules they commended were not practiced by the people, and the norms for oil became a dead letter—as did efforts to ban meat and wine after Rome's destruction of the Temple in Jerusalem (Tostefta Sotah 15.10).[40]

Israel's older and larger covenant with God suffered no such fate. It was accepted because the people could see the wisdom and justice of its principles—which other nations, too, were expected to recognize, a distinctive reality check (Deut 4:5–7). Through its appeal to truth and justice and the clear tilt toward mercy and generosity that its legal rules and moral principles invoked, God's covenant linked all Israel with one another in formal bonds richer and stronger than those of their real or notional shared descent. It made mutual responsibility actionable morally, socially, even judicially. God was guarantor of the norms spelled out in his legislation, but Israel's adherence was the final test. For the Torah was not given to slaves. It presumed the freedom of those who embraced it. Only free persons could make a moral and civil charge their own. And the vitality of the Torah's laws, not least in their open-ended moral expectations regarding obligations to self and others, called for continuous striving and commitment.

So the life of the law rested at once on loyalty to the God who gave it and on every Israelite's commitment to the rest and to humanity and nature: all Israel must love God, love each other, love and sustain the stranger and the helpless. The Torah's narratives, running back to the creation and the histories of the first human couple and of Noah, mankind's second founder, laid out the rightful boundaries of other nations. For it was not just private boundary markers that must not be moved. The Law's first narratives mandated and modeled stewardship for living creatures—the animals God had made (Gen 6:19–20, 7:2, 9:10) and the garden he had planted (Gen 2:15)—animals to be kept from undue suffering (Exod 20:10, 23:5, 11–12; Lev 22:28; Deut 22:4, 6–7, 10,

25:4),[41] trees to be preserved, natural objects safeguarded from wanton destruction, even ordinary objects kept from waste (See B. ullin 7b).

The Torah's covenant idea, as Elazar explains, came to America via the biblicism of the Puritans, reflecting the religious reforms wrought by Huldrych Zwingli (1484–1531), his successor Heinrich Bullinger (1504–1575), and John Calvin (1509–1564). The work of these reformers laid a spiritual foundation in the New World for the biblical commitment to the sanctity of the individual, vested in personal freedom and human dignity, the loci and foci of human rights in a democratic polity. Theorists like Hobbes could ground natural rights in the virtual power of anyone to slay another. Locke could rest civic rights on the natural right of self-protection that anyone might be expected to reserve when seeking shelter in a civil order from an anarchic state of nature. His thesis, answering Hobbes, enshrines the principles of England's Glorious Revolution and anchors the American ideal of inalienable rights. But the older idea of a covenant grounds individual rights existentially, anchoring them in the very life of persons as conscious and conscientious souls. America's founders could call human rights not only inalienable but God given. For it was not the state that gave them.

Enlightenment thinkers spoke readily and fluently of equality—in part because their cause targeted a monarch and the pyramid of class and caste that both sustained and sapped European societies. But if human equality is to be fleshed out with material content, it must rest on the inestimable worth of persons. Robert Cover, a Yale jurist, contrasting the Western, liberal rhetoric of equal rights with the more materially substantive jurisprudence of the mitzvot, where obligations are divinely given duties (and, at the same time, by that very token, blessings for those given those obligations), cites a case in point from Maimonides' discussion of impartiality in his Code of Jewish law:

> It is an affirmative commandment for a judge to judge justly, as it says: "In justice shalt thou judge thy fellow" (Lev 19:20). What is judicial fairness? Impartial treatment of both parties in every way, not allowing one to state his case fully while instructing the other to be brief, not showing courtesy to one and addressing him gently while being severe and harsh with the other. If one party is dressed well and the other poorly, the judge must tell the one respectably attired: Either dress him like yourself, or dress like him, so that you look like equals. Then the trial can begin.[42]

Rights mean nothing or worse than nothing without dignity. We can see the tacit reference to the existential worth of persons, little honored in liberal democratic theory but indispensable to it, if we consider a problem in Kant's moral philosophy.

Kant formulates the categorical imperative in two ways. One looks to the idea of a universal law of nature, the other to the deserts of subjects: persons must be treated never solely as means to an end but always, at the same time, as ends in themselves. The first formulation links fairness with the uniformity that underwrites the idea of written laws in general and constitutionalism specifically. It tacitly acknowledges the golden rule and nods toward the Torah's command to love each other as we love ourselves. But a tip of the hat is not an argument: applying the same rule to all presumes some recognition of human worth but does not vindicate or even define it. Kant's second formulation does impute a special status to the individual as a locus of worth and suggests its basis: each person is a locus of value because each person frames goals, projects, and plans, including projects and plans of self-definition. It's because human beings are moral subjects that they deserve treatment as such. The core of ethical practice, as I've argued, is to treat all beings as what they are.

The resolve and even the legal commitment to treat all persons equally would be empty without the imputation of worth to persons and their projects. Without that, equality becomes a grotesque parody of the goods that moral principles are framed to protect. But despite the moral dependence of Kant's formal rule on the material, the material version does not follow from the formal. It cannot, since there's more to justice than equality.

"Duty itself," G. W. F. Hegel wrote, is "without content." Yet, "ethical life is not abstract like the good." What gives ethics its critical concreteness is the family in the first instance; then, on a larger plane, civil society, forged to unity by the work of the state.[43] Stable families are "the prime unit of civil society," as Maimonides explains. Civil society depends on stable families.[44] Liberal theory tends, so far as possible, to leave the family alone, and rightly so. Likewise with other informal or natural social groups. What is communal—be it tribal or congregational, ethnically organized or built around neighborhoods, schools, or interest groups—neither wants nor needs the heavy hand or still heavier foot of the state, except when things seem likely to get out of hand. Yet culturally there's an all-the-way-downness that liberal states rely on: families, clubs, sports teams, and, yes tribes and clans, faiths and lodges, if fair and open, breed an open society and infuse it with varied versions of the values they canonize and project, most often in the symbols, rituals, and narratives they espouse. In that sense their life is the life of the state, and their rigidity or death can mean death or decrepitude for the state.

John Dewey, who began his philosophical life as a reader of Hegel, saw the importance of thematic unity or coherence in the life of a society. But it was easy for him or for his readers to confuse coherence with univocity and, impatiently, to think thematic harmony must be impressed top down rather than allowed to grow and flourish organically, from the ground. The good health of the state depends on the good health of its families, religious and social communities, schools and universities, even clubs and bowling leagues. But when the state, in recognition (or denial) of that dependence, begins impatiently to tell religions, scouting organizations, families, clans, and schools, bakeries and hobby shops what they shall be, the state has not just put the cart before the horse, it has sapped the ground it stands on and hacked at the branch on which it perches. This is not just a matter of the eggs teaching the chicken. It's more a case of failure to see what's molecular and what's a construct that will be only as stable as its elements and their ordering.

Liberal theorists have balked at even mentioning the ways in which Kant's two principles inform each other. For the end-in-himself formulation is metaphysical, resting on the ontic standing of persons. Viewed from a top-down perspective, the God's-eye point of view the Torah so often adopts and invites, regarding persons as creatures of a loving God, human dignity becomes a religious topic, reflecting our creation in God's image. Even a pagan philosopher like Seneca could say "homo sacra res homini" [man is sacred to man].[45] Liberal thinkers, however, are chary of clouding their rhetoric with too abstract or too pious an expression of moral concerns, and America's founding documents soft-pedal their metaphysical premises and religious motives. The documents are laced with words like "God-given" and "inalienable," as hints or reassurances. But they decline to press a metaphysical or religious thesis. As a result, the American polity relies tacitly on "the background culture" of its people and communities to give practical, positive content to the founders' brief: it could be taken for granted that defendants would defend themselves, that claimants would assert their rights and demand their due. One result of the founders' reticence, practical and welcome but fraught with occasion for future dispute: the basis of human rights remained largely unstated; their content, often unspecified. It seemed obvious to the founders what was meant. To many it still does. But neither they nor we have found consensus about those anchor points or the reach of their demands.

Alexis de Tocqueville keenly saw the problem and its interim solution: American civil and civic life rests on a bed of religious culture: there was, in sternly defended principle, no warrant for confessional conformity. But there was an often unstated, largely unacknowledged reliance on the confessional commitments of the people. There was no overt enforcement of doctrinal conformity, but there was a tacit expectation that action and to some extent belief settle within imperfectly defined but socially visible parameters. Drawing on his experience in America, de Tocqueville can tell his European readers much that the concept of equality alone would never have shown them. Acknowledging the open air afforded by religious freedom in America, he adds:

> But revolutionaries in America are obliged to profess openly a certain respect for the morality and equity of Christianity, which does not permit them to violate its laws easily when they are opposed to the execution of their designs; and if they could raise themselves above their own scruples, they would still feel they were stopped by those of their partisans. Up to now, no one has been encountered in the United States who dared to advance the maxim that everything is permitted in the interest of society. An impious maxim—one that seems to have been invented in a century of freedom to legitimate all the tyrants to come. So, therefore, at the same time that the law permits the American people to do everything, religion prevents them from conceiving everything and forbids them to dare everything. Religion, which, among Americans, never mixes directly in the government of society, should therefore be considered as the first of their political institutions; for if it does not give them the taste for freedom, it singularly facilitates their use of it. It is also from this point of view that the inhabitants of the United States themselves consider religious beliefs. I do not know if all Americans have faith in their religion—for who can read to the bottom of hearts?—but I am sure that they believe it necessary to the maintenance of republican institutions. This opinion does not belong only to one class of citizens or to one party, but to the entire nation; one finds it in all ranks.[46]

Instantiating his observation of the consensus he names, de Tocqueville writes of the warmth and indeed self-sacrifice of those who sustained America's westward movement. Among their motives he finds not only a belief in manifest destiny or an appetite for new opportunities, new challenges, and new freedoms, but also the idea that religion must move westward with the pioneers for America to remain a republic. And, echoing the Torah's values, he finds a union of spiritual with worldly interests that he expects will surprise readers in Europe, where spiritual and earthly concerns were so often seen as rivals, a mistress and a bride, love of this world and hope of the next.[47]

Tocqueville's discovery of the American marriage of worldliness with spirituality was not unrelated to his observations of the dignity expected and to a striking degree (by contrast with what he knew in Europe) accorded to American individuals of all classes and even, in some measure, of all backgrounds. For hope is the seed of dignity. And a worldly religion, where hope need not be dismissed as pie in the sky, helps make hope realistic and allows worldly effort and its fruits to be seen as rungs of a ladder, where personal, familial, communal, and national advancement bear spiritual significance and are not cut off from moral, social, and intellectual advancement. Such a union is evident in the biblical narratives of the lives of Israel's patriarchs. And, despite the risks of confusing worldly success with grace or virtue, de Tocqueville saw that union in the lives and dreams and multigenerational odysseys of the Americans he met. That cultural union of law with love, on which America's success still rests, is anchored in the alliance of humane and liberal institutions with the biblical heritage that has become a common heritage of the West. The same alliance of liberal institutions with biblical humanity is Israel's hope and heritage as well.

NOTES

1. Ann Ward, *Herodotus and the Philosophy of Empire* (Waco: Baylor University Press, 2008), 1.

2. All the passages quoted in this paragraph are in ibid., 2.

3. Ibid., 2–3.

4. Isaiah still speaks for suffering Israel, a people who have long had cause to practice patience: "I gave my back to those who beat me and my cheeks to those who tore my beard. I did not hide my face from scorn and spitting. But the LORD God supports me. So I am unafraid. I set my face like flint. I know I need feel no shame. He who will justify me is near. Who will contend with me? Let us face justice together!" (Isa 50:6–8). The admonition to turn the other cheek is most familiar now from the Sermon on the Mount: "You have heard, 'An eye for an eye and a tooth for a tooth' [Exod 21:24], but I say unto you, resist not evil. Whosoever shall smite thee on thy right cheek turn to him the other too" (Matt 5:38–39). The Gospel maxim, as David Daube writes, "is frequently adduced in favor of a pacifist attitude. Historically, however, that is not its import at all." The Torah's so-called *lex talionis*, the "law of the claw," as the Rabbis understood it, meant that the perpetrator of a physical assault "must pay not only for any damage and for medical expenses but also for the contempt involved (M. Bava Kamma 8.1). Jesus, by contrast, counseled meek acceptance of scorn." A slap in the face was the standard rabbinic example. Jesus advised humble submission to the humiliation: "Put your aggressor to shame by turning the other cheek." Forego compensation for the insult, he urged. But

so did the rabbis: "And to those that curse me let my soul be dumb; yea, let my soul be like dust to all." David Daube, *Civil Disobedience in Antiquity* (Edinburgh: Edinburgh University Press, 1972), 110. Neither the Sermon on the Mount nor its Jewish sources, Daube argues, excludes all forms of forceful retaliation against overt violence.

5. See Lenn E. Goodman, "Democracy in the State of Israel," *Society* 55:2 (March/April, 2018): 170–80.

6. See Jefferson's letter to Charles Yancey, January 6, 1816; see Jennings L. Wagoner, *Jefferson and Education* (Chapel Hill: Thomas Jefferson Foundation, 2004). Jefferson, of course, founded the University of Virginia; Ben Franklin, the University of Pennsylvania. John Quincy Adams won the Federalist battle against states' rights advocates, to use the proceeds of a bequest by James Smithson to establish the Smithsonian Institution, for the "increase and diffusion of knowledge."

7. See Lenn E. Goodman, *On Justice: An Essay in Jewish Philosophy* (Oxford: Littman Library, 2008).

8. We think of the votelessness of women for much of modern history; of slavery, of course, still rampant in much of the world; of Jim Crow, surely; but also of abortion, legalized in the wake of campaigns to deny personhood or real worth to the fetus—and, not least, the failure of the world's liberal democracies to halt or even stem the Nazi Holocaust.

9. See Lenn E. Goodman, *Religious Pluralism and Values in the Public Sphere* (Cambridge: Cambridge University Press, 2014).

10. "Men are also won over by generosity, especially those who lack the means of acquiring what they need to sustain life. But to bring aid to everyone far exceeds the powers and advantage of a private person. For his wealth is quite unequal to the task, and the individual's resources of character are too limited for him to be able to unite in friendship with all men. So the care of the poor falls upon society as a whole." Baruch Spinoza, *Ethica in Ordine Geometrico Demonstrata* (1677) IV, cap. 17 (ed. Carl Gebhardt; Heidelberg: Winter, 1925), 2.271, trans. E. Curley, *The Collected Works of Spinoza* (Princeton: Princeton University Press, 1985), 590–91.

11. The rabbis ruled that even a master who struck his slave hard enough that his death followed must be executed; contrast Plato's apparent presumption in the *Euthyphro* that a slave's death should not have caused serious anxiety to the title character in that dialogue.

12. Hermann Cohen, *Religion of Reason out of the Sources of Judaism* (trans. S. Kaplan; New York: Ungar, 1972), 431.

13. Maimonides, *Guide to the Perplexed* III 39, ed. Munk 3.86ab; all translations from the *Guide* here are taken from the new translation from the Arabic original by Lenn E. Goodman and Phillip Lieberman, forthcoming from Stanford University Press.

14. Philo, *On the Sacrifices of Cain and Abel* 4.123–29 (Loeb Classical Library, 183–87).

15. Daube notes that Shifra's name bears the same meaning in Hebrew as that of Lampito, the Spartan ringleader of the women's strike against the senseless carnage of the

Peloponnesian War, as portrayed in Aristophanes' *Lysistrata*. See Daube, *Civil Disobedience in Antiquity*, 17–18.

16. See Septuagint Exodus 21:22–23 and Philo, *De Specialibus Legibus* 3.108–09.

17. During the reign of Mary Tudor, when 280 Protestants were burnt at the stake, many of the "heretics" fled to Geneva, returning gradually only after Elizabeth was crowned in 1558. William Whittingham, proposed by Calvin (whose sister he married) as the exiles' pastor, found time, as his flock diminished, to prepare a new Bible translation, building on the work of William Tyndale, Miles Coverdale, Thomas Matthews, and John Rogers, one of Bloody Mary's victims. Whittingham's Geneva Bible (1560), well loved by Puritans, saw seventy editions by 1640 and was welcomed by John Knox in Scotland, where it bore a dedication, in Scots, to James VI, future patron of the version that bears his name. But the king took grave exception to a note deeming "lawful" the disobedience of the midwives in Egypt, even though the note conceded that the women did "evil" in "dissembling" about the reason (Exod 1:19).

18. Gerald Blidstein, "Halakhah and Democracy," *Tradition* 32 (1997): 8.

19. See Lenn E. Goodman, *God of Abraham* (New York: Oxford University Press, 1996), 137–38.

20. Nahum Rabinovitch finds in the strict halachic rules of evidence a drive to remove halachah from the penal sphere, shifting its penal laws in general to an educational function. See his *Darka shel Torah* (undated and unpaginated) and *Ma'alei Asor* (Ma'ale Adumim, 1988), cited in Blidstein, "Halakhah," 16. But when procedural rules tilt too far toward lenity to the accused in criminal law, alternatives typically arise, often bearing lighter penalties than those that prompt procedural nicety but also making lighter procedural demands. Plea bargains in America and the bastinado in Ottoman Turkey are cases in point. The division between the penal laws of the State of Israel and halachic procedural strictness and penal severity reflects not only the aversion of secular authorities to a path like that of Saudi Arabia or Iran but also the reluctance of halachic savants to embark on any atavistic path. The secularity of Israel's courts and Knesset relieves them of such an option.

21. For the Talmudic provisions for manumission of escaped slaves (freed by court action, in effect by a kind of eminent domain, their masters reimbursed by a note of hand), see Haim H. Cohn, *Human Rights in Jewish Law* (New York: Ktav, 1984), 60.

22. Samuel Johnson's famous remark, barbed by his hatred for slavery, is from his 1775 pamphlet "Taxation no Tyranny: An Answer to the Resolutions and Address of the American Congress," *Works* (Troy: Pafraets, 1913), 14.144. The pamphlet, written at the request of Lord North's government, was a response to the Continental Congress's resolutions condemning Britain's "Intolerable Acts"—themselves a response to the Boston Tea Party and the colonists' boycott of British goods. Dr. Johnson's pamphlet, toned down somewhat by Lord North before being printed, was heavily plagiarized by John Wesley, the founder of Methodism and an ardent opponent of slavery.

23. James Madison, "Vices," in *The Papers of James Madison*, National Archives Founders Online website: www.founders.archives.gov.

24. See David O. Stewart, *Madison's Gift* (New York: Simon and Schuster, 2015), 80, 93, 108, and Madison's letter of July 26, 1785, to Edmund Randolf.

25. B. Kiddushin 20a, 22a, with Tosefta, Sifra, Behar 7; Maimonides, *MT H. 'Avadim* 1.7; Cohn, *Human Rights in Jewish Law*, 61–62.

26. See Moshe Greenberg, "Some Postulates of Biblical Criminal Law," in *The Jewish Expression* (ed. Judah Goldin; New Haven: Yale University Press, 1976), 18–37.

27. Rabbi Norman Lamm, who long served as the president of Yeshiva University, credited Maimonides with anticipating Freud's thoughts about a death wish "by some seven hundred years" and relates the hidden desire for corporal punishment to a partial suppression of the death wish, as proposed in Karl Menninger's development of Freud's idea, since a death wish might take the form of self-injury or self-mutilation. "While certainly not all, or even most criminal confessions are directly attributable, in whole or in part, to the Death Instinct," Lamm wrote, "the Halakha is sufficiently concerned with the minority of instances, where such is the case, to disqualify all criminal confessions and to discard confession as a legal instrument." Norman Lamm, "The Fifth Amendment and Its Equivalent in the Halakhah," *Judaism* 5 (1956): 59.

28. Steven Resnicoff, "Criminal Confessions in Jewish Law," *Jewish Law Commentary* (Jewish Law Home Page, jlaw.com/Commentary/crimconfess, 2010). See also Samuel J. Levine, "An Introduction to Self-Incrimination in Jewish Law, with Application to the American Legal System: A Psychological and Philosophical Analysis," *Loyola Marymount Law School: International and Comparative Law Review* (Los Angeles: Digital Commons, 2006): 258–59. Levine, like Resnicoff a rabbi as well as a law professor, writes that, "American courts and legal scholars have increasingly turned to Jewish legal tradition for insights . . . and, at times, a contrast case that some have found particularly helpful in illuminating complex, controversial, and unsettled areas of American law." He cites "a substantial body of American case law and scholarship" referencing the Jewish exclusion of self-incrimination. Justice Warren's majority opinion in the celebrated Miranda case is just one instance.

29. In her commentary on John, Adele Reinhartz labels the story an interpolation, since the whole episode is lacking in most of the ancient texts of the Gospel of John. It does, she writes, appear in manuscripts of other gospels, "particularly after Luke 21:38," where, she argues, it fits the narrative much better. Roman law, she adds, "did not permit execution for adultery." See Amy-Jill Levine and Marc Zvi Brettler, eds., *The Jewish Annotated New Testament* (New York: Oxford University Press, 2011), 174.

30. See Ibn Ezra and J. Hertz ad loc.

31. Cohn, *Human Rights in Jewish Law*, 225.

32. Ibid.

33. Livy, *The History of Rome* 9.46, and Daube, *Civil Disobedience*, 119.

34. Cohn, *Human Rights in Jewish Law*, 107.

35. Maimonides, *Guide* I.50.

36. Cohn, *Human Rights in Jewish Law*, 107, citing Deuteronomy 4:35.

37. Maimonides, *Mishneh Torah*, Sanhedrin 10, Perek Helek.

38. Daniel Elazar, *Covenant and Constitutionalism: The Great Frontier and the Matrix of Federal Democracy*, Volume III of *The Covenant Tradition in Politics* (New Brunswick: Transaction Publishers, 1998), 7. In Volume I of his tetralogy, Elazar writes, "*Memshala*, the generic term for governance in biblical and post-biblical Hebrew, implies rule of like by like. . . . From the context we immediately learn that such rule can be shared . . . the sun rules by day and the moon by night; and such rule can be limited, as the sun and moon and stars are limited to their courses." Dictatorship [*redo*] "is not a fitting relationship between humans . . . all having the same parentage. . . . Even God does not rule humans as a *rodan*"—for even God's rule rests on human consent. Elazar, *Covenant and Polity in Biblical Israel*, 99.

39. The Midrash sometimes dwells on the indexical, "This is my God," as if to suggest a visual experience at the sea. But the language more closely parallels the moment of discovery when Adam sees that Eve is the counterpart he has been seeking. But here the matchup is not of two individuals but of Israel as a nation with the God they will find worthy and of whom they will be charged to be worthy. There are homilies, pegged to the phrasing of the language describing Israel's moment at Sinai, where (because the Hebrew tells of the nation standing at the foot of the mountain and uses the Hebraism "under the mountain") some rabbis imagine God raising the mountain over the people's heads and threatening to bury them under it if they reject his law. But these midrashim aim to underscore the centrality of the Torah to God's plan, not to pretend that Israel's acceptance of the Torah was coerced. And even here the choice remains with the governed: It was up to Israel not to frustrate God's plan. Similarly, the timeless relevance of God's law is affirmed in the images of the souls of all future generations of Israel sharing in the epiphany and assent at Sinai. That rabbinic conceit, pinned to the Torah's affirmation that God's covenant embraced not only those present but future Israel as well (Deut 29:13–14), does not undercut but reaffirms the participatory character of the covenant, calling on future generations to commit themselves, recognizing that one generation cannot bind another, but affirming that the covenant sealed at Sinai is rich enough to invite and secure the free consent of all later generations of Israel, whether or not they were literally present when it was first presented for Israel's acceptance.

40. Correspondingly, matters of custom could become not only normative but halachic. See B. Kiddushin 49a; Bava Metzi'a 68b, 86a; Bava Batra 4a, 165a. See the discussion in Cohn, *Human Rights in Jewish Law*, 8–10.

41. See also Namanides at Deuteronomy 22:6.

42. Maimonides, *Mishneh Torah* H. Sanhedrin 21.1–2 (my translation). Robert Cover, "Obligation: A Jewish Jurisprudence of the Social Order," *Journal of Law and Religion* 5

(1987): 72. Cover compares the ruling of the U.S. Supreme Court in Estelle v. Williams that the defendant had a right to appear in his choice of civilian clothing rather than convict garb, but that in the absence of timely complaint he was deemed to have waived that right. Warming to the peroration in his comparison of rights-talk with the language of mitzvot, Cover writes: "Of course, I believe that every child has a right to a decent education and shelter, food and medical care; of course, I believe that refugees from political oppression have a right to a haven in a free land; of course, I believe that every person has a right to work in dignity and for a decent wage. I do believe and affirm the social contract that grounds those rights. But more to the point I also believe that I am commanded—that we are obligated—to realize those rights" (73–74).

43. See G. W. F. Hegel, *The Philosophy of Right* (trans. Alan White; Newburyport: Focus, 2002), §§ 135, 155–57.

44. Maimonides, *Guide* III 41, Munk 3.90b.

45. Seneca, *Epistulae morales ad Lucilium*, 95.33.

46. Alexis de Tocqueville, *Democracy in America* (1835) (ed. and trans. Harvey Mansfield and Delba Winthrop; Chicago: University of Chicago Press, 2000), 280.

47. See ibid., 281.

Monarchy and Polity: Systems of Government in Jewish Tradition

Lawrence H. Schiffman

From earliest Israelite times two parallel lines of debate regarding the political organization of the Jewish people can be traced in our sources. One is the theoretical debate over whether the Torah requires kingship or not. In this debate, it was assumed by virtually all that the powers of the monarch would be constitutionally limited by Jewish law, usually facilitated by means of a council of some kind. From this discussion, there emerged in modern times a variety of traditional approaches to supporting democracy, even as the ideal for a Jewish state. Parallel with this debate was the practical question of how Jews would be governed in a variety of situations, whether independently or dominated by foreign powers. Here a variety of monarchic, oligarchic, and quasi-democratic approaches were followed in different times, places, and conditions. For the most part, these practical considerations led to a situation in which an ever-broadening electorate selected leaders for the Jewish community. These historical experiences, together with the rise of modern nation-states and the concurrent political philosophies, served to guarantee that by modern times, democracy would be assumed by the Jewish community to be the ideal system of government for a Jewish state and the ideal model for diaspora communities.

BIBLICAL PERIOD

There are two ways of approaching the question of Jewish governance in the biblical period: one is to begin with prescriptive texts and to assume that governance was carried out in accordance with these legal codes. The second would be to investigate historical sources and determine from them how the political organization of the Israelites was constructed. We will look at this question from both points of view. It is worth bearing in mind already at this point that later links in the Jewish tradition that sought to base their political philosophy on biblical sources faced the exact same bifurcated approach, and we will see later on how they sought to harmonize the two approaches.[1]

We begin with the prescriptive texts. The main source dealing with political organization in the Torah is Deuteronomy 17:14–23, the Law of the King. While the Torah appears to command the establishment of a monarch upon entry into the Land of Israel, the later debate in Jewish sources as to whether this is an obligation or an option is foreshadowed already in the inner biblical debate. Whereas a plain-sense reading of the material in Deuteronomy seems to make clear that the Torah requires government by a limited monarchy, it is also clear that the author of 1 Samuel 8:10–22 understood monarchy to be an option, not a requirement, and in fact sees a loose tribal confederacy as preferable to monarchy. Indeed, he expects that establishment of a monarchy would lead to abject violation of the very limitations imposed by Deuteronomy and to the abuse of power by the king.[2]

It is not clear how to understand the refusal of the author of the priestly material at the end of the book of Ezekiel to term the ruler of his expected reestablished polity מלך, "king" and his preference for the term נשיא, usually translated as "prince,"[3] a word used later to designate the Roman-period patriarch and in modern times the president of the State of Israel. While this author says little about the authority of this ruler, discussing only his sacrificial role and the limitations on his power (Ezek 46:1–18), we might conclude that avoidance of the term "king" is intended to signal further limitation of the powers of the ruler than is expected by Deuteronomy. Standard modern biblical criticism would argue that Deuteronomy and the priestly material at the end of Ezekiel are essentially contemporaneous and would see this refusal to use "king" as an indication of a fifth century B.C.E. debate over the ideal form of Jewish government. The problem here, however, is that it is necessary for the Deuteronomic Law of the King to pre-date the core narrative (not just the Deuteronomic framework) of the book of Samuel.[4] Furthermore, it is clear from even the most cursory look at the history of the exegesis of Deuteronomy 17 that the Israelites seem to have assumed monarchy as the expected system of government. This, of course, was the norm throughout the ancient Near East.[5]

According to the biblical account, after the Israelite conquest the people were ruled by tribal leaders known as שופטים, usually translated literally as "judges."[6] These officials seem to have come in various shapes and forms: some were actually justices, some ad hoc military leaders in times of crisis, and others tribal chieftains.[7] The system of government in which tribes functioned independently or in loose confederations was insufficient to allow protection against the depredations of the Philistines and other sea peoples who took advantage of their earlier entry into the Iron Age and their chariots to raid and destroy Israelite settlements.[8] With time, according to the Bible, against the recommendations of Samuel, a king was selected. This king, Saul, was essentially a national "judge," ruling with a very minimal bureaucracy but able to defend the people.[9] With his defeat and death, there ensued the classical United Monarchy of David and Solomon with the large-scale building projects, army, taxes, and bureaucracy typical of an ancient Near Eastern monarchy.[10] Attempts to discount the historicity of this monarchy may for now be laid to rest by the excavations at Khirbet Qeiyafa.[11]

This monarchy had been cemented together from southern and northern elements that split apart after Solomon's rule circa 954 B.C.E. with both kingdoms retaining monarchies.[12] However, while the southern kingdom of Judah practiced succession from father to son, the northern kingdom suffered repeated revolutions, although within each of the northern dynasties filial succession was practiced. One has only to look at the positive and negative portrayals of the monarchs to describe the basic powers and limitations of their rule. Kings could collect taxes, raise armies, fight wars, either to defend their kingdom or to expand its borders, engage in large-scale building projects often with corvée labor, judge legal cases, and control religious practice. At the same time, it does not seem that the limitations placed on the monarchy by Deuteronomy were scrupulously observed in either the United or the Divided Monarchy.[13]

Considering the nature of ancient communication and the existence of local elders and priestly religious leaders, we should not see the king as a sort of totalitarian ruler. On the contrary, he ruled through a bureaucracy that itself was often tied closely to the people and would have been in some ways receptive to their demands. Some scholars have argued for the existence of a sort of council termed עם הארץ, literally, "the people of the land," in First Temple times that was a sort of constituent assembly that also would have had considerable influence over the affairs of the monarchy. On the other hand, we find no legal sources describing such an institution.[14]

In both the North and South this system of government ultimately failed the Israelites since it allowed the kings sufficient power to engage in highly unwise foreign policies, flouting the great powers of Mesopotamia. The monarchs risked their kingdoms in order to assert financial and diplomatic independence, first from Assyria and then from Babylonia, resulting in the respective destructions of the Northern Kingdom in 722[15] and the Southern in 586 B.C.E.[16] One has only to look at the complex narratives of Kings, Jeremiah, and Chronicles to realize the complexity of the political maneuvering that surrounded these fiascoes. Nevertheless, the governmental system permitted and provided sufficient support to allow the monarchs to travel down this disastrous path. The attempt of the Babylonians to set up a form of weakened Jewish self-rule under Gedaliah ben Ahikam presaged the fact that the debate over Jewish monarchy would henceforth be conducted in a context in which foreign monarchs appointed those who would rule over the Land of Israel. Only under the Hasmoneans would we again encounter independent Jewish rule.

SECOND TEMPLE PERIOD

With the return of a small number of Judeans after the onset of Persian period in 540 B.C.E., there followed a short period of rule by a Davidic descendant who served as a Persian-appointed governor. Through some unknown combination of circumstances, the land came to be a hierocracy in which high priests ruled over the internal affairs of the Jews within a larger foreign-dominated empire.[17] This situation remained throughout the Persian Empire and under Ptolemies and Seleucids until the Maccabean revolt of 168–164 B.C.E.[18] After the revolt, from 152 B.C.E. the Hasmoneans established a form of rule, eventually termed kingship, that was essentially a blending of the two previous systems—monarchy and hierocracy—so that one individual now held the powers that in First Temple times had resided in two individuals, king and high priest.[19] Despite the fact that the monarchs of the First Temple period dominated religious life, the existence of independent high priests alongside prophets meant at least some semblance of balance of powers, even if unfairly balanced.

Despite this unification of powers, throughout the Hasmonean era, from the consolidation of power by Jonathan in 152 B.C.E. through the end of Hasmonean rule in 63 B.C.E., the *gerousia* [council of elders] served as a representative body and included Pharisaic and Sadducean representatives.[20] This representative body was the ancestor of the later Sanhedrin. Otherwise, Hasmonean rulers had all the powers of the ancient Jewish kings and controlled large bureaucracies, effectively executing all affairs of state: they raised armies, waged wars to expand their territory, and collected taxes.

During the Hasmonean period, the long-standing debate about the nature of Jewish monarchy was raised again as can be seen from the Temple Scroll.[21] Here we find an entire section, titled by scholars the "Law of the King," that parallels, interprets, and expands the Deuteronomic laws (11QT[a] 56–57). In many ways, this material can be seen as a polemic against the

Hasmonean rulers, who were the arch-opponents of the Dead Sea sectarians. The text spells out a series of obligations and privileges of the king. The command that a Torah scroll must be written for the king is meant to indicate that he is to be controlled by the laws of the Torah. All the Deuteronomic restrictions on the king are repeated and emphasized. A council of 12 priests, 12 Levites, and 12 Israelites is to be set up to rule along with the king, who is prohibited from waging offensive war without the permission of the high priest. Most importantly, the text makes clear that the king and the high priest must be two distinct people, clearly opposing the control of both roles by the Hasmonean priest-kings. The text argues forcefully for reform of the political system and for a monarchy even more severely limited than that of the book of Deuteronomy.

However, from 40 to 4 B.C.E. the Romans administered Palestine through a client king, Herod.[22] Rule by client kings emerging from the local populations was tried by the Romans in many areas, although they soon realized that this system of governance did not meet their needs. The experience of Herodian kingship posed numerous challenges. His capricious rule and ignoring of Jewish tradition regarding rights of trial and his donations to pagan rituals must have angered many Jews. However, his paranoia and the resulting execution by him of numerous family members caused widespread disgust and dissatisfaction with his rule.

Curiously, however, the rule of his grandson Agrippa I (41–44 C.E.)[23] was later regarded as a golden age by the rabbis.[24] Herod seems to have been helped in his rule by a quasi-council called the *filoi*, the "friends" of the king. From Josephus (for the most part following the writings of Nicholaus of Damascus, Herod's non-Jewish secretary of state), we can determine that there was great opposition to the rule of Herod and his descendants. Talmudic sources, however, indicate the great generosity of Herod in building projects and relief works as well as in the complete reconstruction and expansion of the Jerusalem Temple.[25] After a short experiment with Herod's son, Archeleus, the Romans returned the country to procuratorial rule, and kingship[26] was never again an active category in Jewish political life.

A number of important Jewish sources from the Second Temple period reflected on the question of monarchy versus other governmental systems. Philo Judaeus discusses this issue in interpreting Deuteronomy 17. He presents a positive view of the king, who was understood to have been chosen by the people, sensitive to their needs, and ruling according to divine law. Essentially, the king of the Bible is seen as the ideal king.[27] Josephus, however, sees hierocracy, that is, the aristocracy of the priesthood, as the best form of government when compared to monarchy, so Josephus sees the laws of Deuteronomy 17:14–20 as essentially a compromise. In Josephus's view, the king there is expected to submit to divine law and to follow the leadership of the high priest and the *gerousia*, the Council of Elders. Josephus understands monarchy as an aberration and sees the Hasmonean period as proving the advantages of rule by an aristocracy. Specifically, in a discussion of various types of government, monarchy, oligarchy, and democracy, Josephus states that the Torah required instead a theocracy, that is, the granting of "sovereignty and authority in the hands of God." He specifies that such a government would actually be led by the priests, with the high priest as the chief authority.[28]

Philo seems to assume that kingship is a required form of government. He understands the appointment of leaders in an essentially democratic manner, stating his opposition to the appointment of magistrates by lot. He also condemns corrupt elections and seems to be criticizing Plato and Aristotle, who had recommended appointment by lots. He emphasized the right of all citizens to participate in electing rulers. He makes no reference to election of kings by prophets. He somehow seems to assume that even though the people elect the king, he is ratified by God. Therefore, he states about Moses that he was appointed by God with the complete consent of the people.

Philo states the duties of the king as ruling and judging in accordance with the Torah, appointing officials, conducting his duties with righteousness, and deferring to legal experts in difficult cases. All these duties are derived from biblical verses, although not necessarily verses regarding the king.[29] What seems to be operative here is that Philo follows the Platonic notion of the philosopher-king, whereas Josephus reads the Bible in accord with the critique of Samuel and understands the ideal biblical form of rule to be the priestly aristocracy, which for him in essence represents the rule of God. Remember, he himself was a priest!

RABBINIC LITERATURE

Rabbinic sources debated the question of the obligation of monarchy, some, most notably the Mishnah,[30] considering it to be an option and others seeing it as obligatory.[31] Those considering it obligatory had to explain how it could be possible for Samuel to oppose it. Two basic explanations were given. Either it was said that the people were not yet ready for such a government or that by asking for a king "like all the other nations" they were seeking what we would call an assimilationist path and, hence, Samuel disapproved. For our purposes, we can point out that rabbinic sources saw Moses in effect as the first Jewish king.

Various opinions existed as to how he was appointed. One view argued that he had been appointed by God and another that he was essentially appointed by the assembly of seventy elders. Saul is said to have been chosen by God as transmitted to the prophet Samuel, but then he is also said to have been appointed by lot. David is said to have been chosen in the same way, by God through Samuel, but then anointed by the men of Judah and later by the elders of Israel. In other words, rabbinic sources seem to identify two basic sources for the authority of the king: divine election, on the one hand, and acclaim by the people or their representatives, on the other hand.

The Tannaim in the Mishnah and Tosefta laid out some basic regulations for the king,[32] effectively naturalizing this position as a part of their overall halachic system.[33] The basic regulations they put forward include: The king is forbidden from serving as a judge or being judged by a court. Nor can the king bear witness or be testified against. The king may not compromise his honor. Various legal procedures may not be effected by the king, and his honor is safeguarded if he should be a mourner. He may lead the people into an optional war only with permission of the court of seventy-one. He has complete power over eminent domain in order to build roads, and gets a large share in war booty. His accumulation of wives, horses, and money is to be limited and the command that he write a Torah scroll is designed to indicate that he rules only in accord with the laws of the Torah.

Various symbols of his authority may not be used by others, and special laws of privacy applied to him to preserve his honor. From the Tosefta we learn that the king's regalia are to be burned after death, so as to make sure that they may not be appropriated by another. Much of the scriptural basis for these laws can be gathered also from the Sifre Devarim.[34] The tannaitic system, as put forward in the Mishnah, speaks of the ideal Jewish society in the Land of Israel, effectively a naturalistic messianic vision. In this ideal, the king, holding executive power, rules alongside a Sanhedrin that serves as the legislative and judicial branch, and these rule alongside the high priest who controls religious affairs. The judicial role of the Sanhedrin is part of an assumed group of Torah sages who are expected to serve as religious authorities and teachers for the people while coexisting with the priestly establishment.

The Babylonian Talmud differentiates two types of kings in recognition of the realities of the First and Second Temple periods. In this way, it attempts to harmonize the prescriptive text in Deuteronomy with the realities of history. The kings of Israel and Northern Israel, and the various Second Temple kings, are seen as those for whom the total set of halachic limitations on the status of the king is fully enforced, specifically regarding the rule that he may not judge or be judged. However, these roles are assumed not to apply to kings of the house of David because the righteousness of this dynasty can be guaranteed. The kings of Northern Israel, the Hasmoneans, and Herodians are seen as only an incomplete fulfillment of the Torah's ideal.[35] Therefore, this latter group of kings eventually served as a model for some modern thinkers for the legitimation of systems of government of a Jewish state other than the Davidic monarchy. These thinkers saw these forms of government as the fulfillment of the Torah's regulations.

MEDIEVAL TRADITION

With the onset of the Middle Ages, the debate over monarchy was framed in a somewhat different manner but continued nonetheless. Although Maimonides (1135–1204) ruled that the establishment of a monarchy was in fact a commandment,[36] other commentators such as Abraham Ibn Ezra (1089–1167) saw the Torah's Law of the King as an option: if you want to appoint a king, these are the rules.[37] This debate was conducted against the backdrop of medieval Jewish life, in which some Jewish communities were governed internally by a system of representative decision making. To be sure, these were oligarchies, not democracies.[38] Of great interest is the emergence of two distinct understandings of local communal authority in medieval Jewish communities. In one view, reminiscent of the Persian-Hellenistic designation of high priests as rulers over the Jews, the authority of local communal officials was traced to authority devolved upon the Jewish leaders by the non-Jewish king or his agents. In this approach, there is no foreshadowing of democracy. On the other hand, a second system of thought understood the authority of local communal authorities to be based upon their election by the electors, namely, those with rights of residence or certain financial status. In this system, authority stems not from above but from below—the community that had elected them.[39] It was just a short step from this approach to the suggestion that democracy might be a legitimate form of government.

The later Middle Ages, no doubt because of trends observable in Christian society, stimulated considerable original thought regarding the significance of monarchy for Judaism and Jewish law. One of the most significant thinkers in this regard was Rabbenu Nissim ben Reuben of Gerona (1320–1376). He observed that according to biblical narrative, it can be concluded that the king had particular rights that went beyond those of the normal halachic system. Based on these texts, he concluded that there existed a *mishpaṭ ha-melekh* [a royal law] that was meant to exist as a completely parallel system along with that prescribed by the Torah. Whereas the first Torah system sought to put forth the moral and ethical ideals of Judaism, the second royal system intended to bridge the gap between these ideals and the reality of life. Accordingly, for example, in his view the king had the right to put to death those who were not permitted to be executed for lack of valid witnesses according to the ideal system of the Torah.[40]

Other commentators explained many of the examples of such nonhalachic behavior in the narratives of Samuel and Kings as violations of God's commands, but Rabbenu Nissim saw them as evidence for the obligation and right of the king to redress evils that could not be handled by the idealistic and impractical system of Torah law. This approach recognized the necessity of the king. However, unlike Maimonides who saw the king as an agent for maintenance of the government according to halachah, Rabbenu Nissim saw the king as providing an entirely separate and parallel system of law to overcome the weaknesses of Jewish law that resulted from its idealistic character. We should contrast this view with that of Yosef Chayoun (sixteenth century), who argued that the purpose of the king was to compel observance of Jewish law.[41]

In the fifteenth century, Jews began to be acquainted with developments in Venice and Genoa where democratic institutions were beginning to grow up in the local governmental arena. This led Isaac Abravanel (1437–1508) to formulate an entire treatise arguing for the superiority of the democratic system of government wherein those who serve in office know that they function at the behest of the people and that if they want to be reelected, they must be responsible to them. Taking his cue from the Talmudic view that the appointment of a king is optional, not a requirement, and from the arguments of the book of Samuel, Abravanel argued strongly for the superiority of democracy over monarchy. One might summarize his point of view by noting that he agreed with the ancient prophet Samuel in seeing monarchy as undesirable. Undoubtedly he was impacted by the beginnings of the emergence of modern democracy and convinced that such a system of government was superior not only for European societies but for a Jewish polity as well.[42]

THE MODERN PERIOD

With the emergence of Europe into modernity, Jews were generally hopeful that democracy would provide just governments in nations in which they could live on an equal footing with other citizens. Democracy promised to bring with it equal civil rights and, indeed, developed in Europe along with the emancipation of the Jews.[43] These two processes went hand-in-hand, and it was not long before the Jewish people as a whole saw democracy as the best form of government. It should therefore come as no surprise that the Zionist movement was, at least outwardly, structured from the beginning as a democracy. That the State of Israel would be a democracy, albeit one with fundamental differences from both the British parliamentary system and the American constitutional system, was clear even long before anyone knew when it would be declared or what it would be called.

Nonetheless, and especially in religious Zionist circles, a discussion of monarchy versus democracy was called forth in the years leading up to and immediately following the independence of Israel. Here the question was not a practical one, but rather concerned how to understand the state from a halachic point of view and how, at least for traditional Jews, to create a bridge between the new reality and the longed-for dream of a renewed Davidic kingdom. Further, and actually of greater practical significance, was the question of how to find a place for Jewish law in the context of a modern democracy.[44] Purposely avoiding the fact that these issues are still plaguing the political and religious leaders of the State of Israel, we will say something about the nature of the earlier debate.

The simplest of the points of view put forward was that of Agudath Israel, representing the Ashkenazic ultra-Orthodox (before the split into two parties). They took the view that the State of Israel is a secular state run by Jews and, hence, that civil law did not have to reflect Jewish law at all. This point of view is similar to that of Rabbenu Nissim in that it assumes two parallel legal systems, since a rabbinic court system functions in Israel as well as the civil judiciary. At the same time, they demanded, with some success, that the state as a whole observe Jewish law in various areas of personal status and public life.

The second approach was that of the Religious Zionists (Mizrachi), who took the view that the state itself, even in the form of a democracy, represented a halachic polity that should observe Jewish law. This vision resulted in various schemes to integrate Jewish law into the state's legal system. Some, in the years leading up to the rise of Israel, thought that it would be possible to put into effect a modified version of Jewish law that could be applied even in a state in which the majority of the citizens were not traditionally observant.[45] Others, taking a more pragmatic approach, and here I am referring to the Mishpat Ivri movement, sought maximum integration of Jewish law into the state's civil system, alongside the British and Turkish law that undergirded it.[46] Of course, for those less connected to traditional texts, democracy was the expected norm that was assumed to be the fulfillment of the ideals of the prophets of ancient Israel.

The possibility that monarchy might actually be the ideal system of government for the renewed Jewish state was entertained by virtually nobody. That democracy was somehow a natural partner of the Jewish tradition, however both Judaism and democracy might be defined, was the natural assumption of all those involved in establishing the state and in advancing their particular visions for it. To the extent that the Israeli parliamentary system imitates that of the British, the president serves the legal and ceremonial role of the British monarch, including selecting the party leader most likely to succeed in forming a parliamentary coalition. However, no one ever dreamt of appointing an actual king.

We have tried to chronicle the long process by which the biblical ideal of monarchy, reflecting the norms of ancient society, even if limited and controlled, has essentially been replaced by democracy. This form of government is now seen virtually unanimously in the Jewish community as the key to the future of the Jewish people and the State of Israel.

NOTES

1. See the discussion of kingship in M. Walzer, M. Lorberbaum, and N. J. Zohar, eds. *The Jewish Political Tradition, Vol. 1: Authority* (New Haven: Yale University Press, 2000), 108–65.

2. Cf. J. Tigay, *Deuteronomy, The Jewish Publication Society Torah Commentary* (Philadelphia: Jewish Publication Society, 1996), 166–69. Tigay understands Deuteronomy as seeing the appointment of the king as optional.

3. See W. Niehr, "Nāśi'," *TDOT* 10.44–53.

4. Contra the valuable discussion of P. K. McCarter, Jr., *1 Samuel: A New Translation with Introduction, Notes and Commentary* (The Anchor Bible 8; New York: Doubleday, 1980), 160–62. Cf. also H. W. Hertzberg, *I & II Samuel: A Commentary* (trans. J. S. Bowden; The Old Testament Library; Philadelphia: Westminster Press, 1964), 74.

5. The classic study of monarchy in the Ancient Near East is H. Frankfort, *Kingship and the Gods: A Study of Ancient Near Eastern Religion as the Integration of Society & Nature* (Chicago: University of Chicago Press, 1948).

6. On the history of this period, see J. H. Hayes and J. M. Miller, *Israelite and Judaean History* (London: SCM Press; Philadelphia: Trinity Press International, 1977), 285–322; and J. M. Miller and J. H. Hayes, *A History of Ancient Israel and Judah* (Philadelphia: Westminster, 1986), 80–119.

7. Cf. A. Malamat, "The Period of the Judges," in *Judges*, World History of the Jewish People (First Series: Ancient Times, v. 3; ed. B. Mazar; New Brunswick: Rutgers University Press, 1971), 129–34.

8. B. Mazar, "The Philistines and Their Wars with Israel," in *Judges*, World History of the Jewish People (First Series: Ancient Times, v. 3; ed. B. Mazar; New Brunswick: Rutgers University Press, 1971), 164–79.

9. For the period of his rule, see Hayes and Miller, *Israelite and Judaean History*, 322–31, and Miller and Hayes, *History of Ancient Israel and Judah*, 135–48.

10. See Hayes and Miller, *Israelite and Judaean History*, 332–80, and Miller and Hayes, *History of Ancient Israel and Judah*, 149–217.

11. Y. Garfinkel, I. Kreimerman, and P. Zilberg, *Debating Khirbet Qeiyafa: A Fortified City in Judah from the Time of David* (Jerusalem: Israel Exploration Society; Hebrew University of Jerusalem, 2016), esp. 199–236.

12. See Hayes and Miller, *Israelite and Judaean History*, 381–421, and Miller and Hayes, *History of Ancient Israel and Judah*, 218–313.

13. On the administration of the monarchy, see R. de Vaux, *Ancient Israel: Its Life and Institutions* (Grand Rapids: Eerdmans, 1977), 87–209, and N. S. Fox, *In the Service of the King: Officialdom in Ancient Israel and Judah* (Monographs of the Hebrew Union College 23; Cincinnati: Hebrew Union College Press, 2000), 43–268.

14. De Vaux, *Ancient Israel,* 70–72, who defines this term as "the body of free men, enjoying civic rights in a given territory." He does not see it as representing an assembly.

15. Hayes and Miller, *Israelite and Judaean History*, 421–34, and Miller and Hayes, *History of Ancient Israel and Judah*, 314–39.

16. Hayes and Miller, *Israelite and Judaean History*, 435–76, and Miller and Hayes, *History of Ancient Israel and Judah*, 340–415.

17. Hayes and Miller, *Israelite and Judaean History*, 514–38, and Miller and Hayes, *History of Ancient Israel and Judah*, 437–75; L. H. Schiffman, *From Text to Tradition: A History of Second Temple and Rabbinic Judaism* (Hoboken: Ktav, 1991), 33–47.

18. V. Tcherikover, *Hellenistic Civilization and the Jews* (trans. S. Applebaum; Philadelphia: Jewish Publication Society of America, 1966), 39–89; Schiffman, *From Text to Tradition*, 60–72.

19. Tcherikover, *Hellenistic Civilization*, 235–65; Schiffman, *From Text to Tradition,* 99–104.

20. See I. Gafni, "Gerusia," *EJ* 7 (1972): 522–23; E. Schürer, *The History of the Jewish People in the Age of Jesus Christ (175 B.C.–A.D. 135),* rev. ed., 3 vols. in 4 (ed. G. Vermes,

F. Millar, M. Goodman, M. Black, and P. Vermes; Edinburgh: T. & T. Clark, 1986), 2.203–31.

21. L. H. Schiffman, *The Courtyards of the House of the Lord: Studies on the Temple Scroll* (ed. F. García Martínez; STDJ 75; Leiden: Brill, 2008), 471–504.

22. For a summary of Herod's rule, see Schürer, *History of the Jewish People*, 1.287–329; M. Stern, "The Reign of Herod," *The Herodian Period* (World History of the Jewish People, First Series: Ancient Times, v. 7; ed. M. Avi-Yonah; New Brunswick: Rutgers University Press, 1975), 89–98.

23. On his reign, see D. R. Schwartz, *Agrippa I: The Last King of Judaea* (TSAJ 23; Tübingen: J. C. B. Mohr [Paul Siebeck], 1990), 107–44.

24. Cf. ibid., 157–71.

25. Listed in Schürer, *History of the Jewish People*, 1.287.

26. Ibid., 1.353–37.

27. H. A. Wolfson, *Philo: Foundations of Religious Philosophy in Judaism, Christianity, and Islam* (Cambridge: Harvard University Press, 1968), 2.325–57.

28. Z. Rodgers, "Monarchy vs. Priesthood: Josephus, Justus of Tiberias, and Agrippa I," in *A Wandering Galilean: Essays in Honour of Seán Freyne* (JSJSup; Leiden: Brill. 2009), 173–84.

29. See E. R. Goodenough, *The Politics of Philo Judaeus* (New Haven: Yale, 1938), 86–100; D. M. Goodblatt, *The Monarchic Principle: Studies in Jewish Self-Government in Antiquity* (Tübingen: J. C. B. Mohr [Paul Siebeck], 1994), 50–52.

30. D. C. Flatto, "It's Good to be King: The Monarch's Role in the Mishna's Political and Legal System," *Hebraic Political Studies* 2 (2007): 225–83.

31. Cf. G. Blidstein, "The Monarchic Imperative in Rabbinic Perspective," *AJSReview* 7 (1982): 15–39.

32. On the king in rabbinic thought, see S. A. Cohen, *The Three Crowns: Structures of Communal Politics in Early Rabbinic Jewry* (Cambridge: Cambridge University Press, 1990), 41–47.

33. M. Sanh 2:2–5.

34. L. Finkelstein, ed., *Sifre on Deuteronomy* (New York: Jewish Theological Seminary, 1969), 208–13 (sections 156–162).

35. Cf. Maimonides, *Hilkhot Melakhim* 1:7–10.

36. A. Ravitzky, *Dat u-Medinah be-Maḥshevet Yiśra'el: Degamim shel 'Iḥud, Hafradah, Hitnagshut 'o Kefifut* (Jerusalem: Israel Democracy Institute, 1998), 19–26. For sources, see 27–44.

37. Commentary to Deuteronomy 17:15.

38. S. W. Baron, *The Jewish Community: Its History and Structure to the American Revolution*, 3 volumes (The Morris Loeb Series; Westport: Greenwood Press, 1942), 2.3–51.

39. D. Guttenmacher, "The Legal Concept of Political Obligation in Medieval Spanish Jewish Law," *Diné Israel* 15 (1989–90): 63–95.

40. Ravitzky, *Dat u-Medinah*, 45–50. For sources, see 50–65.

41. Ibid., 95–102. For sources, see 103–10.

42. Ibid., 67–76. For sources, see 77–91.

43. See, e.g., Berr Isaac Beer, "Letter of a Citizen to His Fellow Jews," in *The Jew in the Modern World: A Documentary History* (ed. P. Mendes-Flohr and J. Reinharz; New York: Oxford University Press, 1980), 107–10.

44. S. Federbusch, *Mishpaṭ ha-Melukhah be-Yiśra'el* (Jerusalem: Mossad ha-Rav Kook, 2005), 19–91; Walzer, *Jewish Political Tradition*, 463–523.

45. Cf. M. Friedman, "The State of Israel as a Theological Dilemma," in *The Israeli State and Society: Boundaries and Frontiers* (ed. B. Kimmerling; Albany: State University of New York Press, 1989), 165–215.

46. M. Elon, et al., *Jewish Law (Mishpat Ivri): Cases and Materials* (Casebook series; New York: Matthew Bender, 1999), 13–57, 389–439.

Democracy, Judaism, Israel, Art, and Demagoguery

Ori Z. Soltes

DEMOCRACY IN THE JEWISH TRADITION

"Democracy" has evolved as a concept since the inception of the word. When Kleisthenes created the idea in Athens in 508 B.C.E., he sought to transfer political power from the self-proclaimed "best" [*aristoi*]— wealthiest—Athenians to the inhabitants of artificially shaped "demes" [*demoi*]. There were 30 of these across the larger Athenian *polis*: 10 in the city, 10 in the mountainous outskirts of Attica, and 10 along the lowlands.[1] The system to accord power [*kratia*] to the demes operated in 10 groups of 3—each group consisting of representatives elected/appointed by a city, mountain, and lowland deme. The point was that the representatives and their constituents had little intrinsically in common, but were forced to find common ground in order to be effective, thus undercutting the traditional governance assumed by socioeconomic class—and thus typically and traditionally serving the needs of the wealthy.

But the franchise was still limited: to free-born adult males native to Athens. Women were excluded. Slaves were excluded. Those known as *metoikoi* ["those who live around"], individuals and their families who had come from elsewhere, perhaps seeking work, and continued to live in and around Athens, sometimes for generations, were excluded. Under Perikles (ca 450–430 B.C.E.), "free-born" was further limited to mean "born of two free-born parents"—thus the child of a slave and a free person was automatically excluded from citizenship, turning citizenship into a closed franchise and democracy to a limited governance proposition.[2] This would all seem to be a far cry from what most Americans imagine has always been our own democracy. Of course, our history was not always so different from what Athens offered. American democracy waited until 1870 to afford African American men the opportunity to vote; Native Americans were not eligible for American citizenship until 1890; women across America had to wait until 1920 to cast ballots. Jews couldn't vote in Maryland until 1828 and in New Hampshire until 1878. Obviously those who couldn't vote couldn't run for office and were clearly not fully enfranchised as citizens of the polity.

An obvious underpinning of voting is that it affords citizens the opportunity to express opinions and to offer dissent from any given majority view without fear of negative repercussions. Within Jewish history, dissent and thus a particular kind of democratic thinking is an essential part of the rabbinic tradition. Many examples may be drawn from midrashic and Talmudic discussions to demonstrate how multiple points of view are entertained on diverse issues. Consider as one example one of the early conversations in the Midrash Rabba on Genesis 1:1 ("In the beginning, God created the heavens and the earth"—referring specifically to the second clause): in which the question is asked whether heaven or earth was created first. The discussion ascribes to the "School of Hillel" the view that the earth was created first; to the "School of Shammai" is ascribed the alternative view, that the heavens were created first—each corroborating its perspective with references to other passages in the Bible. Hillel's view is further supported by Rabbi Judah son of Rabbi Ilai and by Rabbi Hanin. Rabbi Johanan enters the discussion, reporting on the view of the sages, supported by Rabbi Tanhuma, to the effect that heaven was first in beginning the process, but earth was first in completing it.

Into this back and forth discussion steps Rabbi Simeon, expressing surprise at the debate and offering a third view—to wit that both were created simultaneously—before pointing out analogous biblical questions of precedence (honoring one patriarch or matriarch more than another, or Moses more than Aaron, or Joshua more than Kaleb) in order to bring the high-flung discussion down to earth with the observation that we must honor both parents equally (in spite of the commandment that lists "father" first and "mother" second—since the order of terms is reversed in Lev 19:3: "You shall fear every man his mother, and his father.").

The point is that different viewpoints are entertained—although the evidence suggests that not everyone was comfortably included in the process. Women, for example, are not only rarely in evidence, but when one stood out as particularly brilliant—Bruriah, for instance, the wife of Rabbi Meir—a tradition emerged that questioned her moral steadfastness.[3] The rabbinic underpinnings of the Jewish tradition may be called democratic, then, in the sense of diverse perspectives being included, but not necessarily in permitting everybody who is not a rabbinic figure to be involved in the multivalent opinion-expressing process.

The tradition further enjoins us not to oppress those whom our system does not empower to protect themselves—from the criticism offered to the

Judaeans by Jeremiah that they "oppress the stranger, the orphan and the widow, and spill innocent blood" (Jer 7:6, and echoing Exod 22:22)—suggesting in no uncertain terms that to oppress these categories of disenfranchised individuals is to spill innocent blood and that members of a covenantal people are proscribed by God from so doing—to the annual reminder in the Passover narratives that we, who were strangers, should not oppress the stranger (derived from Exod 22:21). This last prescription is underscored by the fact that the phrase "embrace the stranger" appears 36 times in the Torah, more times than does any other injunction. The implication of this is that a limited democracy must not limit an enthusiastically fair treatment of those whose voices are not heard in the discussions of how to be in the world.

The diasporic nature of Judaism helped to facilitate a democracy of thinking with regard to living a Jewish life (which is the primary preoccupation of the rabbinic tradition, as opposed to the issue of belief that dominated Christian patristic and scholastic writing). This is reflected in divergent lifestyle elements—from liturgical details to funerary customs to gastronomic norms—across the Jewish world, even as various Jewish communities within that world assumed autocratic personalities. Thus a German Jew would not even be aware that a Moroccan Jew consumed rice on Passover—*kitniyot* (that also includes corn, millet, and legumes)—so he could not be offended by a norm that would be anathema to him. By contrast, the largely contiguous Christian and Muslim worlds generated a norm in which religious perspective and political power so often interwove that it was easier to generate suppression, often violent, of spiritual dissent.[4]

On the other hand, circumscribed individual Jewish communities could find themselves in thrall to their own rabbinic leadership. No instance of this is more notorious than the evolution of the Sephardic community of Amsterdam in the seventeenth century—much of it direct refugees or descendants of refugees from Spain and Portugal and the brutally suppressive inquisitional authorities that had prevailed across Iberia since the fifteenth century. Two individuals stand out as victims of Sephardic rabbinic cruelty and repression in Amsterdam: Uriel Acosta (1585–1640) and Baruch Spinoza (1632–1677). The prescriptions of excommunication and/or return to the community [more "temporary" *niddui* and more "permanent" *herem*] in the aftermath of their respective trials and condemnations for heresy resonate with an inquisitional tone in terms of both verbiage and methodology. In the end Acosta committed suicide from the mental strain and Spinoza's expulsion led him away from the community toward which he never looked back.[5]

The diasporic Jewish world experienced a most distinctive turn with the advent of modern Zionism and a culmination when Israel was established in 1948. An "ingathering of exiles" offered the chance to shape the first Jewish-governed polity in history. It drew its name from the ancient Israelite Kingdom—underscoring an ideological leapfrog over the centuries of uncomfortable diasporic existence—and it extracted its sense of return from prophetic promises contoured in the context of the destruction of the First Israelite-Judaean Temple and the rabbinic thinking shaped after the destruction of the Second Judaean Temple. The new state, when it finally emerged, derived its sense of self-governance from a combination of rabbinic, Ottoman, and British ideas, ultimately transcending all of them in order to offer a democracy both Jewishly informed and secular, open above all to Jews—and to all kinds of Jews, from ultra-Orthodox to atheists—but open to all.

This sort of perspective is reflected in Israel's Declaration of Independence, which explicitly asserts the intention of the nascent state to "foster the development of the country for the benefit of all its inhabitants [and to] be based on freedom, justice and peace as envisaged by the prophets of Israel [and to] ensure complete equality of social and political rights to all its inhabitants irrespective of religion, race or gender." One could argue that, conversely, the lack of a written constitution reflects the ongoing principles of dissent and disagreement, given that that lack reflects an inability to achieve consensus among its constituent groups as to the very purpose of the state, its identity, and its long-term ambitions. The nature of the Israeli administration is democratic to a fault: the multiparty system often permits small groups with their particular agendas to have more of a voice than they might, say, in the American two-party system, due to the need for coalitions in order for the major power party leaders to govern.

The wrestling match to shape and maintain such a democracy began well before the state was declared and continues to this day. Virtually from its outset, Zionism was fraught with dissent that continued to expand over time: Theodor Herzl's political Zionism was opposed by Ahad Ha'Am's spiritual Zionism, which was abetted by Boris Schatz's cultural Zionism; A. D. Gordon's labor Zionism overlapped but was distinguished from Rav Kook's religious Zionism, all of which were opposed by Ze'ev Jabotinsky's revisionist Zionism.[6] Throughout the twelve decades between the First Zionist Congress in Basel in late summer 1897 and today, the debate has continued regarding what Israel is supposed to be—the center of which debate is a series of questions pertaining to the identity of the state as "Jewish": where do non-Jews fit in who are not entitled to automatic citizenship but can indeed become citizens? How are converts to Judaism and/or the offspring of mixed marriages received? What of Muslim and Christian Palestinian Arabs who remained (or returned) after the War of Independence? Who does or may or doesn't or may not serve in the Israeli Defense Forces and in what capacity?

THE EXPRESSION OF DEMOCRATIC THOUGHT IN THE VISUAL ARTS

In the ongoing expression of opinion, art has served the role that art has often served throughout history: offering political commentary or serving the needs of politics, sometimes with religion as a third leg—from the images of Egyptian pharaohs asserting the divinity that will discourage revolt against their power to images of David against Goliath commissioned by the Medici to represent themselves and Florence struggling against larger powers like the Papal States. In Israel art has continued emphatically to be shaped as a response to the reality of "Israel." Art has affirmed and challenged, defined and dissented from Israel's political-spiritual self-conception: it has thus offered a consummate expression of democratic principles.

Pre-Israel's first public sculpture, Konstantin Melnikov's *Monument to the Fallen at Tel Hai* (1928–1934), offers a roaring lion that combines a Hittite-style mane and Assyrian-style forepaws, but assumes a contemporary, more verticalized position than such forebears did. Melnikov's lion is both indigenous to the region and unique: old and new. Indeed, the very fact of this and other works of public sculpture offers a political statement: it asserts that the Jews are back and in independent control of their land; that they are here to stay, and can thus, for the first time in two millennia, produce visual self-expressions that are large and in the open for all to see. Over the decades, public statuary, particularly memorials—alas, reflecting the war-torn reality of Israeli history—have proliferated across Israel.

Those memorials refer typically not only to the wars in which Israelis have died—from the War for Independence (1948) to the Sinai Campaign (1956), the Six-Day War (1967), the Yom Kippur War (1973), and the Lebanon War (1982), as well as to various more recent military campaigns involving Gaza and less clearly articulated wars, such as the War of Attrition shaped by Egypt in the mid-1970s—but also, beginning some time after the Eichmann trial of 1961, to the millions of Jews who perished in the Holocaust. After fifteen years of statehood, during which Israel, no less and no more than much of the world, was, for various reasons beyond this discussion disinterested in commemorating that event, it began to occupy a central place in the national ideology of memory. In some cases, as in Yigal Tumarkin's enormous public sculpture, *Holocaust and Resurrection* (1975), the intent, in part, is to suggest a trajectory that leads from enormous suffering and the ashes to the rebirth of the Jewish people, miraculously, in its own land. His upside-down pyramid, made of steel and empty space, hovering over and reflected in a small pond with lily pads, offers notions of impossibility made possible, history turned on its head, the idea of regularized geometries contrived by human intellect and effort within the irregularities of nature and of calm within the storm, placed as it is in a park surrounded by the hurly burly of Tel Aviv.

Appositely, among the important canvasses painted more than a generation after Melnikov's sculpture is by Mordecai Ardon, soon after he assumed the directorship of the Bezalel School of Art in Jerusalem. The painting is called *Venus of Beersheva* (1962)—alluding to and including within the depths of his semiabstract, light-within-darkness image the so-named archaeological artifact, (the small fertility figure dates from the very early Bronze Age), treating it iconically and offering it as a testimony to the historical and literal depth of Israeli connection to the Land. This is a crepuscular visual articulation of romantic nationalism.

Within the fifteen years before and the decades after this painting, Israel was confronted by its neighbors and confronted the world in an ongoing series of conflicts, from its initial fight for survival in 1948 to its blitzkrieg victories, over the Egyptians in 1956 and over Egypt, Syria, and Jordan in 1967. The outcome of the first and third conflicts was to increase the outer borders of the state, and in the Six-Day War to acquire administrative control over hundreds of thousands of Palestinians who had been subject for the previous two decades to harsh conditions under the Egyptians and Jordanians, since they had left what became Israel and were trapped, as it were, in Gaza and the West Bank, where they never assumed the status of real citizens in Egypt and Jordan respectively.

If at first it appeared that this situation would achieve resolution—that the Palestinians, Jordanians, Egyptians, Syrians, and others would seek peace with Israel in exchange for the release of Sinai, the Golan, Gaza, and the West Bank—the more so when, a few years after a fourth conflict, in October 1973, yielded further Israeli conquests, Anwar Sadat and Menachem Begin signed a peace agreement in 1979 in which the Sinai was returned to Egypt—yet as tensions remained and as Israeli settlements mushroomed across the West

Bank landscape, some Israelis, artists among them, began openly to ponder how long the "occupation" (for that term would become more and more popular) would persist.

It is a symptom of the vigor of the democratic side of Israel that that question could and did express itself as oppositional to that status quo; artists were among those who queried and protested in their work. Thus in the old building of the Bezalel School an exhibition of posters was organized in 1987 marking the twentieth anniversary of the conquest and occupation of Gaza and the West Bank. By then the first Israeli-Arab war, in Lebanon, to be questioned by a significant number of Israelis had marked the early 1980s; the war was designed to drive the PLO out of the neighborhood. Two of the more obvious noteworthy features of that exhibition were the strident nature of some of the work produced by Israeli artists and the fact that several Muslim and Christian artists were invited to participate. Thus work by well-known figures like Yigal Tumarkin and Raffi Lavie, as well as by lesser known ones, like Dov Haller, Gabi Klezmer, and Yehoshua Borowsky was exhibited. And on the other hand the work of non-Jewish Palestinians was shown.

Among these was Taleb Dweik, (b. 1952, Jerusalem), who eventually became the president of the League of Palestinian Artists (1990–1996) and has exhibited all over the world. Dweik's work, then and since, in spite of living in a Jerusalem that has been such a center of tension and often violence for so long, typically paints with a colorful, often abstract palette so that his imagery tends to lead the viewer away from the ugly politics outside the canvas into a realm of beauty and calm: he offers a kind of visual *tikkun olam* in his work. In recognizing that Jerusalem and its people are his most consistent subject, however, one may also recognize the suggestion of yearning for an earlier, more innocent and childlike pre-Occupation, pre-Wall Jerusalem—particularly in an image in which he has literalized the gerrymandering idea of the Wall by creating a Jerusalem skyline compositionally broken into thirteen vertical slabs that suggest chunks of city broken by chunks of obstruction.

There is certainly some irony to the fact that Israel was the only place in the Middle East at that time where artistic work raising questions about government policy could be exhibited. There is also an obvious contentiousness between what an artist like Dweik recalls as "innocent" and what Israelis of the same generation or older, might recall of the 1949–1967 era, when Jewish access to the Old City was all but forbidden to them—or that, regardless of its negative aspects, the Wall quickly cut down suicide bombings by 90 percent.

If democracy is about expressing different viewpoints, then the fact that these two perspectives can and do coexist in Israel and can be expressed artistically still speaks to an important aspect of its active democracy.

One can follow the issue of political commentary that may or may not be taken as critical into the work of any number of Israeli and Palestinian artists in the decades since 1987. The Palestinian Poster Project is a distinct example; it offers specifically political—and usually critical of Israel—commentary in leading up to the 1987 Bezalel exhibit and continuing to this day. Thus, along conceptual lines paralleling those of Dweik, a 2008 installation by the film-maker Sobhi al-Zobaldi (b. 1961), called *Part-ition*, offers seventy-two playing cards laid out for a game on a table. The cards are made from a cut-up, large-scale, pre-Israel map of Palestine—a map given to him as a young teenager, which adorned the walls of his room as a youth in Ramallah as well as in his home in New York in the 1980s.

He returned to Palestine in 1994 after the Oslo Accords, but felt that he could not display it, for shame: "I felt embarrassed with the map, as though I didn't want it to see me anymore, or see what was going on"—expressing shame and betrayal from the deals made by Arafat with Israel deemed "humiliating and doomed": the map as a symbol of loss. Now cut up as cards on a table with a chair on either side, the map signifies both a Palestinian perspective and a perspective that an Israeli might question—what could Arafat have negotiated that would have been sufficient for Sobhi to feel good about it? It also functions, however, as a symbol of the democratic reality that provided a context for the installation. Can one imagine an analogous sort of installation openly exhibited anywhere else in the Middle East?

So, too, in the case of Nisreen Najjar's (b. 1985, Nazareth) *Route 443* (2010), an installation at Al-Housh [The House of Arab Art and Design)], Jerusalem. The mixed-media sculpture takes its name from the infamous Israeli road that connects Jerusalem to a network of settlements by cutting though Palestinian land. She has shaped it as a grotesquely enlarged toy racing track stuffed into the gallery space, entering from a wall, somewhat randomly rising and falling before exiting into a window grille. So the settlers' roads can go in whatever direction they choose, regardless of topography or the needs of the indigenous population—but it also recalls, with tongue in cheek, the phrase "roadmap to peace" and the "peace process" as understood by Israelis and Americans—as opposed to Palestinians.[7]

In May 2016, an entire conference was devoted to this subject—which took place in Bethlehem, that is, in a city on the West Bank governed by Israeli occupying forces. It was an international conference, in which the contributors came from Palestine and various other countries—but not Israel. So a conference the substance of which was criticism of Israel took place, if not in Israel, yet within the area that the Israelis have administered for half a century. I am not commenting on that criticism as just or unjust—that is beside the point for my present purposes—but rather that there was nobody to offer a counterview to the repeated view of Israel itself as unjust—and of the irony that such a conference could take place in an area occupied and administered largely by Israel, This irony echoes that of the placement of Najjar's installation at an exhibition within Israel proper, in Jerusalem no less.

Questions and comments by Israeli artists have also expanded beyond various overt criticism back in 1987. Particularly photographers, it would seem, capture—or stage—moments that raise issues, whether these pertain to Israeli society in the street and in the home or to the condition of the Palestinians under an Israeli domination that is approaching the end of its fifth decade and of the Gazans in the grip of an isolation enforced by Israel but necessitated by Gaza's duly elected Hamas leaders.

Adi Nes's 2006 chromogenic print *Abraham and Isaac* offers the reality of homeless street people in the country created to provide any and every Jew with a home. The elderly urban street person who pushes his sleeping son in a shopping cart packed with flotsam and jetsam is more akin to Abraham the wanderer than Abraham the founding father of a dramatic new faith, and more akin to the prophet's diasporic descendants than to the still largely rural vision of a century ago in which all Jews coming to the Land would build it and be rebuilt by it. This is a mythic ideal occasionally still trumpeted by the politicians—including the current prime minister in, for instance, his declaration to French Jews that they should all emigrate to Eretz Yisrael, where they will be well cared for and protected.

That same prime minister has presided over an intense response to attacks on Israel from Gazan Hamas in a campaign, "Cast Lead," that underscored, among other things, the doubtfulness of his interest in helping to negotiate a Palestinian homeland. Rita Castelnuovo's photo *Gaza Border* (2009) depicts an Orthodox Jewish Israeli soldier, at sunrise, wearing his *tallit* and *t'fillin* as he recites his morning prayers atop a military tank parked in a grassy field. A stream of black smoke rises from a building in the distance, the end of its plume hovering just over the distant Gazan town illuminated by the newly emerged sun. The issue of piety and religion as it pertains to the politics of defending Israel from Hamas and of devastating Gaza and its inhabitants in the name of that defense would appear to be very much on the artist's mind.

DEMOCRACY AND DEMOGOGUERY IN THE "JEWISH STATE" TODAY

There are two sides to the coin of these forms of expression. One is that the fact of such public critiques of the Israeli reality suggests a robust democracy in action that permits internal commentary and criticism. The other is that, on the one hand, art can be ignored sufficiently by politicians in the mainstream that they can allow visual expressions of protest as not amounting to much or undermining their authority; and on the other, that the expressions are emerging because Israeli society is wandering further and further from democratic values and is in danger of wandering further, so that such artistic expression is essential if the democracy is to survive as a democracy. Is Israel—the "Jewish state"—then, still a vigorous democracy in which diverse expressions of agreement and disagreement with the government and its social and political policies flourish, or is it losing its democratic ethos, against which process of loss artists are desperately trying to push back?

The matter of the ongoing Israeli administration of the West Bank and Gaza raises an obvious practical question pointing toward the future with regard to this issue. If, as it appears, given the ever-expanding Jewish settlements in the West Bank and thus of its Jewish population—together with the extraordinary gerrymandering of the territories in order to accommodate those settlements and with walls whose purpose is to prevent Palestinians with nefarious intent from entering Israel proper—the current Israeli government is apparently content to allow the occupational status quo to persist into the uncharted future, then a simple statistical analysis of the evolving demographics of a "Greater Israel" that functionally and de facto if not de jure includes the West Bank becomes obvious. In not all that many years, the Muslim (and Christian) Palestinians both within and beyond the Green Line will outnumber the Jews. Either the Jewish state will continue to function as the sort of democracy in which each citizen has a vote, or it won't.

Either the non-Jewish West Bank inhabitants will continue not to have a voice as citizens in an Israel that rules but does not legally govern them, in which case a majority of those under Israeli rule will be voiceless, and/or the Israeli Palestinian Christians and Muslim Arabs will in and of themselves begin to vote in sufficient numbers to upset the delicate balance of the democratic multiparty coalition system that has been in place for seventy years. If, however, everyone has a vote, the so-called Jewish state may cease to be "Jewish" or, if it is to remain dominated by Jews, it may cease to be a democracy.

There is a corollary to all of this, regarding potential power and pain: Plato argued against democracy on the grounds that, in leveling the field of participation, it necessarily plays to the lowest common denominator: the polis could be induced to turn away from the "good" by a sufficiently charismatic leader. At its most extreme downside, democracy can become its cognate: "demagoguery"—meaning "to lead the people [*demos*]"—but the term has come to imply a leadership that can and does sooner or later assume tyrannical and opposition-crushing connotations. An astutely manipulative and crowd-pleasing leader can be elected by the crowd. This happened in 1933 in Germany. Adolf Hitler feasted on fear of the Jews and the German concern that their identity was being swallowed, so that he might achieve power. It has evolved more recently in Russia and Turkey, where Vladimir Putin and Recep Tayyip Erdoğan have assumed increasingly long-term roles through the crushing of their opposition by means of arrests and assassinations—and in the latter case, a false coup attempt in July 2016 that afforded Erdoğan the opportunity to quickly round up all those perceived to be in opposition to him—nearly 190,000 people as of this counting.

In 2013, in Israel, Benjamin Netanyahu pulled out a last-minute political victory by a disturbing act of feasting on fear of Arabs and the Jewish Israeli concern that Israel's identity and security were in danger of being swallowed. Admittedly the poster from the Palestinian Poster Project, by an American (Paul Normandia), not an Israeli or Palestinian, offers a strong viewpoint from a strongly nonobjective perspective even if it is that of an outsider. It shows a photograph of Bibi, together with the words in quotes: "Beat them up, not once but repeatedly. . ."—with further words reflecting or commenting on the brutality of his regime. If the words are Netanyahu's own and disturbing, let us suppose that they are taken out of context, placed here in order to present him in as cruel a light as possible. Nonetheless, in any context, they hardly suggest the sentiment expressed in Leviticus 19:34, that "the stranger who resides with you shall be to you as the native among you, and you shall love him as yourself, for you were aliens in the land of Egypt; I am the Lord your God."

Bibi's call to arms at the polls in fear of an Arab takeover was in any case not undemocratic, however ugly. Indeed, one can say that his victory at the polls was a triumph, not only for Likud and for Bibi, but for democracy. That is, the Jewish democracy triumphed in that he was fairly reelected, but, in playing to the uglier side of the human inclination—in bringing to the polls

Jewish Israelis who voted not for Netanyahu but against what he convinced them would be an overly Arabized Israel if his more left-leaning opponents were allowed to win—one might ask whether the price for victory was the defeat of Judaism at its democratically-operative-inclusive-embracing-the-stranger-*tikkun-olam* best and thus of the Jewishness of the "Jewish state." In the time since then, nothing that Netanyahu has said or done, vis-à-vis Palestinian Arabs, Diaspora Jews, or the world at large, offers much hope that in his heart or mind he can any longer distinguish between democracy and demagoguery, Jewish or otherwise.

NOTES

1. Herodotus, *Histories*, 5.62, 69; Aristotle, *Constitution of Athens*, 21–22.2.

2. Thucydides, *History of the Peloponnesian Wars*, 2.65. 8–9.

3. See Rashi's commentary on *Kiddushin* 80B.

4. I am thinking most obviously of the conflict between the Athanasian and Arian views of the nature of God and with it, of Jesus—only partially resolved by the Council of Nicaea in 325 (Arianism, termed heretical at Nicaea, continued to flourish as a thorn in Orthodoxy's side for nearly three centuries); of the Sunni-Shi'i split in Islam regarding proper leadership (Abu Bakr versus Ali) within a year or two of Muhammad's death in 632; of a similar sort of schism that split the Christian world in 1054 between the Catholic West and the Orthodox East; of the Western Schism yielding popes and antipopes between ca 1381 and 1415 within the Catholic world; and of the Protestant Reformation beginning in 1517 that would yield a counter-Reformation and a long period of religious wars between ca 1550 and 1715 between Protestants and Catholics.

5. See Ori Z Soltes, *Jews on Trial: Juries, Prosecutors and Defendants from the Era of Jesus to Our Own Time* (Savage: Bartleby Press, 2013), chapter 4.

6. Arthur Herzberg, ed., *The Zionist Idea* (Philadelphia: Jewish Publication Society, 1997), introduction and parts 3, 4, 6, 7, and 10.

7. For a detailed, pathbreaking discussion of Palestinian art in general, see Gannit Ankori's *Palestinian Art* (London: Reaktion Books, 2006).

Dignity and Democracy: Defending the Principle of the Sanctity of Human Life

Alan Mittleman

The idea of human dignity—of the incomparable worth or, in a religious key, the sanctity of human life—seems fundamental to democracy.[1] Major political and constitutional documents articulate a conception of human dignity in their opening lines. Thus, the Declaration of Independence of the United States of America, after affirming "the Laws of Nature and of Nature's God," famously asserts that "We hold these truths to be self-evident, that all men are created equal, that they are endowed by their Creator with certain unalienable Rights, that among these are Life, Liberty and the pursuit of Happiness." The specific language of human dignity or sanctity is not used, but the belief is nonetheless salient. The reference to the creation of human beings in equality and to their creator limns its contours.

Similarly, and perhaps with greater historical pathos, the German Basic Law [*Grundgesetz*] asserts in Article I: Section 1: "Human Dignity [*die Würde des Menschen*] shall be inviolable. To respect and protect it shall be the duty of all state authority." We see it as well in Israel's 1992 Basic Law: Human Dignity and Liberty. "The purpose of this Basic Law is to protect human dignity and liberty [*kavod ha-adam v'ḥaruto*], in order to establish in a Basic Law the values of the State of Israel as a Jewish and democratic state." The purpose of the law rests on the fundamental principle of recognition of the worth of the human being [*erekh ha-adam*], on the sanctity of human life [*kedushat ḥayyav*], and of the status of the human being as a free being [*hiyyuto ben-ḥorin*].

In the United States, Jewish apologists have sometimes associated the biblical idea of humanity created "in the image of God" with the fundamental conceptual basis of democracy. Thus, Samuel Belkin, in his mid-twentieth century study *In His Image*, writes that Judaism is best characterized as a "democratic theocracy." "It is a theocracy because the . . . entire system of Jewish morality derives from and is founded upon the concept of the sovereignty of God. It is a democracy because, unlike any other legal system, the rabbinic code places all emphasis upon *the infinite worth and sacredness of the human being*."[2] What Jonathan Sarna calls "the cult of synthesis" is at work here—the effort to ground the noblest principles of American democracy in the most sublime theological teachings of Judaism.[3]

In the case of the constitutional documents, as important as their strong, clear statements of principle are, I say that they "seem" fundamental rather than simply "are" fundamental. For there are questions about the role of principles in a legal system or in a constitutional order. What is the relationship between high-level moral or political norms, such as the sanctity of human life, and the day-to-day rules of law? To what extent can bodies of rules, inherited from the past and embedded in their own institutional practices of interpretation and application, continue to operate without reference to the high-level principles that presumably animate them? How important are such principles to the life of a legal system? Legal systems or constitutional orders are not deductive arguments. Conclusions do not flow rigorously from premises. We need not think of principles as major premises in a logical sense from which particular rules are ultimately derived. Although there is a logical difference between principles and rules, modeling that difference upon a deductive argument is too linear.[4] The interplay between principles and rules is more reciprocal, fluid, layered, and heterogeneous than that.

Principles, in Joseph Raz's view, serve as grounds, that is, as metalevel justifications in such matters as interpreting law, changing laws, making exceptions to laws, making new rules, and occasionally as the sole ground for action in particular cases.[5] They are logically distinguished from rules by their generality, that is, they are more comprehensive. They can be used to justify rules, but rules cannot be used to justify them. Principles themselves can sometimes be legislated, but most often they arise out of a public form of life, a culture of political, moral, and religious values to which the principles give selective expression. When embedded in a constitution, the constitution allows the citizens of its life-world to objectify their own principled truths. Once objectified in semantic and pragmatic form, the constitution speaks with authority. It doesn't just describe the ambient norms of a culture; it authorizes them. It acquires authority per se and shapes the normative contours of its world. It guides and constrains the institutions and practices of the actors within its normative order. Principles function within this order as claims indicative of core constitutive values. They are employed as compact arguments on behalf of the integrity and moral soundness of a public form of life.

Thus, it is not clear that principles in isolation mean much. They are semantic and pragmatic moves within an extended, coherent, normative form of life. To take a relevant Jewish example, if the principle of *b'tzelem Elohim* [in God's image]were not instantiated in bodies of halachah, such as those dealing with capital punishment, it would not amount to more than a metaphysical claim. As it is, however, if Yair Lorberbaum's analysis is correct, the theological, philosophical, and legal implications of the concept come together in a dense, mutually supporting web.[6] A principle comes to mean something by the role it plays in a legally articulated public form oflife.

We appeal to principles from inside of a form of life. We employ them to adjudicate conflicts among legal rules, among moral obligations or values, to distinguish between ethical considerations and matters of lesser weight, to rank matters that we care about, or to remind ourselves and one another of our axiological orientations and commitments. But we do not build our moralities or laws upon them brick by brick. As Aristotle, glossing Plato, points out in the *Nicomachean Ethics*, if we had not already been raised with moral habits, we could not even begin to reason about moral first principles (*Ethics* I:4): "We must already be within and, I would say, committed to a moral point of view for principles to play a role in our thought."

This suggests that principles such as human dignity may not play the critical foundational role that we believe, pretheoretically at least, they do.[7] Imagine someone who does not believe that all human beings have worth and are, given that worth, equal in the relevant respects. What could one say in defense or explanation of the principle of human dignity that could convince such a person? If such a person, say a convinced racist or white supremacist or Nazi, truly believed that some classes of human beings lacked worth and hence need not be treated with respect (equality, fairness, and so on), is there a philosophical argument that could change his mind? Would we believe that such a person could even be a discussion partner? Rather than argue with him, wouldn't we want simply to contain or constrain him, making sure that he remained politically marginal?

A counterexample to this is Socrates' treatment of Thrasymachus. Here is a case of fundamental disagreement about first principles, whether injustice is superior to justice. Socrates confidently believes that dialectic might bring mutual enlightenment. He doesn't withdraw from or merely try to neutralize Thrasymachus, but to persuade him through philosophical argument. Socrates takes the only course open to him: to show Thrasymachus that his views are incoherent. Thrasymachus's belief in the superiority of injustice is parasitic upon a suppressed premise in favor of justice. The unjust city, army, bandits and thieves whose exploitation of the just Thrasymachus is wont to praise must themselves behave with some equity and equanimity toward one another in order to accomplish their nefarious common purpose (*Republic* 351c).

Once Thrasymachus sees the incoherence at the heart of his own claim, he abandons the field. But this shows that Thrasymachus was antecedently open, his vehemence and bluster notwithstanding, to rational argument. To participate in a rational philosophical argument, in good faith at least, is already to eschew violence and to affirm a norm of respect. It is implicitly to concede the premise of human dignity. Dignity here entails respect for the rationality of the other, attention to the other's view as that of a rational being, openness to being persuaded by the rationality of the other, and so forth. The principle of dignity, or something very much like it, is presupposed by a discursive encounter. In this sense, an encounter with someone who denies the principle of human dignity must eo ipso fail as a rational conversation.

This suggests that the principle of human dignity has the status of an implicit norm for conversation rather than a principle that can be discursively justified by conversation, that is, by philosophical argument. Perhaps it is comparable to Aristotle's construction of the principle of noncontradiction. It cannot be demonstrated because any argument on its behalf already presupposes it (*Metaphysics*, Book Gamma, section 4). And, indeed, purely philosophical attempts to warrant the principle of human dignity, most eminently Immanuel Kant's, have a circular quality to them. For Kant, a rational being must necessarily find worth in itself and respect its own dignity [*Würde*]. One must already be committed to the concept of human dignity or, more precisely, the dignity of a rational being, for a Kantian argument to acquire traction. If one could coherently maintain the moral irrelevance of rationality and, derivatively for Kant, of human personhood, one would not be persuaded by Kantian ethics.[8]

Dignity cannot be demonstrated; it can only be shown to be a transcendental condition for the moral life. But if one is a cynic or a skeptic about the moral life as such, it is not clear what Kant could answer. If one refuses the call to noumenal selfhood, autonomy, freedom, and respect for the moral law; if one aspired to be a great irrationalist like Friedrich Nietzsche, the circularity of Kant's account of human dignity would prove vicious rather than virtuous. Indeed, Nietzsche's pessimistic precursor, Arthur Schopenhauer, claimed "that the dignity of man . . . became the shibboleth of all the perplexed and empty-headed moralists who concealed behind that imposing expression their lack of any real basis of morals or, at any rate, of one that had any meaning."[9]

I submit that this is becoming our situation today. As the cultural background of Jewish and Christian, ultimately biblical, convictions about the sanctity of human life recedes; as scientific images of man-in-the-world, to use Wilfred Sellars's phrase, replace Jewish (and Christian) ones, human dignity meets formidable conceptual challenges. The principle may be so deeply implicated in our laws, institutions, and practices as to be assumed by our very efforts to defend it. But if we had to defend it, as I think we now do, how shall we do so? What resources do our religious and intellectual traditions offer us in our quest to articulate and sustain the principle? Must we rest content with its status as an ancient if beleaguered tacit norm, or can we give it a full-throated rational justification? Can this be done in the way that Kant aspired to do, namely, without reliance upon religious premises?[10] The question is whether a truly fundamental principle can be sustained only by religious faith—which has an ambiguous status in the discourse of a modern, pluralistic democracy—or whether parallel secular arguments are available. Unlike the apologetic "cult of synthesis," we need not claim that Judaism and democracy are isomorphic. But does the latter need the former for its moral foundations?[11]

CHALLENGES TO THE PRINCIPLE OF HUMAN DIGNITY

The principle of human dignity is challenged, among other reasons, as a consequence of the steady growth of two scientific paradigms: neo-Darwinian evolutionary biology (and its outgrowth, evolutionary psychology) and neuroscience (and its allied philosophical interpretation, "neurophilosophy"). On the one hand, scientific inquiry is premised on the intrinsic goodness of knowledge and is typically conducted with the widening of that good as its premise. The intrinsic good of knowledge attests to the better angels of our nature: our dignity as rational beings. On the other hand, the content of scientific knowledge of the human in the mode of modern evolutionary biology and neuroscience shakes the foundations of the principle of human dignity and problematizes its conceptual coherence. Democratic societies, I would argue, need both free scientific inquiry and the principle of human dignity. The former is iconic of the intellectual and moral freedom that democratic societies are constitutionally designed and bound to protect. The latter underwrites the norms of responsibility, agency, equality, and liberty, as well as the laws that exemplify, objectify, and sustain those values. Let us consider some tensions among these at the point of human dignity.

Challenges to the principle of human dignity arise in at least four ways. The first is perhaps the least worrisome. Human dignity is thought to be a preeminently religious notion and as such its status in a secular society is questionable. It seems to violate the Rawlsian norm of public reason. That might not amount to much except that human dignity, in the eyes of its critics, seems to work against other moral and legal principles, which seem more transparent and urgent from a contemporary secular point of view. Thus, human dignity is at odds with autonomy (a prospect utterly alien to Kant!). The principle of human dignity is often employed by moral and cultural conservatives to exclude the right to die or the right to choose an abortion or the permissibility of stem cell research requiring the discarding of embryos. I will briefly consider a provocative essay by the Harvard psychologist and public intellectual Steven Pinker, "The Stupidity of Dignity," which makes precisely these sorts of claims.

A second, I think more serious, challenge comes from people like the Princeton ethicist Peter Singer. For Singer, the restriction of personhood to human beings—crystallized by the principle of human dignity—excludes consideration of animals as persons. It entails that a distinctively human characteristic, rationality, is allowed to crowd out other characteristics of sentient life, such as suffering, as the only characteristic meriting worth-according treatment. When rationality is not yet gained (as with a fetus or newborn) or when it is lost (as with a patient in a permanent vegetative state), human dignity is generously extended in the absence of rationality. For Singer, there is hypocrisy here. A more valid criterion of worth is the capacity to suffer. Taking that seriously would decouple dignity and humanity. Taking that seriously would allow for the mercy killing of the irreversibly comatose, for example, and prevent the slaughter of chickens and cattle for food. I will consider Singer's view in more detail below.

Third, there is a complex of views arising from evolutionary biology that, like Singer, erases any significant line between human beings and animals. We are confronted with a scientific image of man-in-the-world that accounts for human features, such as sociality, rationality, and ethics, as emergent properties of evolutionary adaptation. Once ethics, for example, is traced to the reciprocal altruism of higher primates and, presumably, of our hominid ancestors, a distinctive and valuable feature of the human is fully naturalized. Chimps are also moral beings. Nothing is particularly special about us in this respect. So too for rationality. If rationality is an adaptive mechanism for enhancing the effectiveness of the fight or flight response, the development of tool usage, and so on, then human rationality becomes a matter of degree not kind vis-à-vis that of other primates. The ascription of a peculiar dignity to the human seems arbitrary, a form of "speciesism," in Peter Singer's phrase.

Neuroscience and neurophilosophy provide an additional challenge to human dignity. To sustain the latter, one needs more than something emphatically valuable about human beings; one needs human selves. These selves have to be capable of moral agency, of responsibility, of freedom. But some strains of neuroscience hold eliminative views of the self. All conscious activity, "mind," reduces to brain activity and brain activity—the electrochemical pulses of a hundred billion neurons linked in a trillion synaptic networks—reveals no single executive center. There is no self in any reified sense. Rather along the lines of David Hume's view, there are just different functions, executed by different "software," realized in different pieces of organic "hardware," constructed according to a genetic blueprint. The self is a kind of narrative, organized by the left hemisphere, ultimately generated because of the survival advantages that it bestowed on our early hominid ancestors.[12] The related problem is the elimination of free will. If all mental activity is brain activity and if the brain is a physical object, as it surely is, and if physical objects behave according to laws of physics, then free will turns out to be another kind of illusory narrative. Our belief in it, based on our first personal self-experience, must also have been generated through evolutionary happenstance. Hominids who thought that they had choices and behaved accordingly spread their genes more effectively than their more zombie-like competitors. The neuroscience story may yet have the greatest impact on moral and legal institutions. Let us consider each one of these in a little more detail and offer, as well, the beginnings of a critical response.

In "The Stupidity of Dignity," Pinker follows an earlier, seminal assault on the concept by the bioethicist Ruth Macklin.[13] Macklin argued that "dignity is a useless concept in medical ethics and can be eliminated without any loss of content." The content that would be preserved when the allegedly vague, religion-laden notion of dignity is jettisoned is "respect for persons: the need to obtain voluntary, informed consent; the requirement to protect confidentiality; and the need to avoid discrimination and abusive practices." Macklin believes that "dignity" adds nothing—but detracts something—from these core principles of medical ethics. Its use is semantically otiose. It is a "vague" usage that cashes out at "nothing other than respect for autonomy." She does not see it as indicating a deeper justificatory ground for autonomy. Pinker builds on this view. The occasion for his essay was the publication of a long report by President Bush's Council on Bioethics titled *Human Dignity and Bioethics*. After a remarkably ad hominem attack on the Council's chairman, Leon Kass, and a condemnation of what Pinker takes to be its conservative

Catholic-dominated political bias, he offers a more substantive argument against dignity.

The argument is, pace Macklin, that dignity is inherently vague and adds nothing. It does, however, detract and distract from democratically appropriate moral argument. First, "dignity is relative" to cultural prejudice. What Victorians found undignified, we find entirely acceptable.

Thus, dignity does not get at anything deep. But wait, one might object: these surface signs of dignity *are* culture-relative, but that is not what a proponent of dignity truly means by it. Pinker acknowledges that for some, like the Vatican, dignity is a "sacred value," never to be compromised. But he thinks that this is cant. "Dignity is fungible," that is, we routinely trade off our dignity by submitting to things like prostate exams or airport body searches. Thus, "dignity is a trivial value, well worth trading off for life, health, and safety." Finally, "dignity can be harmful." Pinker sets out a parade of horribles, instances of dictators cowing their populations with ostentatious displays of their grandeur to enforce their dignity; fatwas condemning those such as Salman Rushdie to safeguard the dignity of Islam and so on.[14]

Pinker concedes that dignity has a role. Donning his official psychologist's cap, he explains how certain sensory signals convey dignity and dispose us to treat the dignified generator of those signals with respect. Thus, just as a baby's face moves us to protect it, features that convey "composure, cleanliness, maturity, attractiveness, and control of the body" elicit "a desire to esteem and respect the dignified person." But this is a very limited ethical epiphenomenon hardly able to bear the weight the proponents of human dignity ascribe to it.

Indeed, dignity may become pernicious. The "gap between perception and reality makes us vulnerable to dignity illusions." We are back to tin pot dictators flaunting their dignity in pompous public displays.

What Pinker has done here is conflate different senses of dignity. By reducing the concept of dignity to typical instances of proper deportment in some given society or to displays of self-importance or public role play, he has slighted the deeper significance of the concept. For both Macklin and Pinker, dignity remains superficial; what is deep and important are values such as autonomy, which are strangely unconnected to dignity on these principled postreligious accounts. If one were to put this to Pinker, he would not be persuaded. He would argue that dignity does not stand for something deeper; it remains vague and therefore useless as a precise concept. The worth of human beings, which we want to preserve, is amply protected by more precise concepts such as autonomy, which play out in the relevant bioethics context as informed consent.

There is more than a semantic wrangle going on here. In cashiering dignity, these views seek to cut the cord with the history of Jewish and Christian normative theological anthropology and fully empower a secular image of the autonomous human being as a creature of self-evident worth. This is the Kantian project, taken several steps beyond Kant. I don't see this as a profound challenge to human dignity because it seeks to preserve those values that religious persons affirm with reference to dignity. It remains parasitic on them, unable to generate an argument of its own, taking the self-evidence of human worth as a given. It is more a sign of cultural drift and secularization, one might say, than of "depravity." But if depravity in these matters is real, then views such as Pinker's and Macklin's, which rhetorically disparage dignity, arguably weaken its content and its cause in the long run.

Singer presents a graver challenge. His aim is to efface the distinction between human life and other forms of (at least higher) sentient life such that prohibitions on killing biologically defective humans are lifted and allowances for killing animals are eliminated. Singer's approach rests on the argument that any relevant distinction between humans and at least some animals is mere prejudice and is fundamentally akin to racism. "The doctrine of the sanctity of human life," he writes ". . . has at its core a discrimination on the basis of species *and nothing else*."[15] Sometimes discrimination is appropriate, as when one teaches a human child to read but not a dog (his example). But if one were to say, I will teach only white children to read but not black children, one would be invidiously discriminating because race has nothing to do with the ability to read. Similarly, species membership in Singer's view has nothing to do with claims to special treatment, that is, claims to solicitude, respect, protection, or deference. Any such claims must be made on the basis of some characteristics other than sheer belonging to the species *Homo sapiens* as such. What are those characteristics? Let me quote Singer at length:

> Now what is the position when we compare severely and irreparably retarded human infants with nonhuman animals like pigs and dogs, monkeys and apes? I think we are forced to conclude that in at least some cases the human infant does not possess any characteristics or capacities that are not also possessed to an equal or higher degree, by many nonhuman animals. This is true of such capacities as the capacity to feel pain, to act intentionally, to solve problems, and to communicate with and relate to other beings; and it is also true of such characteristics as self-awareness, a sense of one's own existence over time, a concern for other beings, and curiosity. In all these

respects adult members of the species I have mentioned equal or surpass many retarded infant members of our own species; moreover some of these nonhumans surpass anything that some human infants might eventually achieve even with intensive care and assistance.[16]

Singer takes these enumerated features to be the main indicators of "personhood" or "humanhood." If one grants that they are shared by other species, then the umbrella of personhood ought to extend to those species. Similarly, "humanity" ought to be understood, as we sometimes do, as an evaluative term, not solely as a biological classification. We might therefore understand mature dogs and pigs, monkeys and apes as "human" in an extended sense, certainly as persons. The burden is on proponents of the sanctity of human life, in a biological, species-bound sense to show why only human beings are deserving of protection. Singer believes that burden cannot be met. We have "huge prejudice in favor of the interests of our own species and a corresponding tendency to neglect the interests of other species."[17] But that is all that it is—a huge prejudice.

This was not always the case. Back in the era when Christianity dominated Western intellectual life, people thought that they had sound reasons for their "prejudice" in favor of human over animal interests. But Singer is convinced that this is a bit of pre-Enlightenment, pernicious, intellectual immaturity. He approves, for example, of the near universal ancient practice, endorsed by no less than Plato, Aristotle, and Seneca, of killing deformed or defective infants. This was banned under Christendom in the name of the supposed sanctity of human life. Theological ideas, which today are patently ridiculous (in Singer's view), such as possessing an immortal soul or damnation to hell fire, swayed men's minds. Abortion and infanticide were condemned because of their consequences for immortal souls. If a fetus, for example, were aborted, its soul would go to hell eternally because it had not been baptized. As a carrier of original sin, through no fault of its own but simply through the sheer fact of its human status, it was damned, unless it was saved through the sacrament of baptism. The agent of the abortion would have committed an unimaginably great sin in damning its soul to eternal torment. Singer does not trace the sanctity of human life back to the Hebrew Scriptures (e.g., Gen 9:26) but dwells on the medieval Christian appropriation so as rhetorically to heighten the foreignness of the idea. He is unsparing: "My brief historical survey suggests that the intuitions which lie behind these laws are not insights of self-evident moral truths, but the historically conditioned product of doctrines about immortality, original sin, and damnation *which hardly anyone now accepts; doctrines so obnoxious, in fact, that if anyone did accept them, we should be inclined to discount any other moral views he held.*"[18]

Singer's argument rests on a set of claims about personhood. He wants to free personhood and the moral implications it entrains from humanity in a narrow sense. In order to do this, he has to decouple personhood from traditional criteria such as rationality and moral responsibility. For Singer, personhood, with apologies to John Locke, is not a forensic term. He accomplishes this marginalizing of rationality and responsibility by focusing on human infants, who do not yet possess these traits, as well as on severely deformed infants who will never possess them. That we consider such infants—as well as severely senescent adults—to be persons for him speaks to the secondary or epiphenomenal nature of rationality and responsibility. We are willing to suspend them, betting that infants count because they will grow into them (except for severely retarded ones who won't or terminally comatose or senile adults who have lost the traits forever). But this only shows how shaky these criteria for personhood are.

Other characteristics that are shared with nonhuman animals are stronger candidates for the criteria of personhood. Singer's views might not be as controversial as they are if he fought shy of rigorous consistency. That is, one might agree that animal suffering should be minimized, that an ethic of care toward animals be maximized, and so on. It is the principled elimination of any line of normative differentiation between humans and animals that is provocative, as is his rigorist conclusion that human life has no claim to protection if animal life has no claim to protection. He rejects the sanctity of human life as a prejudiced, invidious claim to human specialness. If humans are special, they are so in degree rather than kind. This removes an absolute barrier to infanticide. If a human infant fails the test of personhood on the basis of the new set of criteria, then its life should be ended as a preemptive act of mercy, just as one might put a wounded animal down to spare it further suffering. Singer dispels any prejudiced sentimentality about human life.

What is disquieting about Singer's views, in addition to their substance, is the dissonance at the core of his method. He sidelines rationality as a decisive characteristic of humanity and therefore as a leading criterion of personhood but pins his whole approach on rational argument, as a philosopher must. He must persuade us rationally to overlook the centrality of our rationality and liken ourselves to dogs and pigs. We are to reconstruct our personhood so as to treat our canine and porcine brethren as persons. But we must do so, of course, in a uniquely human conceptual way that is utterly alien to our friends Fido and Babe. And yet we are not supposed to be, in a relevant respect, radically different from them.

Nor do we deserve treatment that is different in kind. Is this a coherent view? Furthermore, he sidelines moral agency and responsibility—which dogs and pigs do not possess—while calling us to exercise our moral agency with respect to a concept of responsibility that assumes the personhood of nonhuman animals. I do not see how his expansive view of personhood can be coherently reintegrated with our ordinary experience of what it is to be persons and consequently what personhood can credibly mean. There is certainly a case to be made for minimizing the suffering of animals [*tza'ar ba'alei ḥayyim*] or for vegetarianism, but doing so on the basis of a radical attack on human dignity seems self-defeating to me.[19]

Singer is a moral philosopher and his project of "unsanctifying human life" is located in the discourse of bioethics. Darwinian philosophers drive views such as these into other domains. Darwinism can be, in Daniel Dennett's phrase, a "universal acid." It dissolves our ingrained and cherished ideas of human difference. Darwinism's global explanation for the diversity of organic life presses down into the origins of life itself and then bridges the gap between the organic and inorganic realms. Self-replicating carbon-based molecules straddle the line between the living and the nonliving. No divine spirit breathed life into clay. Darwinian philosophers see adaptation through natural selection as a universal explanatory framework, relevant not only to the evolution of species but also to the coevolution of culture. Under paradigms such as sociobiology, now called evolutionary psychology, human sociology and psychology are fully analogized, even reduced, to animal social organization and behavior. Primatology weakens or erases the lines between humans and other primates. Human moral behavior roots back, in Frans de Waal's view, to the empathy, altruism, fairness, and consolation behavior of chimps.[20] Of course, there are significant differences between human moral action and pongid behavior, but, if one is convinced by the evolutionary paradigm, these are differences of degree not kind. The same emergent laws of evolutionary biology, genetics, and cognitive science account for the basic features of human life no less than those of other animals.

Developments such as these have convinced some biologically minded philosophers that human morality has to be put on a new basis.[21] Human dignity, which entails the view that humans are different in kind from other animals and the rest of nature, has got to go. "Evolutionary theory does not directly contradict the doctrine of human dignity," philosopher Steve Stewart-Williams writes, but "it undermines the foundations upon which it rests and the worldview within which it makes any sense."[22] Stewart-Williams argues that radical human difference can only be the case if one or both of these claims were true: (1) there is a God in whose image we were created, and (2) we and we alone possess rationality. As to the former, many contemporary philosophers in the analytic and scientific tradition seem incapable of construing the concept of God as anything other than a failed attempt to explain natural processes. Now that we can better explain such processes through sound science, the concept of God has no explanatory role and therefore no cognitive status.

If one were to object that the religious person is doing something other than attempting a causal explanation of how some feature of the world, like human beings, came to be, the contemporary philosopher would find that activity no less occult, wooly-minded, and misconstrued. Thus, Stewart-Williams parries a sophisticated theology like Paul Tillich's: "And if God were some weird abstract principle, we could not have been made in God's image. What could it mean, for example, to say that we were made in the image of the Ground of All Being?"[23] The appeal to God as the ground of values or the model of moral perfection that humans ought to imitate would be dismissed as suppositious and unnecessary, given likelier explanations for morality and mundane reasons to practice it. God can never be, inferentially, the best explanation for anything.

As to rationality, Stewart-Williams and others view it as an adaptation that conferred a survival advantage early in our evolutionary history. Other animals, in particular higher primates, share rationality albeit to a lesser degree. But why should the possession of rationality in any degree be dignity conferring or confirming? Once you accept the "universal acid" of Darwinian explanation, the elevation of this trait seems arbitrary. "We like to think that reason is the supreme adaptation," Stewart-Williams writes, "that rational animals deserve preferential treatment and that non-humans, because they don't have reason, have no intrinsic moral value."

However, after Darwin, this is no different and no more convincing than, say, an elephant thinking that *trunks* are the supreme adaptation; that animals with trunks deserve preferential treatment and that nonelephants, because they don't have trunks, have no intrinsic moral value."[24] Just as we would dismiss an "elephant-biased view of the world," we ought also to dismiss a "human-biased or anthropocentric" view.

Thus, Darwinism leaves human dignity without "intellectual foundations." "With the corrective lens of evolutionary theory, the view that human life is infinitely valuable suddenly seems like a vast and unjustified over-valuation of human life."[25] After lengthy reflection on the unnecessary suffering caused to animals (which he likens to the Holocaust), as well as to suffering humans whom our law deprives of the option of voluntary euthanasia, Stewart-Williams concludes that "the effect of the doctrine of human dignity is to increase the sum total of suffering in the world."[26]

As in Singer, one must point to an odd, almost willful blindness in Stewart-Williams's argument. He suggests a lively thought experiment to get us to consider the elephant's point of view vis-à-vis its trunk. But elephants, after all, don't think about their trunks; they simply use them. They don't think, because they can't think, of their trunks as adaptations, let alone supreme adaptations. They don't, properly speaking, have a point of view. They have interests, which we should consider; but they don't have perspectives. If they could be said to have an "elephant-biased view of the world," there is nothing that they could do about it. They couldn't choose to suspend it to take the interests or perspectives of other creatures into account. The very fact that we can, in thought experiments and in moral practice, take on a point of view that relativizes our own interests attests to our profound differences from other creatures. Chimps may treat other chimps within their kinship group fairly, but they can't think about fairness, articulate it as a principle, or apply it to beings outside of their kinship group. These are differences in kind not degree. To shovel all of these differences into the bin of "adaptations" is to obliterate them. It is to these differences, which Darwinian explanations must elide, soften, or distort, that the principle of human dignity responds and fixes as axiologically central.

A final challenge to human dignity is found in neuroscience. As mentioned, neuroscience discredits the concept of selfhood where self implies a reified entity. The modern folk-psychological concept of a self descends from an earlier conception of the soul. Self and soul were both held to be composed of occult mental stuff, different in kind from the extended physical stuff that made up the external world. This kind of thinking, famously propounded by René Descartes, begins to unravel with Thomas Hobbes and later with David Hume. Mental stuff, memorably derided by Gilbert Ryle as the ghost in the machine, has no place in empiricism. Today, mental functions that cannot be reduced to neuronal activity have no place in the physicalist universe of brain science. The experience of self, self-consciousness, qualitative states, and so on must be reduced from a first-person ontology to a third-person object-language.

To pass muster, any concept of selfhood must entail conscious awareness of unity and persistence through time, phenomenological experience of agency and of embodiment, and relatedness to the outside world.[27] These characteristics naturally imply a single being, a subject in possession of these properties. But there is reason to doubt the cogency of this intuition even pretheoretically. We do speak in ordinary language of "not being myself" if one is out of sorts, or "I hurt myself" when one means that one hurt one's body, or "I talk to myself" when one carries on an interior dialogue. Thus, we often entertain a nonunified, pluralistic, flexible concept of selfhood on a pretheoretical level. Neuroscience theorizes that concept: "What the nonsystematic character of [ordinary language] suggests is that the self is not a thoroughly coherent, unified representational scheme about which we have thoroughly coherent unified beliefs."[28] The neuroscientific claim is that the self designates an ensemble of representational capacities that are always in play.

The self amounts to such capacities of the brain as the ability to map the internal homeostatic states of the body, the position of the body at rest and in motion in space, its responses to internal and external stimuli; the ability to initiate muscular exertion, to notice feelings; to become self-aware on a meta-level of neuronal activity at a more primary level, and so forth. The self captures a vast plethora of brain activity occurring in parallel processed information states; there is no unified, executive center, no internal "Cartesian theater," as Daniel Dennett calls it.[29] Consciousness per se is not a unified process but a "multitude of widely distributed specialized systems and disunited processes."[30]

We feel that we have—that we are—a unified center of thought, decision, memory, and executive function, however, because one of those specialized systems, the "left hemisphere interpreter" as Michael Gazzaniga calls it, has been selected by evolution to produce such a representation. This interpreter infers causal connections among events, thereby generating explanations. When we perceive a fresh scar on someone's face, for example, we immediately jump to speculate about how it got there. Or at least our left hemisphere interpreter does. We can't leave striking facts isolated from a potential causal-explanatory narrative. Selfhood is a kind of narrative explanation arising from the information shaping activity of the left hemispheric interpreter. It brings coherence to the parallel, diverse, ramified activities of the brain. Without its coordinating, simplifying activity, we might become overwhelmed by the chatter of a million modules running programs clambering to crack into consciousness. "Our subjective awareness," Gazzaniga writes, "arises out of our dominant left hemisphere's unrelenting quest to explain these bits and pieces that have popped into consciousness."[31] Presumably, those prehistoric hominids who, as a result of random genetic mutations, acquired the illusion of having an executive control center in their heads fared better than their competitors and reproduced more effectively. The genes that coded for the neural architecture that supported the left hemisphere interpreter function were passed on. Every human being who thinks she has a self is the descendent of those lucky hominids.

Is selfhood then like Otto von Bismarck's quip about politics and *Wurst*, that is, one shouldn't look too closely at how they are made? I don't think that a neurological account of the constructed, neural nature of selfhood necessarily undermines our phenomenological experience of selfhood. Analogously, a neurobiological account of vision doesn't alter how we see things. But there is a level at which it is problematic, namely, the dismissal of phenomenological experience per se. This occurs through the global equation of mind with brain, the reduction of mental states to neuronal synaptic activity, the elimination of the bedrock ontology of thoughts, beliefs, desires, and intentions in favor of firings, processing, computation, and function.[32] There is a relentless march against the integrity of the first-person point of view. This was not begun by neuroscience. We find it in very different ways in Marx (false consciousness) or in Freud (the Unconscious)—any view that tries to be scientifically credible tends to be reductionist. All the arrows of causality, the physicist Steven Weinberg says, point downward to physics. It is unclear how the integrity of the first-person point of view, with which human dignity is intertwined, can be conceptually maintained.

A special and critical instance of this is found in the renewed debate over free will. This hardy perennial of philosophical and theological argument flourishes anew in the age of neuroscience. Hume paved the way with his compatibilist analysis of free will. No choice is uncaused, on Hume's account. Desires, beliefs, and other motivations play a causal role; they determine choices. Any claim that we make that our choices are free must be compatible with the claim that they are caused by such things as desires and beliefs. What we really mean when we say we have free choice is that we acted deliberately, not by accident—we broke the vase because we threw it down on purpose, not because we slipped and dropped it. Free-willed decisions are decisions made within a subtler network of causes, not within a cause-free universe.

Neuroscience pushes the causal network, in which "free" choices are made, down to a neurobiological level. Thus, we may feel—in the largely illusory world of first-person phenomenological experience—that we made our choices in a cause-independent, libertarian way, but that is never actually the case. Our decisions are the product of long chains of causation, but not all causes are created equal. The decision to raise my arm has a different causal history than someone's taking my arm and lifting it for me or putting an electrode on my arm and zapping it, and so forth A relevant piece of support for this view is the famous experiments of Benjamin Libet. Using fMRI scans, Libet showed, arguably, that "decisions" are made at a neuronal level before the conscious mind becomes aware of them. We do not formulate desires and then enact them; we become conscious of incipient action up to five seconds after it has been initiated preconsciously. We do not have freedom of will but we do have "freedom of won't." That is, "We don't quite initiate voluntary processes; rather, we 'select and control them,' either by permitting the movement that arises out of an unconsciously initiated process or 'by vetoing the progression to actual motor activation.'"[33] Just as the self has been diffused into an at best contingently coherent collection of capacities, free will has been translated into a filtering mechanism that functions ex post facto to modulate preconscious brain activity.

Neuroscientists and philosophers who theorize along these lines want to preserve responsibility even if they have weakened or eliminated free will as the conceptual backdrop to agency. One way to do this is through an evolutionary biological strategy. Just as other social animals, such as chimps, rely on punishment, exclusion, shunning behavior, and so on, to enforce social norms—which contribute to and are necessary for group survival—so too human beings are genetically programmed to maintain such practices. We are not troubled by the metaphysics of free will with respect to other primates. We accept that their policing practices, which register approval and disapproval of one another's behavior, are entirely natural and confer a survival advantage. We should thus naturalize the social policing of human action, the ascription of praise and blame, the fixing of responsibility, and so forth, as what our kind of highly social, highly developed primate does. There is nothing metaphysically mysterious about this. Responsibility and determinism are compatible.[34]

Gazzaniga, Churchland and others, like David Hume before them, want to maintain the salience of human responsibility in the absence of free will, at least free will of a metaphysical, libertarian sort. Gazzaniga argues that agency and responsibility are social categories. The level of the individual brain is the wrong place to look for them. "Responsibility is not located in the brain. The brain has no area or network for responsibility," Gazzaniga writes. "The way to think about responsibility is that it is an interaction between people, a social contract."[35] There is good sense in this transposition. Holding agents responsible is necessarily a social practice, a public feature of a shared, normative form of life. And perhaps the practice is not weakened by a compatibilist account of free will any more than our conviction of the solidity of tables is weakened by an atomic account of matter (in terms of which tables are mostly empty space). Perhaps it is a category mistake to class features of a shared moral life under the rubric of individual subjectivity. If the story of subjectivity, of consciousness, of mind should turn out to be a physicalist, reductive one, perhaps we could still maintain responsibility and agency at the emergent level of sociality.

If we are able to sustain reductions of selfhood and free will to neural, bioelectrical activity while continuing to take selfhood and free will seriously, I suspect that we will do so not because we need to affirm the basicality of social life but because we continue to believe in the reality, durability, and dignity of human beings. How could society and the humane survival of the species that it facilitates matter if human beings did not matter? How could the commitment to human flourishing within society, of which the search for scientific knowledge is a principal part, matter if human beings did not? If we were really to bracket all of those profoundly axiological concomitants of personhood out and reconstruct human beings along purely biological and neurological lines, would we come up with a picture of persons as distinct from highly complex things? Would we come up with beings that have worth? Would we come up with creatures about which we should care on other than brute conative grounds? I very much doubt it.

CONCLUSION

It is an empirical question, a question about an unknowable future, whether emphasizing our animality, deemphasizing our capacity for rationality, eroding the differences constituted by our humanity, and eliminating the foundations of our experience of selfhood and free will threaten our moral principles and practices, among those ordered by human dignity. I am inclined to believe that this course, if followed, would have that effect, but this is only a worry, an apprehension. Human dignity may prove so fundamental that it cannot be dislodged or displaced. Or it may be that human dignity, as a robust moral and legal principle, is so tied to Jewish and Christian religious traditions that a fully secularized, amnesiac culture would become unmoored from it. I have tried to argue for human dignity indirectly through probing the weaknesses of counterarguments and exposing, tu quoque, their covert assumption of what they overtly reject. As with a Socratic elenchus or Kantian argument, however, one must already be committed to the claims of reason to care that one's violation of them matters. Reason is already biased in favor of human dignity.

This seems to me as robust a defense of dignity as robust secularism can offer. If dignity is fundamental to a decent democracy, biblical conviction about indefeasible human value may well be necessary. Absent the continuing cultural power of "Jerusalem," the claims of reason might ring hollow.

NOTES

1. I use the terms "human dignity" and "sanctity of human life" interchangeably in this paper. By doing so, I ignore other concepts of dignity, such as social status and gravitas. I also elide the ancient Stoic concept of *dignitas* as indicative of the singular worth of "the whole human race" with the biblical concept of *b'tzelem Elohim*, of humanity made in the image of God. See note 14 for the various other senses and sources of dignity.

2. Samuel Belkin, *In His Image* (New York: Abelard Schuman, 1960), 18.

3. Jonathan Sarna, "The Cult of Synthesis in American Jewish Culture," *Journal of Jewish Social Studies* 5:1–2 (Fall 1998–Winter 1999): 52–79.

4. The contemporary attention to the role of principles in law owes much to Ronald M. Dworkin. See his influential article, "The Model of Rules," *University of Chicago Law Review* 35:1 (Autumn 1967): 14–46.

5. Joseph Raz, "Legal Principles and the Limits of Law," *Yale Law Journal* 81:5 (April 1972): 823–54.

6. Yair Lorberbaum, *Tzelem Elohim: Halakha v'Aggadah* (Jerusalem: Schocken, 2004), esp. chapter 3.

7. Alan Mittleman, "No Fear of Foundations: Reflections on Human Rights in Contemporary Jewish Philosophy," *Heythrop Journal* 50 (2009): 923–29.

8. One of the features of Kant's ethical thought is his strong distinction between "rational being" and "human being." This opens the door to nonhuman persons, if such there are, having precisely the kind of dignity or worth that Kant ascribes to rational beings, a class now currently exhausted by human beings. An indication of where this might go is Allen Wood's openness to Peter Singer's claim that animals that are capable of suffering be included in the class of persons in what Wood calls "an extended sense." See Allen W. Wood, *Kantian Ethics* (New York: Cambridge University Press, 2008), 290.

9. Schopenhauer quoted in Michael Rosen, *Dignity: Its History and Meaning* (Cambridge: Harvard University Press, 2012), 1.

10. For a keen analysis of how Kant fell short of his goal and remains deeply entangled with religion see John Hare, *God and Morality* (Oxford: Blackwell, 2009), 122–83, and John Hare, *The Moral Gap* (Oxford: Oxford University Press, 1996), 7–37.

11. There is a strong historical case to be made that the founding generation of Americans drew inspiration from the "Hebrew Republic" that they found in the Bible. See, for example, Eran Shalev, *American Zion: The Old Testament as a Political Text from the Revolution to the Civil War* (New Haven: Yale University Press, 2013); Daniel Dreisbach, *Reading the Bible with the Founding Fathers* (New York: Oxford University Press, 2017); and others. This is a different matter, however, from the normative question of whether a human dignity–respecting democracy is conceptually dependent on a biblical idea such as imago dei.

12. Michael S. Gazzaniga, *Who's In Charge? Free Will and the Science of the Brain* (New York: Harper Collins, 2011), 102.

13. Steven Pinker, "The Stupidity of Dignity," *New Republic* (May 11, 2008), http://richarddawkins.net/articles/2567-the-stupidity-of-dignity. Ruth Macklin, "Dignity Is a Useless Concept," *BMJ* 327:7429 (2003): 1419–20. All subsequent citations are from these articles.

14. Pinker conflates separate senses of dignity. As Rosen points out, Latin *dignitas* could indicate intrinsic worth, a position advocated by the Stoics and Cicero (roughly comparable to the biblical idea of *b'tzelem Elohim*), as well as status and rank in a social hierarchy (a nobleman would have *dignitas*; a slave would not), and impressive appearance, behavior, and bearing. See Rosen, *Human Dignity*, 11–62. In this essay, I am using the first sense of "dignity," that is, the one closest to *b'tzelem Elohim*.

15. Peter Singer, *Unsanctifying Human Life* (ed. Helga Kuhse; Malden: Blackwell, 2002), 221 (emphasis added).

16. Ibid., 219–20.

17. Ibid., 225.

18. Ibid., 230 (emphasis added).

19. For a qualified argument on behalf of vegetarianism, see the posthumous theological anthropology of Rabbi Joseph B. Soloveitchik, *The Emergence of Ethical Man* (Jersey City: Toras HaRov Foundation, 2005), 31ff.

20. Frans de Waal, *Primates and Philosophers: How Morality Evolved* (Princeton: Princeton University Press, 2006).

21. As E. O. Wilson pungently puts it: "Above all, for our own physical well-being if nothing else, ethical philosophy must not be left in the hands of the merely wise. Although human progress can be achieved by intuition and the force of will, only hard-won empirical knowledge of our biological nature will allow us to make optimum choices among the competing criteria of progress." Edward O. Wilson, *Human Nature* (Cambridge: Harvard University Press, 1978), 7.

22. Steve Stewart-Williams, *Darwin, God, and the Meaning of Life* (New York: Cambridge University Press, 2010), 262.

23. Ibid., 263.

24. Ibid., 263–64. Edward O. Wilson offers a thought experiment from the other direction. Imagine highly advanced aliens coming to earth and finding human beings primitive, undeveloped, uninteresting, and therefore, from an alien-biased point of view, lacking in value. Nothing would prevent them from eating us, if that is what they chose to do. Wilson, *Human Nature*, 17.

25. Stewart-Williams, *Darwin, God, and the Meaning of Life*, 266.

26. Ibid., 279.

27. Walter Glannon, *Bioethics and the Brain* (New York: Oxford University Press, 2007), 32.

28. Patricia Smith Churchland, *Brain-Wise: Studies in Neurophilosophy* (Cambridge: MIT Press, 2002), 63.

29. John R. Searle, *The Mystery of Consciousness* (New York: New York Review of Books, 1997), 101.

30. Gazzaniga, *Who's In Charge?*, 102.

31. Ibid., 103.

32. For an example of this, see Paul M. Churchland, *The Engine of Reason, The Seat of the Soul* (Cambridge: MIT Press, 1996), 322.

33. Libet is cited in single quotation marks by Tallis in an excerpt from Raymond Tallis, *Aping Mankind: Neuromania, Darwinitis, and the Misrepresentation of Humanity* (Durham: Acumen, 2011), 56.

34. This is the basic strategy of Patricia Churchland; see Churchland, *Brain-Wise*, chapter 5. For a biting critique, see Tallis, *Aping Mankind*, 51–59.

35. Gazzaniga, *Who's In Charge?*, 193.

"The Will of the People" or "The Will of the Rabbis": Democracy and the Rabbis' Authority

Shlomo Abramovich

PREFACE

A well-known secret is that if any candidate wants to earn the votes of several Jewish communities in Brooklyn, he does not need to go visit any bar mitzvah parties or take pictures with Jewish children. All he needs is to meet with their rabbi and convince him to order his followers to vote for him, and what the rabbi decides, they will do without any doubt.

This description might be a simple answer to the common question "Is Judaism democratic?"[1] In these kinds of communities, the answer is a definite "no." Without getting into the different ways to define democracy, the free will of the individual in the society is an essential part of it. Therefore, the Jewish ultra-Orthodox communities, which emphasize the value of obedience to the rabbis, cannot be considered democratic communities.

However, as we see in this essay, the truth, as always, is much more complicated. We will examine various sources as well as some research that was done on Jewish ultra-Orthodox communities, in order to present the different motives for obedience to the rabbis. We will create a scale of democracy and see the differences between the approaches in terms of closeness to democratic values.

We will focus on Jewish ultra-Orthodox communities from the end of the nineteenth century to the present. Of course, there are big differences between the communities in this spectrum—a Chasidic community in Brooklyn is not the same as a Sephardic community in Jerusalem. Yet, the differences are going to be presented in the different ways to explain the obedience to the rabbis, as we will see.

The decision to focus on this period was made because during this time there was a huge growth in the importance of this value: obedience to the rabbis. The rabbis had an important role in the Jewish communities for ages, and they were involved in their followers' lives in many ways, but in this period something had changed.

Described in the short and exact words by Haym Soloveitchik: "What is new in the contemporary scene is the unprecedented frequency, scope and authority currently ceded to them [the rabbis]."[2]

The role of the rabbi was no longer limited to typical halachic topics. Rabbis were asked questions about business and financial issues, as well as marriages and divorces. In several communities, the members ask the rabbi whom to marry, where to invest their money, and whether to renovate their houses. Another important aspect of the obedience to the rabbis is politics.[3] Rabbis are involved in each decision of the political representatives of their communities, and they are the real leaders of ultra-Orthodox political parties.

The political aspect of obedience to rabbis is another aspect of the change in the role of the rabbis during the period with which we are dealing. The political institutions, with the authority of the rabbis, strengthened their power and influence. The rabbis became much more famous as they got exposure from the political party and thus gained many more followers who looked for their advice and obeyed their decisions. Furthermore, they got the opportunity to directly influence a wide variety of issues, with national and even international significance.

This value became very important in ultra-Orthodox communities, and in some ways, we can say that it defined and separated them from other Jewish religious communities. We can see how some groups in Religious Zionism define themselves by resistance to the involvement of rabbis in wide aspects of life, as happened in the ultra-Orthodox communities.[4]

Other developments in the obedience to the rabbis during this time are the theoretical explanations for it that were discussed and written by the rabbis, who gave this value deeper and more diverse meanings. The theoretical explanations for the meaning of obedience to the rabbis will be the basis for our discussion in this article.

FOUR MOTIVATIONS FOR OBEDIENCE TO THE RABBIS

We can arrange and divide the explanations for obedience to the rabbis into four different concepts: political-social, mystic, halachic, and rational.[5]

THE POLITICAL-SOCIAL CONCEPT

Usually, the political-social concept will not appear in internal Orthodox sources—although we can find some expressions of it, as we will see. However, according to some research, this is the main cause for the growth of rabbinic obedience in this period.

According to this concept, obedience to the rabbis is a way to deal with the weakening of the traditional Jewish community. Modern influences led some Jewish leaders to fight back by strengthening the borders of Jewish communities. This is the foundation of Jewish Orthodoxy, in which obedience to the rabbis is considered one of the main characteristics of this process.[6]

This obedience to rabbis created a system that requires members of the community to keep close relations with the rabbi and leaders of the community. If you are taught to ask the rabbi about every step in your life, you cannot leave the community. Strengthening this value became a way to prevent abandonment of the Orthodox community.

In addition, the empowerment of the rabbis' position reduces the independence of individuals, and it is therefore easier to keep them away from new ideologies that may be opposed to Orthodox ideology.

Furthermore, as mentioned before, this value became a way to define and separate Orthodox communities and Orthodox parties from other groups in Jewish society. The difference between who accepts the authority of the rabbis and who does not emphasized the uniqueness of Orthodox identity and helped to strengthen the borders of these communities.

In this concept, obedience to rabbis is not described as a Jewish value—or as a value at all. It is a political and social tool that is used to promote several concepts and targets. Therefore, we do not expect to find this concept in any internal Orthodox sources. We can assume that it will be displayed and explained in much more ideological ways.

However, we can find traces of it in some rabbis' writings. For example, an interesting explanation of the importance of total obedience to rabbis was given by Rav Avraham Yeshaya Karelitz, known by the name of his book—Chazon Ish.[7]

In his book, he talks about people who do not trust the rabbis and think that maybe they have private motives in their decisions—just like any other people. In response, he does not talk about the greatness and holiness of the rabbis, which makes them think and act differently from other people. Instead he speaks about the danger of this thinking. He explains that if we do not trust the rabbis, it will break the entire social and juridical system and will cause anarchy. He claimed that without total obedience the generation will become orphans, without any leadership.[8] According to his explanation, obedience to the rabbis, without any doubts in their motives, is a way to keep order in the community and maintain social stability.

An interesting comparison was made by Gershon Bacon between obedience to the rabbis in ultra-Orthodox communities and the decision regarding papal infallibility made by the Vatican Council at the end of the nineteenth century.[9] According to some research, the motive for this decision was to "enhance his sovereign power as the head of the church," as Brian Tierney termed it.[10] We can see in both cases how religious decisions and values can be used for political and social needs.

THE MYSTIC CONCEPT

According to this concept, the rabbi is considered to be closer to God and to have special spiritual powers. His decisions represent God's will, and therefore ordinary people must obey them.

By this concept, obedience to the rabbis has significant importance. It is not only a matter of keeping community order or the regular halachic obligation. The rabbi's decisions represent God's will, and so disobeying is actually resisting God. This concept gives unlimited power and authority to rabbis and encourages followers to widen the involvement of rabbis in their lives—who does not want to have direct guidance from God in every step of his life?

Researchers argue about when this concept started to be popular as an explanation to rabbinic obedience—after the Holocaust or maybe after the establishment of the State of Israel.[11] However, many agree that its origin is the Chasidic concept of the *Tzadik*—the spiritual religious leader—and the expansion of this concept is an expression of the influence of the Chasidic movement on the entirety of Jewish Orthodoxy.[12]

One way to identify the mystic concept of obedience to rabbis is when the rabbis give their answers and orders without any explanations or sources. In regular rabbinic writings, rabbis base their decisions on traditional sources or previous cases. This sort of writing gives other rabbis and followers the ability to discuss the conclusions and to argue about the way the rabbi understood the sources. According to the mystic concept, the source for the rabbis' decisions is their closeness to God, and therefore there is no need to bring in other sources or explanations, and it is also impossible to disagree with their decisions.

There is a similarity between this concept and the Catholic dogma of papal infallibility that we mentioned before. If the rabbi has close relations with God and if his decisions represent God's will, then it makes sense that he cannot be wrong. Some researchers claim that we can find sources for this idea in Jewish ultra-Orthodoxy, in the argument about rabbis' leadership during the Holocaust.[13]

However, most rabbis avoid using these kinds of terms and do not describe rabbis as totally infallible. Followers should obey rabbis without any doubts, and their decisions have a highly spiritual significance, but not in the same way that happened within the Catholic Church. The common explanations talk about the huge distance between the rabbis and regular people. Therefore what seemed to be the rabbi's mistake is actually the follower's mistake—the assumption that the rabbi can never be wrong is usually not stated.[14] This can be explained by a reluctance to relate total divine abilities to a human being in Orthodox Judaism—even when he considered to have special spiritual abilities.

THE HALACHIC CONCEPT

This concept seems to be the most conservative concept because it bases obedience to rabbis on the traditional halachic obligation to the rabbis, which is mentioned in the Torah and the Talmud. However, this concept is radical due to the unlimited number of topics considered to be part of halacha, which made every kind of question part of the rabbis' responsibility—from political decisions to personal finance questions. According to this concept, members of the religious community should ask their rabbi who to marry or where to build their home in the same way they should ask him how to make kosher food and observe the rules of Shabbat.

This concept is based on the theological idea that everything can be found in the Torah—every aspect of life, every question we have. Benjamin Brown wrote a comprehensive study about the roots of this idea and showed its various origins in Maimonides' philosophy, as well as in Nachmanides' kabbalah.[15] According to this concept, rabbis should use traditional sources as a base for explaining their decisions. It requires them to provide a creative reading of the sources and to use varying sources to find answers to many different questions.

An example for this creativity can be found in an answer written by Rav Moshe Sofer, known by the name of his book Chatam Sofer, considered to be one of the founders of Jewish Orthodoxy. He was asked if it is allowed to build the bimah, or stage, at the front of a synagogue. This question was an argument between Orthodox rabbis and the new Reform movement, which chose to place the stage at the front in their new temples. He answered that it is forbidden to do it and used extremely unusual sources with remarkable creativity to support his decision for this simple architectural question.[16]

Decisions made according to this concept result in open discussion—the same way it happens in any other halachic decisions. Another interesting result of this concept is the connection, or perhaps better to say disconnect, between their decisions and reality.

We previously discussed the claim that rabbis cannot be wrong according to the mystic concept. In the halachic concept we can find similar claims, that the rabbis' decisions cannot be tested by their results in reality. The Chazon Ish, who was mentioned before, was quoted saying that "success is not Halacha." This slogan means that the halachic goal is to figure out the Jews' duties, what God is expecting them to do in each situation. Therefore, the practical result of what they do is irrelevant, as long as they believe it is God's will.

An example of this way of thinking can be found after the establishment of the State of Israel, when the ultra-Orthodox rabbis were asked if the success of the Zionists was God's will, and if the rabbis who opposed Zionism were wrong. The answer given by Rabbi Izhak Soloveichik, the Rabbi of Brisk—one of the most important ultra-Orthodox rabbis in Jerusalem in the first years of the State of Israel—was the same: that success means nothing if what they are doing is against halachah, as he believed.[17]

This concept is a great example for Jewish Orthodoxy. The essence of Orthodoxy is the claim that nothing has changed—they observe the traditional Jewish way of life, which always included obedience to rabbis.[18] Indeed, great changes had occurred when obedience to the rabbis began to cover all aspects of life, and halachah itself grew new and wider meanings.

THE RATIONAL CONCEPT

Unlike the halachic concept, according to this concept there is a difference between ordinary halachic questions and all other questions rabbis were asked, which are not considered to be part of halachah. The main question is, why should rabbis be involved in nonhalachic questions? If marriage, finance, and politics are not considered part of halachah—why should people obey rabbis' decisions in those areas?

The answer, according to the rational concept, is that the rabbis have clearer thinking and better logic than the ordinary person has, and therefore their decisions should be followed. The reason that the rabbis have these special abilities is the Torah they studied. Some sources talk about how studying the Torah helps to shape rational skills and logical thinking. Other sources focus on the moral influence of the Torah, which purifies the minds of learners and enables them to make decisions without external influences, from desires to social concerns. This claim about the influence of Torah studying has roots in the Talmud and even the Bible, but the implication of it in total obedience to rabbis is a unique development.

We can understand that the commitment to the rabbis' decisions here is lower, according to this concept, in comparison to the others. The rabbis are considered to be good advisors, and it can be useful to consult them in any aspect of life, but their decisions in nonhalachic topics are only advice.

Therefore, rabbis and other writers were trying to encourage people to obey rabbis, even in nonhalachic matters. Certain famous quotes sharply describe the huge difference between the rabbis' way of thinking and ordinary people.[19] We can see the difference between this concept and the others in the way it was presented. In practice, the result may be the same—the rabbis lead their communities with absolute control. This concept can give followers a sense of willingness and understanding of their rabbis' leadership in their society, but does not necessarily mean that their obedience to the rabbis was different.

THE SCALE OF DEMOCRACY

After examining the four main concepts of obedience to the rabbis, we can examine their level of democracy. As mentioned at the beginning, we are not talking about full democracy in the way we usually understand this phrase. We are still talking about ultra-Orthodox communities, where rabbis make most important decisions for their followers.[20] What we are trying to do is to build a scale of democracy, and examine the differences between these concepts, to examine their proximity to democracy—or maybe we should say to examine their distance from democracy.

The main criterion in our scale of democracy will be the individual's status in society, relative to the position of the rabbis. The heart of democracy and the basis for many democratic values is the importance of each member of a society, which is expressed in his or her independence and freedom. Therefore, the more the individual is worthless and meaningless in society, the more this concept will be considered as nondemocratic.

By this criterion, we can find a difference between the first two and last two concepts described above. The basis of the political-social concept was the weakening of individuals in society. The strengthening of the rabbis' position was part of a process of fortifying the boundaries of the Jewish community, in order to resist modern theories that were considered a threat to Jewish tradition.

According to this concept, the less free will the individual has and the less he or she makes decisions independently, the less ability an individual has to make changes in his or her life. And the more social institutions, represented mostly by the rabbis, have the power to control their members' lives, the more possible it is to keep them away from any external influence.

Therefore, this concept can be considered extremely nondemocratic. As mentioned before, this political-social concept was mostly described by researchers who examined ultra-Orthodox communities, and not by the rabbis themselves. However, as we stated before, we can find examples of this concept in their writings.

The second concept, the mystic concept, also presents a total weakening of individuals, though from a different perspective. According to this concept, the rabbis have special spiritual abilities, they are closer to God than anyone else, and their decisions represent his will. Therefore, the individual has to obey the rabbis and has no right to decide on his own or even to think independently—everything is cancelled in the presence of godliness. Unlike the political-social concept, the purpose is not specifically to weaken individuals. However, the emphasis on the rabbis' greatness and uniqueness leads to the insignificance of the regular members of society. Therefore, this concept can also be considered as nondemocratic.

In the next two concepts, however, we find a different status of individuals in society, despite their total obedience to the rabbis. We can see it clearly in the rational concept. As mentioned before, in the rational concept the rabbis are considered expert advisors, with special rationality and clear minds, and therefore their orders should be followed. The individuals in the society have full freedom to choose their way—and they choose to obey the rabbis because they appreciate their wisdom and their advice.

Of course, some might claim that it is a fake freedom, because the encouragement to obey the rabbis is actually brainwashing, and the social consequences for disobeying rabbis in these communities does not give a chance for true free will. As mentioned before, we are not dealing with the psychological aspects of obedience to the rabbis, and we are not examining the practical motives, but rather the way it is explained in the sources. We can assume, however, that in a society that educates its members according in this manner, it will be easier for an independent individual to choose differently and to make his own decisions in life.

The halachic concept of obedience to rabbis is different in many ways, but the position of the individual is similar. According to this approach, all aspects of life are considered to be part of halachah, and therefore the rabbis, who are the halachic authority, are in charge of every kind of decision in each person's life.

The individual, who chooses to be committed to halachah chooses to obey the rabbis. We can consider the rabbis as experts in the field of halachah, and the regular person, who is not qualified enough in this area, needs the help of the rabbis' expertise. We can compare it to other aspects in life, such as medicine, finance, or technology, where most people defer to experts in these areas—doctors, bankers, or engineers. Obedience to the rabbis is not because they are greater than other people, but because it is their expertise.

We can see in both the halachic and rational concepts that the individual's status is different, in comparison to the mystic and political concepts. Their obedience to the rabbis is made by their own decision to count on the rabbis' expertise in halachah or on their wisdom. According to the democratic scale we describe before, we claim that these concepts are more democratic than the other two.

We can still claim that the decision to give up on your free will and let other people make your decisions cannot be considered democratic in any way. However, we all choose to give up our own free will in many aspects of our life and live our lives according to the decisions of different experts. The fact that this is our own choice to count on other people's decisions is what makes the difference.

Another way to describe the scale of democracy of these concepts is by the distance between the rabbi and his followers. According to the political concept, the purpose of obedience to rabbis is to create a distance between leadership and individuals, to keep them away from any external influence, and build boundaries for Jewish society.

In the mystic concept, there is also a huge distance between the rabbis and their followers. The rabbis have a high level of spirituality, and regular members of the community are way behind. Therefore, we can, again, describe these concepts on the democratic scale as closer to dictatorship.

On the other two concepts, we can see that the distance between the rabbis and their followers is much smaller. The rabbi is an expert in his field—halachah or rational thinking—but he is not entirely different from his followers. Theoretically, anyone in the community can study Torah and reach his level—the focus is not on the rabbis' abilities or their social position, but on the Torah they studied, which is open to everyone to study. This social structure, where the distance between the leader and followers is limited and open to change, creates a different society in comparison to the other two approaches. This is a less hierarchical society, and therefore it can be considered more democratic.

SUMMARY

In summary, we have seen four different ways to explain the total obedience to rabbis in ultra-Orthodox communities in the last century. We divided the four approaches into two main groups, according to their proximity to democratic values. Our main argument was that the lower the status of the individual in the society and the greater the distance between the individual and his rabbi, the more we can consider the approach as nondemocratic.

Understanding the differences between these different motives for obedience to rabbis is extremely important for understanding ultra-Orthodox communities and their way of life. In modern-day Israel, understanding these communities is very important, especially because their population growth has made them an important factor in Israeli politics and economy.

The Israel Democracy Institution has conducted interesting research about obedience to rabbis in ultra-Orthodox communities in Israel in order to understand processes happening in this field and to predict where it is going to take these communities. Their title was a question: "Are we going towards democracy in the ultra-Orthodox leadership?"[21]

From these sources, we can answer that if democracy means that the ultra-Orthodox will no longer obey their rabbis, then the answer is probably "no." This value is part of these communities' identity, part of their DNA. But, even though obedience to the rabbis will remain, the motives for it can be changed to more democratic motives, and that may impact Israeli society.

In the end, we can learn from this case about the importance of taking a closer look, with an open mind, of any social phenomenon. If we just look deep enough, we will find the differences and the complexities, and maybe we will see that the reality is different than what we thought before. Even an ultra-Orthodox community, with total obedience to the rabbis, should not necessarily be considered as wholly nondemocratic.

NOTES

1. This topic became very popular after the establishment of the State of Israel. See for example, Joseph E. David, *The State of Israel: Between Judaism and Democracy* (Jerusalem: Israel Democracy Institute, 2003).

2. Haym Soloveitchik, "Rupture and Reconstruction: The Transformation of Contemporary Orthodoxy," *Tradition* 28:4 (1994): 67.

3. An important discussion about the beginning of the involvement of the rabbis in modern Jewish politics can be found in Gershon Bacon, "Daat Torah and Birth Pangs of the Messiah," *Tarbiz* 52c (1983): 497–508 [Hebrew].

4. Yosef Achituv, "Non Illusionary Religious Zionism," in *100 Years of Religious Zionism*, vol. 3 (ed. Avi Sagi and Dov Shwartz; Ramat Gan: Bar Ilan University, 2003), 7 [Hebrew].

5. Various sources for the following explanations and concepts can be found in the comprehensive research of Benjamin Brown: Benjamin Brown, "The Daat Torah Doctrine: Three Stages," *Jerusalem Studies in Jewish Thought* 16 (September 2004): 537–600; Benjamin Brown, *Toward Democratization in the Haredi Leadership? The Doctrine of Da'at Torah at the Turn of the Twentieth and Twenty-First Centuries* (Jerusalem: Israel Democracy Institute, 2011). Brown arranged the concepts in a chorographical order and arranged some of them differently. We focus on the meaning of each concept and its closeness to the democratic values and not its historical background.

6. Bacon, "Daat Torah," 501. Researchers are arguing about the timing of the growth of this value, according to the political and social conditions in Jewish society. Some of them are talking about the beginning of the twentieth century, as part of the establishment of Agudat Israel; some of them refer it to the crises in Orthodox leadership after the Holocaust; and others refer it to the struggle against the Zionist movement, and especially the Religious Zionist parties, after the establishment of the State of Israel. Benjamin Brown, "The Daat Torah Doctrine," 539.

7. He was one of the most important ultra-Orthodox leaders in Israel from the middle of the twentieth century. Comprehensive biography can be found in Benjamin Brown, *The Hazon Ish: Halakhist, Believer and Leader of the Haredi Revolution* (Jerusalem: Hebrew University, 2011) [Hebrew].

8. Avraham Yeshaya Karelitz, *Hazon Ish—Faith and Trust* (Jerusalem: 1996), 40 [Hebrew].

9. Bacon, "Daat Torah," 502.

10. Brian Tierney, *Origins of Papal Infallibility* (Leiden: Brill, 1972), 1.

11. Brown, *Toward Democratization,* 16.

12. Brown, "The Daat Torah Doctrine," 570, 593.

13. Ibid, 582–83.

14. For example, Eliyahu Eliezer Dessler, *Michtav Me'Eliyahu* (Jerusalem: 1978), 75–77 [Hebrew].

15. Brown, "The Daat Torah Doctrine," 542–45.

16. Moshe Sofer, *Shut Chatam Sofer—Orach Haim* (Jerusalem: 1972), 28 [Hebrew].

17. Brown, "The Daat Torah Doctrine," 548, 585–86.

18. Ibid., 594. Brown claims that this case can be a proof for the deep connection between Jewish Orthodoxy and premodern communities because this concept, which is usually presented as an Orthodox development, has deep roots in the traditional communities.

19. One of the most famous quotes is the saying of Rabbi Joshua Falk in his commentary to the *Shulkhan Arukh* that the decisions of regular people are totally the opposite of the decisions of the rabbis. Joshua Falk, *Sefer Me'irat Enayim—Hoshen Mishpat* (Jerusalem: 1955), 3:13 [Hebrew].

20. As mentioned, this extreme description is not happening in all types of ultra-Orthodox communities, which are separated also in the extent of obedience to the rabbis.

21. The predication of this research was that ultra-Orthodoxy in Israel is going to develop a new type of rabbinic leadership—not democratic but more pragmatic and less total. Brown, *Toward Democratization,* 106–11.

The Jewish State and the End of Democratic Judaism

Meirav Jones

The question of this volume, "Is Judaism Democratic?" seems to be missing a word, *state*.

Since before the formulation of Israel's declaration of independence, and increasingly in the last twenty-five years, the question of how to settle the apparent tension between Jewish state and democratic state, or the demands of Judaism with those of a democratic state, has been the subject of books, articles, position papers, educational programs, rabbinic responsa, university courses, yeshiva arguments, and more.[1] It seems that with so much effort having been put into exploring Judaism's approach to democratic governance—or how Judaism might be compatible or incompatible with democratic governance—there would be little more to be said.

But the question "Is Judaism democratic?," absent the term *state*, provides a new challenge. It asks of Judaism itself whether the highest authority is in the people. And as we see in the array of essays in this volume, Judaism itself is and has been many things.

In this essay, I will ask a political theorist's question: what difference does a state make to the locus of power in Judaism? If the case can be made—and has often been made—that Judaism itself, as lived in many places and times in the Diaspora, was in some sense democratic, with the ultimate authority in the hands of the people who constitute their own community and leadership, how does the fact of a Jewish state change, preserve, or challenge this? What does a state—particularly a modern state of the sort conceived in the sixteenth and seventeenth century by Jean Bodin, Thomas Hobbes, and their contemporaries, a state constituted by the people for their protection—do to the locus of power in Judaism?

The essay is in three parts. The first is a brief discussion of Judaism before the state or without the state. As this is not my area of expertise and some of the contributors to this volume have spent years studying Judaism throughout the ages, I will keep this section to a talmudic story that sets the terms for thinking about Judaism as democratic, and I will focus on one particular Jewish practice—ritual immersion in a *mikveh*—to explore how the highest authority being "not in heaven," translated to the people administering their own religious lives. In looking at the *mikveh* and other aspects of Jewish life, I introduce a little-known text from around the time the modern state was being consolidated, which confirms my understanding. I will offer a view that Judaism before the state or without the state belonged to the people, as a legacy they preserved, and this had an effect on the diversity that developed within Judaism.

The second part of the essay is about the modern state: the Westphalian state established at the heels of Christendom, formally in 1648, but consolidated in the centuries that followed, and still the key ordering principle of world politics today. What I'm particularly interested in engaging here is what the modern state does with religion and what it sought to change about Europe and particularly European religious life when it came into being. My choice to discuss the European state model founded in the seventeenth century is based on the fact that will be explored in the third part of the essay, that this was largely the model adopted by Zionism and then by the founders of the modern State of Israel.

The third part of the essay explores what modern statehood does to Judaism when a "Jewish state" is founded on the seventeenth century model. I claim that at the establishment of the Jewish state in 1948, Israel's founders applied the idea of the modern state to a Jewish state without addressing the need to theorize Jewish statehood or consider how a Jewish state might differ from a "regular" (or "Christian") state. Of course, the case can be made that the modern (even the modern Christian) state is built on Jewish models, and scholarship in the field of political Hebraism has explored the extent to which this is the case.[2] But whatever Jewish models and ideas were employed by the founders of modern sovereignty, the state was ultimately established to resolve a Christian problem, and interpretations of Jewish sources and models were carried out by Christians for Christians, often with little regard for Jewish exegetical traditions. When the founders of Israel applied the modern state model to their state, without conceiving a particular type of state suited to the needs of the Jews, this was set to affect the locus of power in Judaism. I identify how the Jewish state on this model undermines the democratic character of Judaism—its belonging to the people—by offering itself as a higher authority, and then present some alternatives that were available to the founders of the Jewish state and may still be available today. I argue that Judaism is less democratic today than ever due to the role played by the Jewish—even the Jewish and democratic—state.[3]

The question of whether democracy is an end worth preserving or whether the democratic characteristics of Judaism are worth preserving remains a question. I end the essay with a reflection on teleology, messianic times, and the state, refracted through John Milton's understanding of what Judaism had to contribute to the argument for free speech and multiplicity of voices at the dawn of modern politics. My reflection on the telos of democratic Judaism will be an addendum to my main argument which will run as follows: (1) Diasporic Jewish life could be described as democratic in certain respects, as an ideal and in practice, in the sense that practices and institutions belonged to the people participating in them; (2) the nature of the modern state is such that it purposely limits the role of the people in constituting religious life when it sets a single sovereign over civil and religious matters; and (3) that if Israel does not define its statehood otherwise, Judaism will cease—and in some areas has already ceased—to be ultimately in the hands of its constituents.

JUDAISM BEFORE THE STATE

Any discussion of locus of authority in Judaism before the state has to contend with the background story of the "oven of Achnai." In this remarkable story recounted in *Babylonian Talmud*, Bava Metziah 59b, Rabbi Eliezer claims the truth of his halachic position against the position of the sages on the question of whether a particular sort of oven can be defiled. He calls upon the heavens to support him when the other sages will not. He calls out: "If the halachah [religious law] is in accordance with me, let this carob tree prove it!" The carob tree moves, but the sages reply that nothing can be proven by a carob tree. R. Eliezer then calls out on the channel of water to prove him correct, and though the channel of water flowed backwards, the sages responded together, "No proof can be brought from a channel of water." He then calls on the walls of the house to prove him correct, but when the walls tilted as if to fall, R. Joshua rebuked the walls, saying, "When disciples of the wise are engaged in a halachic dispute, what right have you to interfere?" According to the story, the walls did not fall in deference to R. Joshua but they did not resume their upright position in deference to R. Eliezer; they are still standing aslant. Finally, R. Eliezer says to the sages, "If the halachah agrees with me, let it be proved from heaven." A divine voice is then heard crying out, "Why do you dispute with R. Eliezer, with whom the halachah always agrees?" R. Joshua stands up and protests: "'The Torah is not in heaven!' [Deut 30:12]. We pay no attention to a divine voice because long ago at Mount Sinai You wrote in your Torah, 'After the majority must one incline' [Exod 23:2]." God finally rejoices in his sons defeating him. The Torah is not in heaven.

What is remarkable about this story when it comes to democracy is that "the majority" overrule God when it comes to religious law. What is less remarkable, and what might be used against the argument that the story represents an inclination toward democracy, is that the majority that overruled God was not a majority of men, but rabbis. Of course, this does not preclude democracy: only a certain class of Greeks were included in Greek democracy, and there were modern democracies before women had the right to vote. But a situation in which the law is in the hands of the majority of rabbis is different from a situation in which the people—even some classes of men—is the highest authority. The move away from divine authority to human authority, even the authority of sages, is certainly a move toward democracy, but it is not definitive. We would want to see that the rabbis are not understood as representing God, or as kings or prophets. We would want to know how rabbinic authority is constituted. And we would want to know how texts such as this were understood by Jews administering their public lives.

Many of the essays in this volume discuss Jewish political life in diaspora communities and accounts of such life found in rabbinic responsa that support the understanding that ultimate authority was in the people or those viewed as representing the people, rather than in God or in those viewed as representing God. We find examples of how Jews in diaspora communities built and maintained their communal institutions, how they represented themselves to non-Jewish rulers of the states via elected officials, and how they allowed for popular constituency with the prominence of the idea of covenant. The fact that there were occasionally "states of emergency" where such protodemocratic practices were curtailed serves as an exception to the rule that Judaism was generally run bottom-up rather than top-down, belonging to the people. For present purposes I refer to the contributions of my colleagues and teachers.

But because I intend to explore the difference a state makes to the locus of power in Judaism, I will look to a concrete Jewish practice that persists today, which was part of Jewish life from ancient times and which I believe exemplifies the extent to which Judaism belonged to the people—even radically so—before the state. The example is the *mikveh*, the Jewish ritual bath in which women immerse monthly in observation of "the laws of family purity."[4] The *mikveh*, I suggest, properly belonged to the people, which meant that the people were the highest authority and ultimately that the women of each community were its custodians. The *mikveh* is thus brought to exemplify how Jewish life was run democratically, as Judaism had the women owning this institution, bottom up, before women were granted the rights to be part of democratic society, top-down. This will be shown to be in stark contrast to how this institution is run in the Jewish state, to which I will return in the third part of the essay.

In what sense did the *mikveh* belong to the people; to the women?

First, in terms of belonging to the people, the *mikveh* was built by the community through the collection of taxes, so it was built bottom up, by the people with their funds. While this has been likened to the way a state collects taxes and then builds institutions for the people to use,[5] there is a key way in which the building of institutions outside the state differs, and this is the fact that without a state presiding over religion, the *mikveh* in the diaspora belongs to the diverse Jews, with their diverse practices, who contributed to the building or to its fund. We see this clearly in a twentieth century ruling of R. Moshe Feinstein, who was asked to rule about whether a *mikveh* that was built by an Orthodox community with funds gathered both from within the community and outside of it should be available for use by Reform and Conservative rabbis for conversion purposes. R. Feinstein ruled that the *mikveh* properly belonged to all those who had participated in building it.[6] This meant that not only must non-Orthodox women be welcome to use the *mikveh* for postmenstrual immersion, but also Reform and Conservative rabbis should be able to use the *mikveh* for conversion purposes if they contributed funds for the construction of the *mikveh*.

If we look now at the sense in which the *mikveh* belonged specifically to women, we can observe that once built by the community, the structure itself was handed over to the women of the community as custodians of the postmenstrual immersion practice. The few artistic renditions we have of the practice show bathhouses resembling women-only spas, with no men in sight. As the artwork is not by women, this shows a male acceptance of such a female realm. In searching for a female account, I found a wonderful recent book in which a secular Israeli woman with a religious background describes herself letting go of the preconceptions with which she entered the *mikveh* to find herself enjoying a "supreme physical pleasure," of being pampered by other women who she likens to "bacchantes in a Dionysian orgy." It is described as an essentially feminine encounter, an ancient female ritual, and in that vulnerable and spiritual time of nakedness, there is no higher authority present, and no intermediary.[7] The idea that Judaism allows and encourages such a feminine encounter in which men have no part other than to build the structure and enable women contributes something to our understanding of what exilic Judaism looked like—and in some places still looks like—and how it was run.

Interestingly, rabbis have long related women's administration of the practice to the way the halachah on postmenstrual immersion was constituted. Most interpretations of *Babylonian Talmud*, Nidah 66b, where it says "the daughters of Israel were stringent upon themselves," find that the root of the current-day practice is in the stringency women placed upon themselves, which was later adopted approvingly by the rabbis. Both Maimonides and Nahmanides find women to have constituted the mandated practice through their custom, though some rabbis hold a different opinion and interpret the halachah to have been brought about by rabbinic interpretation of the Torah.[8] If indeed women constituted the halachah by their own stringency, then we see the law itself being shaped by the people over whom it became law, even when the people were women, marking a form of democratic legislation.

The administration of the practice by women, and their ruling of this realm of their lives also comes out in accounts of the "*mikveh* rebellion" in Egypt at the end of the twelfth century, in Maimonides' time, and also in a similar period in Byzantium. The rebellion was a well-coordinated refusal of women to attend the *mikveh* and to rather turn to the Muslim bathhouses, the hammam, which were common in Egypt and which may have been cleaner with better access to hot water than the *mikveh*. The influence of Karaism was also likely a factor. The rabbinic response was extreme and mostly ineffective and included threatening *Ketubah* [marriage contract] money.[9] The fact that men—even rabbis—could do little to enforce this aspect of Jewish life attests to the extent to which it belonged to women. One of the few questions rabbis discuss and disagree on regarding women's immersion is whether it is permissible to bathe after the *mikveh*. This discussion is said to have been rooted in the period of rebellion, as apparently a common misunderstanding (or disagreement) developed, that what purified women was not the water of the *mikveh* but the mere act of washing, such that any baths were adequate.

Finally, we can find evidence of the extent to which the *mikveh* belonged to women by the dearth of rabbinic discussion about it. While recently there has been some excitement about the rise of *mikveh* scholarship among rabbis,[10] perhaps there should be more positive reflection, in retrospect, at the halachic void that left space for women to constitute their practice prior to the recent surge in interest among men in this area, which curiously coincides with the Jewish state's rulings on religious matters, including on the *mikveh*.

The result of women running the *mikveh* for themselves, according to a legal regime they initiated and with little observation, enforcement, or rabbinic discussion, was that the practice of ritual immersion was observed distinctively in different communities and became reflective of the character of the women in those communities. In a fascinating account of Jewish life in North Africa in the early modern period, English Anglican author Lancelot Addison discussed the *mikveh* as one of the aspects of Jewish life practiced differently in Barbary and in Europe. While much of his work, titled *On the Present State of the Jews (More Particularly Relating to those in Barbary)* and written following his travel in that region,[11] draws on accounts of Jewish life and laws that Addison read in Hebraist works merged with his observations and accounts heard in North Africa, in his account of the *mikveh* he drew a distinction between North African Jewish life and Jewish life as reported in Hebraist sources. Addison wrote of the "discrete matrons" responsible for the "tabila" [*tvilla*, immersion] in Barbary and described the practice they were in charge of carrying out, comparing the women of Barbary to the women described by other Hebraist authors. He found that the young Jewish women of Barbary were more modest than Jewish women he had "heard of" elsewhere (likely in Johannes Buxtorf's *Synagoga Judaica*) and would not have paraded with the young bride on their way to and from the "bath," which would have been contrary to their modest ways.[12] Here we have testimony to a variety of ways in which *mikveh* was practiced by women, and there is no mention of male involvement or mandate over the practice, even when a male rabbi described the female practice in Barbary to the male author (Addison) who recounted it and compared it to another male Hebraist's account.

Addison's work is more than an account of the practices of women in Barbary. It is also an account of Jewish life there, and the account gives a strong impression that despite the restrictions on the Jews that amounted to forced separation from Muslims and separate living quarters, within their quarters Jews lived as they always had, with their own legal codes and institutions. Their separation by external symbols and walls was only a forced physical expression of a separation Jews themselves would otherwise have maintained without physical symbols. The book ends up being about Jewish life as governed by custom and text. About the *mikveh* and the prayers, about the Sabbath and about trade. The Judaism Addison describes was an inherited tradition—a comprehensive way of life—that Jews in different places accommodated to their time and place. This was in line with the seventeenth century perception of the Jews in general, that would have the Jews as a people who observed and preserved their own texts and traditions in distinct teachings and practices.

This—Judaism belonging to the people wherever they lived—was an aspect of Judaism that seventeenth century thinkers correctly understood. James Harrington, an influential English republican thinker, proposed settling the Jews in Ireland because "The Jews of all people never incorporate."[13] Even if placed in the same space with non-Jews, Jews would choose to take part in their own distinct form of life. But the modern state could not tolerate a people that wouldn't incorporate. The modern state didn't section off land for people to be different and to rule themselves, not in the seventeenth century or in the French Revolution, or in the nineteenth century colonies or nation-states. When we look at the meaning of the modern state, we understand the necessity of incorporating—becoming one with the people and its religion—in the eyes of the founders of modern sovereignty. The fact that the modern state requires conformity becomes a primary justification for a Jewish state, but it also means that a modern Jewish state, on what has become known as the Westphalian model that will be explored in the next section, contains an inbuilt threat to a Judaism in which the highest authority is the people.

THE NATURE OF THE MODERN STATE

In 1576, Jean Bodin first published his work *Six Books of the Commonwealth*, which is well known for its founding the idea of modern sovereignty that has become synonymous with the modern state. But what exactly was Bodin's idea of modern sovereignty, why was it needed, and what change did it propose from what came before? Most students of the history of political thought these days aren't able to answer these questions well. The only full English translation of Bodin's *Six Books* was published in London in 1606. Since then, Bodin's theory of sovereignty has been promoted in an abridged translation published in 1955, which can be found online, but most commonly in four chapters in a very thin book titled *On Sovereignty* published by Cambridge University Press.[14]

What is hard to tell from the abridged editions of Bodin's *Six Books* was the extent to which the modern state was initially conceived to resolve a Christian problem that rose at the beginning of the Protestant era. The onset of Protestant Christianity brought Europe sudden and quite intense religious heterogeneity—or diversity—radically transforming a largely homogenous Catholic world. Europe's wars of religion followed, and Bodin was the first in a series of authors, and political theorists in particular, who would consider heterogeneity a cause of war and would offer a political resolution—a form of state—to end the conflict. This form of state, needless to say, was imagined as largely homogenous, and the homogeneity was in the form of uniform public religion.

And so, while the modern state, in line with Renaissance ideals that predated Bodin, sought to create lasting and peaceful political units that would not be destroyed from within and that would protect those within them from threats without, modern sovereignty sought to achieve this with a single sovereign who was to be the undisputed highest order of command, created by the people themselves by covenant, who would rule over civil and religious matters. That the sovereign was to preside over religion is generally underemphasized, but the meaning of this is that Christian Europe, at its first moment of religious diversity, sought to tame it. The sovereign would be the highest authority on religion, state religion would support his authority in all areas, and Bodin cited "all wise men and lawgivers" on the importance of religion serving the sovereign.[15] The successful sovereign—even the sovereign who could best protect his constituents' lives—would be the sovereign who could preserve his own sovereignty and thus demonstrate stability, and religion was a key ingredient for preserving sovereignty. Whereas religious diversity was a cause of discord, religious unity under a sovereign was a way of maintaining peace.

Thomas Hobbes's *Leviathan* follows from Bodin's *Six Books*, developing the idea of modern sovereignty while addressing specifically English problems. "My highest priority was to absolve the divine laws," wrote Hobbes in his correspondence on the question of why he chose to write *Leviathan*—a work about sovereignty—at the time he did, during England's wars of religion.[16] Hobbes was concerned about the divine laws being used to undermine sovereignty. English preachers, some even speaking from the pulpit in parliament, promoted the idea of England as a new Israel, justifying using political means to reach salvation or the kingdom of God. Hobbes found these preachers to be the cause of England's civil war, as they presented themselves representing and promoting a spiritual kingdom that could be at odds with the ends of the civil kingdom, which were for Hobbes first and foremost self-preservation.[17] For Hobbes, unity between the spiritual and the civil under one sovereign was imperative for the sake of peace. This unity would be achieved by the sovereign determining the religious canon—namely, which books of the Bible were to be considered God's word—and there would be no higher appeal on matters of religion or state.[18] The sovereign would be, quite explicitly, like God over the Israelites.[19] For those who did not truly believe, Hobbes affirmed freedom of conscience, meaning freedom to believe internally whatever one liked, but the sovereign could command any ritual or law with the highest authority. And Hobbes was quite possibly not ignorant of what Judaism certainly knew, that ritual had the power to create something that looked very much like conscientious belief.

While there were other ideas of politics floating around early modern Europe and a very different idea of Church-State relations that developed in America,[20] Bodin's idea of the state that Hobbes affirmed and enriched, with religion serving the sovereign, reflected and guided the actual formation of modern European confessional states. The modern state was characterized at the peace of Westphalia in 1648 in the same terms as the peace of Augsburg in 1555, *cuius regio eius religio* [he who holds the region holds the religion]. The Peace of Westphalia, in 1648, was defined as "a Christian and universal peace" that sought to end "Christian wars" between "Christian king" and "Christian majesty" mostly by setting a religion over each territory: Catholic, Lutheran, or Calvinist.[21]

Interestingly, this idea—in fact the modern state itself—in Hobbes's *Leviathan* is portrayed as temporary. Temporary until the second coming of Christ when the kingdom of God would be restored. Until that messianic moment, Hobbes tells us, we need a Leviathan—an earthly sovereign. The commonwealth is described as mortal; it will die when God comes to rule in person. Until then, the sovereign rules over civil and religious matters, not in order to bring about the messianic moment—which Hobbes found humans could not know how to do—but in order to protect life and strengthen the sovereign who protects life.

Thus far the modern state. A commonwealth constituted by covenant—social contract—to protect the lives of its constituents partly by presiding over religion and preventing religious warfare from within or without.

It may seem odd that I am about to end a description of the nature of the modern state and its approach to religion in the middle of the seventeenth century, particularly as I am about to move to the implementation of the model of the modern state in a Jewish state. Should we not move now to consider the nation-state model of the nineteenth century? My position is that there was no new state model proposed in the nineteenth century, but that the nation-state was a direct development—in some respects a secularization—of the Westphalian model. "Westphalian sovereignty" is still the form of sovereignty honored by the United Nations, and when the idea of sovereignty is being scrutinized today, it is the seventeenth century idea that is being scrutinized.[22] If we are to consider the founding of the state of Israel, the seventeenth century provides as much background as the nineteenth. Not only was there was actually a proposal for a modern Jewish state framed in the seventeenth century that is strikingly similar to nineteenth century proposals (I will discuss this in the next section), but the justification early Zionists found for a Jewish state in the nineteenth century was grounded in the justification for states in the seventeenth: protection of life, religion, and liberty. Theodor Herzl famously sought a state to protect the Jews, and his diplomatic interlocutors in the nineteenth century spoke in no novel terms about their desire for homogeneity.

A JEWISH STATE AND THE LOCUS OF AUTHORITY IN JUDAISM

Just as I ended the discussion of the modern state in the seventeenth century, I begin my discussion of the modern Jewish state in the that same period, two centuries before the rise of modern Zionism. For contrary to common perception, the first proposal for modern Jewish sovereignty came not with the Zionist movement in the nineteenth century, but with the sovereignty theory of the seventeenth. When they conceived of the modern state partly to resolve religious conflict, early modern political theorists considered the implications of their approach for politically resolving the problem of Jewish diversity, which was largely theoretical. Should Jews be tolerated or encouraged to coinhabit states with Christians, or should they live in separate political entities?

Jean Bodin, writing in France where Jews were prohibited from living but where crypto Jews were victims of the violence of the wars of religion, considered the implications of the statelessness of the Jews. He explained that it was quite natural for men to be jealous of their religion, and that the Jews' insistence on preserving their "strange religion" would cause others "to hate and condemn them."[23] Bodin speaks of the "great poverty of the Jews themselves, who in no place of the world may possess any lands, means that they need the less and are indeed the less able to fight for their religion and liberty."[24] In the absence of land, according to Bodin, the Jews are unable to protect themselves or their religion, as they cannot be included in the lands of others. While Hugo Grotius, writing in a Dutch context, differed and found Jewish difference not so essential as to mean the Jews' exclusion from political society or even from a minimal civil creed,[25] Thomas Hobbes agreed with Bodin, referencing the fact that the Jews were the only religion not allowed in the Roman republic.[26] The Jews, as I quoted from Harrington above, didn't "incorporate." It is worth considering that the Dutch context was one in which Jews lived, de facto, when Grotius wrote, whereas there were no open Jews in England or France. This brings us back to Harrington who, in 1656 when Cromwell was consulting on the reintroduction of Jews to England, first proposed giving the Jews land and arguably sovereignty or statehood. His proposal, which he lamented hadn't been "thought of in time," was that the Jews should be settled in Ireland, in perpetuity, under their own laws and institutions.[27] Harrington's discussion of the Jews, and even his proposal for Jewish sovereignty, was very much in line with the discussion and the terms set by Bodin and Hobbes.[28]

Why this matters to the present discussion of the democratic nature of Judaism and the question of what statehood does to the locus of authority within Judaism is that it highlights the type of state the modern state on the Westphalian model is. Even when discussing a Jewish state, non-Jewish sovereignty theorists at the onset of modernity conceived of a Jewish *confessional* state. The model then was *cuius regio eius religio*—he who holds the region holds the religion—only that the religion held in the lands imagined for Jews would be Jewish. On this state model, diversity within Judaism would be no more a virtue in the Jewish state, no more a contribution to stability, than diversity within Christianity was to a Christian state. The same sovereign constituted by the people who would decide on civil matters would decide on Jewish religious matters, at least for the purposes of outward religion.

Two hundred years later, when Herzl sought a state for the Jews, his theoretical and utopian writings opened up various possibilities for encountering difference other than the possibilities imagined by early modern sovereignty theorists. Herzl imagined, for example, preserving the unique character of diverse Jewish communities and a mutually enriching relationship between the Jews and other inhabitants of the land.[29] But still, Herzl considered religion an important factor for maintaining social cohesion in the state, and he imagined Jewish religion playing this role just as sovereignty theorists in the seventeenth century had imagined the role of Christian religion within the states they conceived.[30] Herzl was also wary—as were the founders of modern sovereignty—of what religion interpreted in certain ways could do to society, only that unlike the founders of modern sovereignty, Herzl's approach was not to suppress or exclude difference, but rather to meet it with radical toleration and to recognize the dangers of doing otherwise.[31]

Whatever Herzl's ideal and whatever its deviation from the early modern encounter with religious difference was, his successful diplomacy appealed to a European Christian—even a Westphalian—mindset. Herzl wrote in and for a world in which the Jews were unprotected in their absence of a land and for a Europe that understood the state as sustained by a single public religion to which the Jews were outsiders.[32] It is interesting to note that Herzl's appeal to representatives of the Ottoman Empire was not successful, even when the Ottoman model for encountering difference was treated with great respect in *Altneuland*.[33] Rather, Herzl was successful in appealing to Europeans—markedly the English—and Russians interested in reducing heterogeneity in their states by sending the Jews elsewhere.[34]

The partnering of Herzl with other organizations and individuals in the Jewish world, the split between territorialism and Zionism, and the settling of Palestine in the early twentieth century must largely be set beyond the limits of this essay, so as to allow me to reengage the foundations of Jewish sovereignty with how the state eventually defined—or in some cases did not define—its relationship to lived Judaism in its founding years and again today. Yet it is important to acknowledge the extent to which the partnering of Herzl with his Westphalian mind frame, and religious Zionists who sought not only to protect the Jews and facilitate their cultural flourishing but also to begin the long-awaited redemption, was among the complex of positions that became the Zionist movement constituting the State of Israel. The joining together of post-Catholic European secular political ideals and messianic-religious ends in the early years of the state meant that various arrangements were made by the secular establishment to create common cause with religious Zionism. Set beyond the pale were Jewish voices, religious and nonreligious, that warned of the dangers of statehood for Judaism and who called for separation of religion and state. If in *Altneuland* Herzl had considered the dangers messianic ends could pose to political life and imagined a society in which the problems the modern state had with religious difference would not apply, partly due to some degree of separation between religion and politics, separation was out of place in the Zionism that came to build the state. The British Mandate's governing of religion through status quo agreements, and not the nature of Judaism in the Diaspora, was the starting point for relating religion and state in Israel.

Exemplifying the extent to which separation of religion and state was beyond the limits of Zionist discourse in the founding years of the state, we find the correspondence between R. Isaac Halevi Herzog and R. Haim Ozer Goroditzky. Herzog would become Israel's chief rabbi, whereas Goroditzky was the head of Moetset Gdolei Hatorah [Council of Rabbis] in Europe before the Holocaust. The rising religious leader in Palestine had turned to the European Jewish leader to consult on the relationship between Jewish law and state law in Israel. Goroditzy proposed that the state set up two parallel sets of laws, thus continuing a relationship that Jewish law had had to state law outside the Jewish state. Herzog was apparently surprised by Goroditzky's response and would not accept his recommendation. To Herzog, it was crucial that Jewish law be expressed in state law.[35]

Yet when Herzog was appointed to the position of chief rabbi, it was under the state and under a secular administration in which many presumed that Judaism itself, as religion, would become redundant once Jewish life was protected in the state.[36] Jewish law, then, could not simply (or in any complex adaptation) become state law, and the relationship was never clearly defined. It is well known that Israel does not have a constitution, and over the years the Knesset and Supreme Court have sought to balance the desire of Jewish statehood—with such agreed-upon ideas as Shabbat and the Jewish calendar being expressed in the public sphere—with the needs of a modern society and a large secular population.

There is surely some irony in the fact that in the Jewish state, from its founding, the agreed-upon framework for the balance between religious and secular legal realms was based upon status quo arrangements that would continue the British Mandate's approach to religion rather than seeking a Jewish approach. But together with the formation of a state rabbinate and with the state's providing of religious services, religion-state relations in Israel today actually resemble neither pre-state Judaism or Mandate arrangements. Rather, they exemplify the Westphalian principle of *cuius regio eius religio*: a top-down power structure, with rabbis appointed by the state and serving the sovereign, the chief rabbinate and local rabbinic council being arms of the state.[37] Religious pluralism has been enabled through lack of definition and purposely left loopholes, but recent rulings and proposed laws have revealed a closing-in on this pluralism in a manner made possible given the definition—and lack of definition—of the relationship between religion and the state. With the sovereign today being bolder than ever in legislating religion,[38] the locus of authority in Judaism is changing on account of the state, which is problematic both for the state and for Judaism more broadly.

Before returning to the *mikveh* as an object of parliamentary legislation, I state my understanding that when the Jewish state positions Judaism politically, this affects not only the locus of power in Judaism within state borders, but the locus of power in Judaism itself. For, certainly the fact that conservative women who attend *mikvaot* in the United States will not find one to attend in Israel could be described as a local issue, to do with how Judaism is practiced in different locations. It could be argued, indeed, that when the state of Israel owns Judaism within its borders, this is equivalent to a large community owning its Judaism without this affecting other communities. But this is not presently the case. The fact that Israel was established as a national home for the entire Jewish people, with the potential for Jews to gather there at any time as necessary or desirable, means that Jewish religious authorities throughout the world will administer their affairs such that their constituents will be able to conduct their lives in Israel. Any rabbi conducting a conversion, for example, will want the convert to be able to move to Israel and marry an Israeli. This means that if the Israeli rabbinate sets particular standards for conversion, rabbis abroad will likely abide by these standards as a service to their constituents.

A recent incident demonstrates the extent to which Israel's rabbinate, a body appointed by the sovereign in the Jewish state, is a higher authority beyond the Jewish state, in its own perception and in the perception of rabbis around the world. The incident was the leaking of a "black list" of rabbis put together by the Israeli rabbinate. Whatever the purpose of this contentious list, its existence conveyed a simple message: rabbis worldwide were expected to understand that if they want their decisions and authorizations to be respected in Israel—even the conversions and marriages they conduct and the letters they write—they are to abide by and respect the standards of the rabbinate in Israel, even with a degree of trepidation.[39] This means that a rabbi appointed by a community in New York, who is part of the Orthodox Union, or local rabbinic council, in such a way that reflects the traditional democratic nature of Judaism and its belonging to the people, cannot simply rely on the democratic basis of his authority. He must, for full authority and credibility, even among his own constituents, bow to the standards set by the Israeli rabbinate that serves under the sovereign state of Israel.

We return now to the *mikveh*, and to how this aspect of Judaism that once belonged to the people—even in a sense to women—became (though perhaps not irreversibly) a tool in the hands of the state, marking a move away from democracy in Judaism.

In Israel, the *mikveh* is a state institution built with taxpayer dollars. It is run by municipal councils in accordance with their understanding of the makeup of their community and always within the framework of Orthodox Judaism. There have long been—and increasingly over recent years—accounts of women feeling uncomfortable with the way in which their local *mikveh* was run. Recently in Ramat Beit Shemesh, women opted to drive far from home to avoid being handled by the Haredi [ultra-Orthodox] women running their local *mikveh* in a stringent, and reportedly physically painful, manner.[40] In response to such complaints and others, an organization called ITIM, which rose to assist Israelis in their encounter with state-administered religion,[41] filed a request with Israel's Supreme Court that women in Israel be permitted to use their local *mikveh* without an attendant, which had not been previously possible.[42] The Chief Rabbinate and Religious Council agreed to the change, and the response came from the State Attorney's office, though the rabbinate made clear that its halachic ruling was still that women should bathe with an attendant. What is important in this ruling is that it was up to the state to make a decision about how the *mikveh* would be run and what the limits of this practice are in the state. The state was able to broaden the scope of permissible practice beyond what the rabbinate would have liked, but this political decision could be changed by the state too.

Indeed, the state currently appears to be moving towards enforcing more stringency on the way the ritual baths are used in the state. The Torah Judaism party in Israel's Knesset recently proposed a "*mikveh* bill," according to which regional religious authorities (all of whom are Orthodox and serve under the Chief Rabbinate) would have the discretion to bar individuals from using state ritual baths, regardless of any previous agreements.[43] The impetus was a Supreme Court ruling requiring the state to allow reform and conservative bodies to use the *mikvaot* provided by the state for their conversion purposes. To the court, this was a matter of taxpayer dollars serving the general public. In the past, rabbinic authorities might have ruled like the Supreme Court—as we saw with R. Moshe Feinstein—that those who contributed to building the *mikveh* should be allowed to use it. But in the Jewish state, the *mikveh* is a state institution, funded by the state. The logic of *cuius regio eius religio* means that the fact the state is funded by the taxpayers does not require it to provide equal religious services that serve all. A Catholic state might use taxpayer dollars for Catholic institutions but not for Lutheran or Jewish ones, and if Catholics were divided, the state could choose a position. The fact that *mikveh*, once built by a community and handed over to women, is a state-provided service in a state with a particular understanding of Judaism set by coalition politics marks a real change in the institution, away from popular authority and toward state authority.

There have recently been a number of other examples of the state legislating on religious matters, not only to restrict secular or non-Orthodox ways of life but also to limit the diversity within orthodoxy. A conversion bill now on hold seeks to make the Orthodox Rabbinate the only body in Israel legally allowed to conduct conversions in Israel. The question of whether any shops will be allowed to open on the Sabbath or any modes of public transportation will be allowed to run have long been in the hands of the Knesset. For the nature of Judaism, these all mark a fundamental change, away from the people administering their own religious lives and toward the state administering Judaism. Religion, in Israel, is very much governed by the sovereign. But if at the founding of the state the sovereign was a secular leftist establishment that assumed religion would disappear, today the sovereign itself is strongly invested in religious interests. Initial concessions made to religious authorities under the state, primarily over matters of marriage, divorce, and burial, initiated a process by which the state changed the locus of authority for rabbis and Jewish institutions in Israel and around the world.

Is there an alternative that would allow the locus of authority in Judaism to remain with the people, while still having a Jewish state? Separation of church and state that became the principle for relating religion and politics in America is the alternative Western politics has to offer to the confessional state, but this developed in the American colonies through Christian evangelical and local political concerns. Any alternative conceived for Israel will more likely be rooted in Jewish concerns and local Israeli concerns.

Such concerns were very recently expressed by a prominent rabbi in Israel. In a rare and bold interview published in *Makor Rishon*, R. Shlomo Riskin of Efrat described how the rabbinate in Israel has become corrupt to the extent that there are five municipalities in Israel in which it is not possible to get kosher food. Riskin, interestingly, writes that in such a situation it would be preferable to separate religion and state, sounding a voice—even a political possibility—for returning Judaism to its constituents. This is a voice that has been long suppressed in Zionism and no less in religious Zionism.

Indeed, there have long been rabbis who sided with a separation of religion and politics, such as R. Goroditzky, who was discussed earlier. But such rabbis generally did not identify as Zionists, and their concerns have generally been kept out of mainstream Israeli and Jewish public discourse. Even the mere desire for continuity between pre-state Judaism and post-state Judaism is generally seen as a denial of one of the key principles of Zionism: the need to overhaul Judaism and overcome the Diaspora. But it may be time to consider that negating exilic Judaism may not be a necessary component of Zionism.[44] After all, it is the Westphalian state of *cuius regio eius religio* that changes the locus of authority in Judaism, and not a particularly Jewish form of state.

The idea that there might be an alternative to state-owned religion for Judaism and for the Jewish state first occurred to me when reading Herzl's works. Herzl's initial vision was that: "Every group will have its rabbi, traveling with his own congregation. Local groups will afterward organize themselves around their rabbi, and each locality will have its own spiritual leader." Herzl imagined communities maintaining their difference in the state. Further, he wrote the following:

> Anyone who has seen anything of the world knows that just these little daily customs can easily be transplanted elsewhere. . . . There are English hotels in Egypt and on the mountain crests of Switzerland. Viennese cafes in South Africa. French theatres in Russia. German operas in America, and the best Bavarian beer in Paris. When we journey out of Egypt again we shall not leave the fleshpots behind. Every man will find his customs again in local groups, but they will be better, more beautiful, and more agreeable than before.

It is enough to compare Herzl's fleshpots to Ben Gurion's melting pot to understand the extent to which Israel's founders sought homogeneity over diversity and to relate this to the singular Judaism developing as state-Judaism in Israel. The state currently follows Hobbes: it chooses the canon, the extent of rabbinic authority, and the rabbis who run the *mikveh*; even the women who supervise are public servants. Accountability is not to the people, but to the state. How distant from a Jewish world of communities living in accordance with their rabbis, who are accountable to them. How distant, indeed, from diaspora Judaism as it is still lived in the United States and elsewhere.

It may be worth reflecting on the fact that not all of Judaism as lived in Israel is distant from community lived and run Judaism. The Haredi establishment continues to run its own courts and schools and continues a more diasporic, people-owned Judaism in Israel, largely in private. To an extent, it lives a separation of religion and state by not accepting religion as interpreted by the state. This is true even when Haredi politicians are among the most vociferous arguing in the Knesset for religious laws: for public transport not to be run on Shabbat, for *mikvaot* to allow only the Orthodox, for secular schools to teach Judaism as religion. The way Haredim live in Israel offers a view into the possibility of living out a separation of religion from state, even a communal existence with representation in a greater state framework. Imagining this is beyond the scope of this essay. But such a framework could be created in the Jewish state today, which would contain the possibility for returning some of the democracy to Judaism, some of Judaism to the people.

AFTERWORD: THE END OF DEMOCRATIC JUDAISM

In the introduction, I promised to end the essay with a reflection not only on the bringing-to-an-end of democratic Judaism, which I have claimed is the result of administering a particular kind of Jewish state, but also of the end—in the sense of a "telos" or teleological end—of democratic Judaism. What end does democratic Judaism serve, such that it might be justified to preserve this aspect of Judaism, even if this means changing the ways in which the Jewish state currently relates to Judaism?

When we think of the telos of Judaism, we may think of messianic times, and there is a complex relationship between Jewish statehood and messianic times, since before the establishment of the state, some religious Jews considered the return of the Jews to the biblical land to mark the onset of messianic times, while others considered the return to Jewish statehood a sin, until messianic times, and there are many positions in between. In fact, insofar as a messianic end is part of the way some branches of religious Zionism understand the state itself, it has become part of what justifies the "bringing to an end" of democratic Judaism.

But messianic times as an end can be interpreted in many ways, as there are multiple conceptions of messiah within Jewish tradition, many of which do not involve a progressive idea of history that would involve bringing traditional Jewish life to an end at a messianic moment. The idea that Judaism as we know it ends with the coming of the messiah—that messianic times supersede life in this world—is a quintessentially Christian idea that many of the rabbis actively rejected. Maimonides, for example, famously argued that messianic times—marking the time at which God would once again dwell with the people—would not fundamentally mean changing Judaism or Jewish life, but only changing the king. God's intention for the way Jews should conduct themselves in the world would not change. We saw that in the Talmud, the Oven of Achnai story has the people constituting the law in the direct presence of God, just as they did in his absence. Democratically lived Judaism, in which the constituents hold the highest authority, seems according to the rabbis to itself fulfill God's intentions, both in his absence and his presence.

I would propose, then, that the end of Judaism as lived democratically be detached from conceptions of change or progress or even messianic times and that we focus, rather, on the human ends about which there is generally agreement. God bequeathed his law at Sinai to the people, who accepted it as one voice and committed to continuing to transmit, adapt, and legislate in continuing God's work. Man, through owning the law, comes to live in as close as possible proximity to God's intentions; both God's intention for man and God's intention for the world. Living in accordance with God's intentions, and in proximity to God himself through the legislative work that was once God's own, is an end in itself. Such a life also encourages a certain humility, as man recognizes the tentative nature of his legislation, bequeathed to future generations, and realizes the timelessness and greater perspective of God.

John Milton, the seventeenth century poet and political writer, understood Judaism in this way, and his work allows us to explore how Judaism lived democratically might be compatible with modern politics. In *Areopagitica*, a pamphlet in favor of freedom of the press published in 1644, Milton argued that the closest we can come to the rule of God in the absence of the kingdom of God—in the meantime—is to allow for a plurality of voices, even false voices, in public space. His argument was that freedom of the press and the human encounter with a variety of opinions and positions allow truth to emerge, and this is God's intention for how men should recover truth in the world.[45] While recovering truth through encountering multiplicity, Milton also finds that men leave space for the return of God's rule, as no one usurps God's authority in the meantime. In another text, Milton found multiplicity to be the way of rabbis, as he argued with his interlocutor by siding with some rabbis over others, acknowledging that there is no single rabbinic viewpoint that is authoritative, but multiplicity.[46] Milton of course was a Christian, and the idea that God would eventually return and end the human search for truth was integral to his understanding, but his idea of human politics was very much compatible with both the human constitution of truth and law and with a state that allows such pursuit to occur within it—a state that does not promote a single truth at the expense of all others.

It is interesting to contrast Milton's ideas with those of Hobbes on this matter. Both Milton and Hobbes consciously wrote for a period in which God was absent, and both authors considered the meaning of human rule for the interim period between God's kingdom over Israel in the past and his future kingdom promised in messianic times. Yet Hobbes had human rule mean that men authorized a sovereign to make decisions for them, while Milton considered the continuous acts of men constituting and considering texts and truths to be a godly activity in which they were supposed to participate. The difference between Hobbes's idea and Milton's can be analogized to the difference between R. Eliezer and the sages in the Oven of Achnai story. R. Eliezer would like to be the highest authority, and he has every reason to believe his title to be true, only that God himself authorized not a single highest authority, but the people. Once God placed the law in the hands of the people, the people are not authorized to return the law to heaven. This is not the nature of the Torah or God's law. There is not a single truth to be obeyed, but it is through multiplicity that God intends for men to reveal truth themselves in his image. This may be read to imply that not only may men not return the law to heaven, but they may also not relinquish their ownership of it to a sovereign, Hobbes's mortal God.

If we consider the situation in the state of Israel, where the state is the highest authority on matters of religion, we see state-appointed authorities leaving little space for dissenting voices and practices or for people to constitute their own laws and practices. The result is the alienation of many traditional Jews from the state and the alienation of many within the state from Judaism. The end of democratic Judaism may have been a human end, to allow Jews to engage the laws and participate in Torah discourse, while at the same time leaving space for divine authority. The end may simply have been to live in accordance with God's intentions. The end of state-run Judaism abandons these ends of democratic Judaism in favor of strengthening the sovereign—the end of state religion for Hobbes—and this is a high price to pay.

Judaism, we have learned from history, is capable of leaving space for the state. It allows the law of the state to be the law, *Dina Demalchuta Dina*, and provides a realm for the Jewish people to own, each in their communities; a realm where they are the highest authority. The question now facing the Jewish world is whether the Jewish state is capable of leaving space for Judaism as it has been lived for generations. A Judaism where the highest authority lies not in a state or even in God, but in its constituents.

NOTES

1. Regarding the increase of interest in the combination between "Jewish" and "democratic" over the last 25 years, a search on scholar.google.com (search conducted August 7, 2017), reveals that only 58 scholarly books and articles were published mentioning "Jewish and democratic" between 1948 and 2001, whereas 2,980 scholarly books and articles mentioning "Jewish and democratic" were published between 2002 and 2017. The rise of interest in "Jewish and democratic" as paired principles followed the legislation of two laws by Israel's High Court of Justice in 1992, which were specifically justified as reflecting Israel's "Jewish and democratic" character. Prior to the legislation of these laws, the pairing of "Jewish and democratic" was not to be found in official state documents, and most scholars employing the phrase were considering the general incompatibility of the ideas in the Israeli context or not speaking of the Israeli context at all. The two laws that

raised interest and scholarship on this construct were "Basic Law: Human Dignity and Freedom" and "Basic Law: Freedom of Occupation." Israel's Declaration of Independence, contrary to common belief, does not mention the democratic nature of the state, though its references to "benefit of all its inhabitants," "freedom, justice, and peace as envisaged by the prophets of Israel," and "complete equality of social and political rights to all its inhabitants" as well as "freedom of religion, conscience, language, education and culture" and its offer to Arab inhabitants of "full and equal citizenship and due representation in all its provisional and permanent institutions" were understood as referring to democracy.

2. See the introduction and chapters of Gordon Schochet, Fania Oz Salzberger, and Meirav Jones, *Political Hebraism: Judaic Sources in Early Modern Political Thought* (Jerusalem: Shalem Press, 2008). See also Eric Nelson, *The Hebrew Republic: Jewish Sources and the Transformation of European Political Thought* (Cambridge: Harvard University Press, 2010).

3. Here I sidestep the question of whether the Jewish state is properly described as democratic in its current form and what type of democracy it is, including the debate on ethnic democracy, which notably began before 1992, even when it alluded to the "Jewish and democratic" claims of the state. See, for example, Sammy Smooha, "Minority Status in an Ethnic Democracy: The Status of the Arab Minority in Israel," *Ethnic and Racial Studies* 13:3 (1990): 389–413; Sammy Smooha, "The Model of an Ethnic Democracy: Israel as a Jewish and Democratic State," *Nations and Nationalism* 8:2 (2002): 475–503; Yoav Peled, Ethnic Democracy and the Legal Construction of Citizenship: Arab Citizens of the Jewish State," *American Political Science Review* 86:2 (1992): 432–43; Ruth Gavison, "Jewish and Democratic? A Rejoinder to the "Ethnic Democracy" Debate," *Israel Studies* 4:1 (1999): 44–72.

4. Conservative rabbis have recently offered alternative names for the ritual of immersion, including the laws of sanctification of marriage or the laws of sanctifying the family, taking the emphasis away from purity and impurity and towards sanctity.

5. Benny Porat, "Five Jewish Concepts of Israeli Democracy: Opening Essay," in Benny Porat and Aviezer Ravitzky eds., *Thoughts on Jewish Democracy* (Tel Aviv and Jerusalem: Am Oved and the Israel Institute for Democracy, 2010), 19 [Hebrew].

6. For more on this, see J. David Bleich, *Contemporary Halakhic Problems*, vol. 3 (New York: Yeshiva University Press, 1989), 102–5. R. Moshe Feinstein's rulings from *Iggerot Mosheh, Hoshen Mishpat* II:24, and *Iggerot Mosheh, Yoreh Hadeah* II:125 are cited.

7. Varda Polak-Sahm, *The House of Secrets: The Hidden World of the Mikveh* (trans. Anne Hartstein Pace; Boston: Beacon Press, 2009). To experience the *mikveh* in this way in the State of Israel, the author had to shed not only clothing, childhood memories, and preconception, but also thoughts of the watching eye of the state

8. See Rambam, *Hilchot Isurei Biah* 11:10; Ramban, *Hilchot Niddah* 1:19. For rabbinic authorities that see *hilchot niddah* of seven days a stringency of the rabbis, rather than a custom of the women later agreed upon by rabbis and much later codified, see Tosefot

Megillah 28b, which says that the rabbis would not enact something that was not in the Torah, implying the role of the women to have been insignificant.

9. For the rebellion and the rabbinic response, see Avraham Grossman, *Pious and Rebellious: Jewish Women in Medieval Europe* (trans. Jonathan Chipman; Waltham: Brandeis University Press, 2004), 109–11.

10. Hillel Goldberg, "The Efflorescence of '*Mikveh*' Studies," *Tradition: A Journal of Orthodox Jewish Thought* 43:3 (2010): 73–79.

11. The first edition of this work was published under the title *On the Present State of the Jews (More Particularly Relating to those in Barbary). Wherein is Contained an Exact Account of Their Customs, Secular and Religious. To Which is Annexed a Summary Discourse of the Misna, Talmud, and Gemara* (London, 1975). The second edition of the work was published under the same title only without reference to the Jews in Barbary, reading *On the Present State of the Jews, Wherein is Contained an Exact Account of Their Customs, Secular and Religious. To Which is Annexed a Summary Discourse of the Misna, Talmud, and Gemara* (London, 1976). Both editions contain a frontispiece of an American-Indian looking "barbarian" with the short title "On the Present State of the Jews in Barbary."

12. Lancelot Addison, *On the Present State of the Jews* (London, 1675), 47–48; Elliott Horowitz published an important article documenting the ways in which Addison clearly read and drew on Buxtorf's *Synagoga Judaica*, which was published in 1603 but made its way to England in a largely plagiarized work by Alexander Ross, published as *A View of the Jewish Religion* (London, 1656). See Elliott Horowitz, "'A Different Mode of Civility': Lancelot Addison on the Jews of Barbary," *Studies in Church History* 29 (1992): 309–25.

13. James Harrington, *The Commonwealth of Oceana* (London, 1656), Introduction.

14. Jean Bodin, *On Sovereignty* (ed. Julian H. Franklin; Cambridge: Cambridge University Press, 1992).

15. Jean Bodin, *Six Books of the Commonwealth* (London, 1606), 4.7.

16. Thomas Hobbes, *Autobiography* [Thomas Hobbes malmesburiensis vita carmine expressa, in *opera philosophica*, ed. Molesworth, London, vol. 1, pp. lxxxi–xcix], cited in Skinner, *Hobbes and Republican Liberty* (Cambridge: Cambridge University Press, 2008), 125.

17. Hobbes writes: "I am sure that experience teaches, thus much, that the dispute for [precedence] between the *spirituall* and *civill power*, has of late more than any other thing in the world, bene the cause of ciuill warres, in all *places of Christendome*." See Noel Malcolm, ed., *The Correspondence of Thomas Hobbes* (Oxford: Clarendon Press, 1994), vol. 1, 120.

18. The frontispiece of Hobbes's *Leviathan* (London, 1651, multiple editions) is a powerful image of an "artificial man," made of numerous men, presiding over church and state. This is in line with the subtitle and content of the work, which speaks of a commonwealth "ecclesiastical and civil."

19. Hobbes offered the Ten Commandments as teachings the sovereign would do well to teach his constituents and in general offers the kingdom of God over Israel as a model commonwealth. See Hobbes, *Leviathan* (London, 1651), Book 2, chapter 30. See also Meirav Jones, "My Highest Priority Was to Absolve the Divine Laws: The Theory and Politics of Hobbes' *Leviathan* in a War of Religion," *Political Studies* 61:1 (2017): 248–63.

20. While there is a vast literature on church and state in America, which is structured on a different model than the European confessional state, which sowed the seeds for the European nation-state, I found Teresa Bejan's recent work on Roger Williams's idea of toleration and its roots in Evangelical Christianity particularly interesting as a view into how religious politics can yield diverse interpretations on how the state should relate to religion. For Bejan's account, see Teresa M. Bejan, "Evangelical Toleration," *Journal of Politics* 77:4 (October 2015): 1103–14.

21. Avalon Project at Yale Law School. n.d. "Treaty of Westphalia; October 24, 1648," Lillian Goldman Law Library. http:// avalon.law.yale.edu /17th _century/westphal .asp (accessed January 8, 2015).

22. There is a vast and growing literature that is revisiting "Westphalian sovereignty," or the seventeenth century model. See, for example, Andreas Osiander, "Sovereignty, International Relations, and the Westphalian Myth," *International Organization* 55:2 (2001): 251–87; Christopher Rudolf, "Sovereignty and Territorial Borders in a Global Age," *International Studies Review* 7:1 (2005): 1–20; James A. Caporaso, "Changes in the Westphalian Order: Territory, Public Authority, and Sovereignty," *International Studies Review* 2:2 (2000): 1–28; Stephane Beaulac, *The Power of Language in the Making of International Law: The Word Sovereignty in Bodin and Vattel and the Myth of Westphalia* (Leiden: Martinuc Nijhoff, 2004); and many more.

23. Bodin, *Six Books*, 3.7, 4.7.

24. Ibid., 3.8.

25. On this see Jacob Meijer, "Hugo Grotius' 'Remonstratie,'" *Jewish Social Studies* 17:2 (1955): 91–104.

26. Hobbes, *Leviathan*, 1.12.

27. Harrington, *Commonwealth of Oceana*, Introduction.

28. For a more detailed account of the discussion of the Jews' political predicament and the possibility of Jewish sovereignty among modern sovereignty theorists, see Meirav Jones and Yossi Shain, "Modern Sovereignty and the Non-Christian, or Westphalia's Jewish State," *Review of International Studies* 43:5 (2017): 918–38.

29. In *The Jewish State*, Herzl imagined communities continuing as they had outside Israel, insofar as this was considered desirable by the members of the communities, and even languages preserved in a "federation of tongues." In *Altneuland*, the visitors to Palestine are introduced to a Muslim member of the Jewish "New Society" and are introduced to Jewish Palestine not as a "state" in the European sense, but rather a society where all are treated as "men," though religion is preserved and seems to serve an important role,

both in territorial parsing, in terms of where communities live, and also in the identities that are preserved in and by the greater society. See Theodor Herzl, *The Jewish State* (1896) http://www.jewishvirtuallibrary.org/quot-the-jewish-state-quot-theodor-herzl; Theodor Herzl, *Altneuland* (1902), Book 3, Chapter 1, http://www.jewishvirtuallibrary.org/quot-altneuland-quot-theodor-herzl.

30. Shlomo Avineri wrote on the religious element in the portrayal of Jerusalem in *Altneuland,* that for Herzl, "religion, and certainly the Jewish religion, was to be respected in the future of the Jewish state. Religion was an important force for social cohesion on the symbolic level. It was not, as Protestant tradition would have it, only a matter of inner personal faith." See Shlomo Avineri, *Herzl: Theodor Herzl and the Foundation of the Jewish State* (trans. Haim Watzman; London: Weidenfeld & Nicholson, 2013).

31. It is worth considering the place of Rabbi Dr. Geyer, in *Altneuland,* Book 3, who is described as having brought the prejudice of Europe to the New Society.

32. The secularization of this idea is beyond the bounds of this essay, but it is possible not only to understand religion as something from which the Jews were outsiders, but also irreligion and nationhood as well.

33. The Muslim member of the Jewish society in *Altneuland,* represented by Reschid Bey, offers the insight that he did not learn toleration from the Europeans, but that Muslims had long tolerated the Jews, whereas Christians had not.

34. In February 1897, *Die Welt,* the Zionist newspaper edited by Theodore Herzl, visionary of and diplomat for the establishment of the modern Jewish state, published an interview with Prince Dimitrie Sturdza, former prime minister of Romania. The Prince said: "I consider Dr. Herzl's idea to be excellent; in fact I may say the one and valuable way of solving the Jewish question. . . . The Jews are the one people who, living in foreign countries, do not assimilate with the inhabitants as others do." Translated in Avineri, *Theodor Herzl,* 153.

35. Aviezer Ravitzky, *Religion and State in Jewish Thought: Models of Unity, Separation, Clash, or Subjection* (Jerusalem: Israel Democracy Institute, 1998), 11–18 [Hebrew].

36. A poignant critique of this position of the secular Left, not only among Israel's liberationists but also among the leftist liberationists of India and Algeria, active at roughly the same time, can be found in Michael Walzer, *The Paradox of Liberation: Secular Revolutions and Religious Counter-Revolutions* (New Haven: Yale University Press, 2015).

37. This had long been ambiguous, and religious courts tended to rule beyond their official state jurisdiction, as many considered these courts continuous from Diaspora rabbinic courts. Recent Supreme Court rulings, which limited the jurisdiction of rabbinic courts based on the fact that they are an arm of the state, have more clearly defined the relationship between church and state in Israel, while creating controversy and spurring a religious resistance in the form of resort to private courts. On this see Arye Edrei, "Judaism, Jewish Law, and the Jewish State in Israel," in *The Cambridge Companion to Judaism and Law* (ed. Christine Hayes; Cambridge: Cambridge University Press, 2017).

38. While the focus of the discussion here is the role of the Knesset in legislating religion, often spurred on by challenges from the Supreme Court based on appeals by citizens, still there is a place beyond this essay to discuss the extent to which the Supreme Court itself has been involved in legislating religion, even in seeking to shape halachah for today's world. Arye Edrei's work in this area is fascinating, and I direct the reader to his recent article, "Judaism, Jewish Law, and the Jewish State in Israel."

39. The "blacklist" was reported and transcribed on many news sites in Israel and abroad. The Chief Rabbi apparently had not authorized its release, nor did he acknowledge the existence of it. For present purposes, it is enough to note that the Israeli rabbinate keeps an organized list of rabbis abroad and follows their conduct, and that there is an expectation that rabbis will meet whatever standards the Israeli rabbinate sets, if their authority is to be accepted. This is very distant from pre-state Judaism. For some sample news reports, see online reports from *Haaretz*, the *Jerusalem Post*, NPR, and *The Forward*, respectively: "The Complete List of Rabbis Blacklisted by the Israeli Chief Rabbinate," *Haaretz*, July 10, 2017, http://www.haaretz.com/israel-news/1.800651 (accessed August 4, 2017); Jeremy Sharon, "Israeli Chief Rabbinate Blacklists 160 Diaspora Rabbis," *Jerusalem Post*, July 9, 2016, http://www.jpost.com/Israel-News/Politics-And-Diplomacy/Chief-Rabbinate-forced-to-publish-rabbinical-blacklist-of-160-rabbis-in-Diaspora-499171 (accessed August 4, 2017); Daniel Estrin, "Have Israel's Religious Authorities 'Blacklisted' 160 Rabbis?" *NPR*, July 9, 2016, http://www.npr.org/sections/thetwo-way/2017/07/09/536270818/have-israels-religious-authorities-blacklisted-160-rabbis (accessed August 4, 2017); Ben Sales, "Israeli Rabbinate 'Blacklisting' American Rabbis," *The Forward*, July 9, 2016, http://forward.com/news/breaking-news/376546/israeli-rabbinate-blacklisting-american-rabbis/ (accessed August 4, 2016).

40. Ruth Eglash, "Ramat Beit Shemesh Jostle Over Control of Mikva," *Jerusalem Post*, April 25, 2010, http://www.jpost.com/Jewish-World/Jewish-News/Ramat-Beit-Shemesh-residents-jostle-over-control-of-mikva.

41. See http://www.itim.org.il/en/about-itim/about-us/.

42. Ben Sales, "At Israel's Mikvehs, Women Claim Verbal Abuse, Unwanted Touching," *Times of Israel*, March 29, 2016, http://www.timesofisrael.com/at-israels-mikvahs-women-claim-verbal-abuse-unwanted-touching/ (accessed August 4, 2017); "Israel's Chief Rabbinate Agrees to Mikveh Immersion Without Attendant," *Jewish Telegraphic Agency*, June 22, 2016, http://www.jta.org/2016/06/22/news-opinion/israel-middle-east/israels-chief-rabbinate-agrees-to-mikvah-immersion-without-attendant (accessed August 4, 2017).

43. Marissa Newman, "Knesset Approves Law to Bar Non-Orthodox from Ritual Baths," *Times of Israel*, July 26, 2016, http://www.timesofisrael.com/knesset-approves-law-to-bar-non-orthodox-from-ritual-baths/ (accessed August 4, 2017). Interestingly, in the discussions surrounding this law, the United Torah Judaism MK, Moshe Gafni, who proposed the bill, vociferously argued that Reform Jews in the United States did not seek *mikvaot*, and only in Israel they wish to attend. This demonstrates an unsurprising ignorance of what has been considered a "*mikveh* revival" in the American non-Orthodox,

and particularly Conservative, community. On this, see Johanna R. Ginsburg, "Dipping into Tradition: The Mikveh Makes a Comeback," *Jewish Theological Seminary Magazine* 10:3 (2001); Diana Stevens, "The Growth of the Mikvah Movement," *United Synagogue Review* (2001); "Mikveh and the Sanctity of Family Relations," Rabbinical Assembly, https://www.rabbinicalassembly.org/sites/default/files/public/halakhah/teshuvot/20052010/mikveh_introduction.pdf (accessed August 4, 2017).

44. Salo Baron, in a 1928 article, offered the perspective that a lachrymose view of Jewish history was not necessary for Zionism. He implied that there could be a Zionism without *shlilat hagalut* [denial of the exile], but did not expand on how such a Zionism would relate to religion and state. See Baron, "Ghetto and Emancipation," *Menorah Journal* (1928).

45. John Milton, *Areopagitica* (London, 1644), in John Milton, *Areopagitica and Other Writings* (Indianapolis: Liberty Fund, 1999), 19. Milton cites the Hebraist and Talmudist John Selden approvingly on this matter.

46. John Milton, *Defense of the People of England*, in Milton, *Political Writings* (ed. Martin Delzainis; trans. Claire Gruzelier; Cambridge: Cambridge University Press, 1991), 98–99.